Management Career Progress
in a Japanese Organization

Research for Business Decisions, No. 24

Gunter Dufey, Series Editor
Professor of International Business and Finance
The University of Michigan

Other Titles in This Series

Management Career Progress in a Japanese Organization

by
Mitsuru Wakabayashi

RESEARCH PRESS

Produced and distributed by
UMI Research Press
an imprint of
University Microfilms International
Ann Arbor, Michigan 48106

Library of Congress Cataloging in Publication Data

Wakabayashi, Mitsuru, 1942-
    Management career progress in a Japanese
organization.

    (Research for business decisions ; no. 24)
    Bibliography: p.
    Includes index.
    1. Organizational behavior—Longitudinal studies.
2. Middle managers—Japan—Longitudinal studies.
3. Organizational change—Japan—Longitudinal studies.
4. Success—Longitudinal studies. 5. Industrial management—Japan—Longitudinal studies.   I. Title. II. Series.
HD58.7.W25   658.4'09'0952   80-23789
ISBN 0-8357-1108-0

Contents

Tables

Figures

Acknowledgments

A longitudinal study on the "Role Making Processes within Japanese Organizations" was started in 1972. This study, upon which the present work is based, was initiated by the joint efforts of Professor Katsuo Sano of Keio University, Tokyo, and Professor George Graen, formerly of the University of Illinois and now a professor at the University of Cincinnati. I have incurred great debts to both professors who gave me opportunities for serving as an apprentice and sometimes as their colleague since the start of the research project.

Throughout the three-year research period (1972–1975), young managers and their supervisors in three large business organizations in Japan have been aiding us as invaluable informants to our research. They performed their part of the research responsibilities far better than we did. We can never repay them adequately for their kindness and the inconveniences that we caused them. We can only hope to prove worthy of their time and effort by displaying their organizational lives as accurately as we know how, without sacrificing their anonymity. To these unnamed managers, especially to those of the DEPART company upon which the present work is based, we express our deepest thanks.

We owe special thanks to the personnel people in three Japanese companies also. The companies themselves wish to remain anonymous. During the three-year research period, personnel people actually administered a part of the research procedures in their organizational fields. Without the efforts and patience of many of these personnel staff members, our study would not have been possible. We are indebted to Mr. Yamada, Mr. Hirata, Ms. Matsui, Mr. Hanaoka, Mr. Iwasaki, Mr. Kurei, and Mr. Yoshimi, to mention only a few.

I extend my heartiest thanks and friendship to the three researchers with whom I worked in Japan while administering complicated procedures for the long-term research project: questionnaire development, data collection and coding, analyses, interviews, and publication of the preliminary results. The most difficult position for the project was filled by Professor Takao Minami who paved the way for a method of longitudinal investigation for me. Then, Mr. Masao Hashimoto and Mr. Shūsuki Konomi took the office successively, after I came to the University of Illinois for graduate study. To me they were always good teachers, coworkers, and friends. It must be noted that all of us are indebted to the assistance given by the hard working students of Professor Sano's seminar at Keio University. The group effort of those students constitutes the single most important contribution to the successful completion of the study. Without their time and energy, we would have been left with a tremendous pile of unprocessed papers and questionnaires at the end of the research period.

Members of my dissertation committee made significant contributions in bringing their ideas to bear on the subject of the study. Professor George Graen enabled me to find the street of management progress research from a blind alley with a heap of data. But, he always gave me the freedom of inquiry and testing on each corner point. Professor Walter Franke contributed heavily of his time, his patience, and his understanding. Professor Kendrith Rowland helped clarify a number of key theoretical issues regarding management progress. His attempts to impart his insights to me led the study to a quality that would never have been possible otherwise. I owe methodological refinements of the study to Professor James Terborg. Extra analyses that I attempted based on his suggestions produced results indicating improvements or very often limitations of the study.

The Japan Society for the Promotion of Science (JSPS) supported my graduate study from Summer 1974 to Fall 1975. Then, the University of Illinois Research Board financed my graduate study from Spring 1976 to Summer 1977, as did the Institute of Labor and Industrial Relations for the periods thereafter. The Research Board at the University of Illinois and the Fukuzawa Research Foundation at Keio University, Tokyo, provided research grants for our Japan Role Making project. The Institute of Management and Industry at Keio University also helped us in many ways to complete the project successfully.

At the University of Illinois, Professor Maurice Tatsuoka offered his insight in the analysis of variance design that was used extensively for this study. My fellow graduate students, Lee Stepina, James Browne, Ronald Seeber, Michio Fujiwara, and Basu Sharma were most free with their criticisms and teachings. Especially James Browne who read all of the early drafts and helped to polish the work in various ways. I express my deepest thanks to Phyllis Stout who worked on the voluminous and difficult draft to produce the final thesis with her professional typing skills. I will never forget those beautiful trips that I made to a nice little house in the cornfields during the crisp midwestern fall. Finally, any errors are the responsibility of the author.

Part I

Approaches to the Study of Managerial Career Progress

Chapter I

Introduction

The research in the area of managerial resource development has been underdeveloped despite the pressing need for research in the area: the high turnover rate among young managers, a relative shortage of professional managers, human productivity, development of effective human organization, and so forth. It was only in 1970 that Campbell and his associates conducted the first comprehensive study on *Managerial Behavior, Performance, and Effectiveness.* In this book, the authors reported that the contemporary situation in the practice of managerial development might be characterized as "man-power chaos." For their survey, Campbell and his associates (1970) defined an ideal, comprehensive program of managerial development as one that integrates three key personnel areas: selection, training, and motivation. But, they reported that even in organizations known as practicing such advanced ideas of managerial development, most of the programs examined were found falling far behind their criterion of comprehensiveness. Also, the authors were very disappointed by the fact that so little ongoing research on managerial effectiveness was reported by the firms they interviewed. The authors hinted that even those select organizations might have based their managerial development practices mainly on fads and such fashions rather than on evidence derived from their research.

For our study, the term managerial career development, is used to imply any personnel movement along or across the organizational hierarchy that will lead to the greater aquisition of organizational resources, regardless of differences in an occupational or career line pursued by each individual in the organization. One of the basic assumptions for managerial development programs is that the organization and its members maintain their relations over a considerable period of time, in which interactions for development will take place. In our study, data for analyzing the process of managerial progress was derived from the longitudinal investigation of the college graduates recruited by one of the large industrial organizations in Japan, where the idea of lifetime employment is practiced. This situation provided us with an excellent setting to conduct research. However, it is obvious that the lifetime employment *per se* does not mean a superior system for managerial career development. On the contrary, this practice might be easily turned into a system that discourages development by installing a rigid seniority principle, lenient selection procedures, a hardened habit system that resists change, and hindering adult learning and development. These features may imply that human resources tend to be underutilized, hoarded, and mislocated in a system that counteracts the outside pressures demanding the effective human organization. It is not a major interest for the present study to examine the Japanese managerial system based on the cross-cultural perspective. Instead, the purpose of our study is in testing, based on a Japanese organization and its people, a set of hypotheses derived from theories of managerial career development in the formal organization where integrating given human resources into the effective human organization is a strong concern for both the individual and the organization.

Following Mills, we will state that the purpose of studying human resource development rests in our conviction of "developing and managing our human resources at work toward new goals of greater sharing of personal, social, and economic values" (Mills, 1975, 123). In this introductory chapter, a set of key concepts will be defined to build a basic model for the study of managerial career development. From the development point of view the organization is conceived of as a system of collaboration in which each individual is allowed to utilize resources of the system for performing his task requirements while enhancing the development of himself simultaneously. Therefore, under this assumption the system is faced with problems of how to establish the internal structure of resource allocation such that limited resources will be best utilized (a) by the organization for promoting effectiveness of human collaboration, and (b) by the individual for attaining his career goals. For the individual, career development implies establishing, investing, and shifting his career roles through interaction with the environment of his organization.

1. Basic Changes

Human development after adolescence is often called adult socialization, or socialization after childhood (Brim and Wheeler, 1966; Becker, 1964). The underlying notion for this conceptualization is that men are socialized throughout the life cycle, through childhood as well as adulthood. The individual faces relatively novel situations through life (e.g., family, school, occupational and organizational situations) in which he will be required to learn a set of new behaviors. Especially, the pressure for new learning will become stronger in occupational situations where the effective role learning is pressed by the structure of the organization and the institution. Brim pointed out that the role acquisition may be the key aspect in the socialization after childhood. He stated that,

> our emphasis is on the acquisition of habits, beliefs, attitudes, and motives which enable a person to perform satisfactorily the roles expected of him in his society. The acquisition of role is not viewed as the entire content of socialization, but role learning is the segment of socialization that we propose to analyze, and role acquisition is probably the most important aspect of adult socialization (Brim and Wheeler, 1966, 5).

According to Brim, the content of learning in adult socialization must vary from what is learned in the preceding socialization periods. He pointed out six basic changes in the content of adult socialization. First, the most important change which occurs represents a shift in content from a concern with values and motives to a concern with overt behavior. Early-life socialization usually emphasizes the content of primary drives (learning of basic values and motivation), while socialization in later stages deals with secondary or learned motives generated by the expectations of significant others. Brim stated that this change is directed toward the acquisition of knowledge and abilities: (a) one must know what is expected of him both in behavior and in values, (b) must be able to meet the role requirements, and (c) must desire to practice the behavior and pursue the appropriate ends. The second characteristic of adult socialization, he continued, is that the objective of training in adulthood is in enabling one to practice a new combination of skills already acquired, to combine elements into new forms, to trim and polish existing material, rather than to learn wholly new responses as is required for childhood socialization. Brim stated that the content acquired in adult socialization comes from the synthesis of old material, "the synthesis of elements from a storehouse of already learned responses" (Brim and Wheeler, 1966, 28).

Third, Brim emphasized that adult socialization is characterized by the transformation of idealism into realism: early learning encompasses the formal status-role structure, whereas later learning takes into account the actual or informal structure that makes the system work effectively under realistic environmental pressures. The fourth type of change is an emphasis of learning to resolve conflicts. Brim indicated that the role-set members for an individual keep increasing as he becomes involved in broader segments of social life. The expanding population connected with one's roles, then, tends to create interrole as well as intrarole conflicts for the focal individual in the set. Therefore, he will be required to learn methods of conflict reduction such as avoiding the situation, withdrawing, scheduling conflicting demands, compromising, and rationalizing his decisions using *metaprescriptions*, and the like. The fifth characteristic is the emphasis of specificity. Brim stated that socialization in the later phases of one's life cycle tends to be practical and role-specific. The final aspect that characterizes the adult socialization is that the learning situation would involve fewer of the "I-me" type of self-other relationships and more of the "they-me" components. According to Brim, this change will take place because in adulthood, search for significant others, "they," to establish self-identity, "I," — becomes more active. Moreover, with the growth of power as a result of maturity, one increases the degree to which he is the initiator of the action and consequently is engaged more frequently in the "I-them" relationship.

The above discussion suggests that the changes in the content of adult learning will lead to the shift in the pattern of role behavior. According to Parsons and Bales (1955), in an adult role one channels his behavior more on the basis of *affective neutrality* rather than *affectivity*. He will face more often the situation in which the *universalism* rather than *particularism* is the principle which defines the relationship between him and other people. Also, he will have to limit himself to a *specific* position in his behavior to, and relationship with, others instead of putting himself in a *diffuse* position to them. Moreover, the most characteristic pattern of adult behavior may be that he will become more *collectivity-oriented* rather than *self-oriented*, because his activities will involve more aspects of organizational role requirements that are, by their very nature, group-oriented. One will be asked to be affectively neutral in one situation and to be affectively involved in another. His role position may require the combination of neutrality-universalism (like a scientist's role) on the one hand, and affectivity-particularism (as a member of his informal group) on the other. The pattern of behavior and change will become more complicated as one increases the area of role involvement. This suggests that role achieving in adulthood requires differentiation in the repertoire of behavioral patterns and specialization in one or several of them as a primary area of his social commitment.

The process of development after basic socialization periods has been studied in connection with the occupational achievement of the individual, because studies on development would be more meaningful if they focused upon the concrete occupational and organizational settings in which the individual is going to attain his specific career goals. Past studies have disclosed the mechanism of role acquisition and development unique to the specific occupational groups: doctors (Becker, et al., 1961), nurses (Davis, 1968), school teachers (Becker, 1952), scientists (Glaser, 1964,; Hinrichs, 1964; Pelz and Andrews, 1966), forest rangers (Kaufman, 1960; Hall, et al., 1970), priests (Hall and Schneider, 1972), soldiers (Janowitz, 1960; Stouffer, 1949; Dornbush, 1955), managers (Berlew and Hall, 1966; Jennings, 1967 Bray, et al., 174), and so forth. However, occupational studies like those cited above have long been concerned only with documenting occupational specificities (e.g., aptitudes, occupational values and beliefs, uniqueness of the occupational institutions, etc.) rather than being oriented toward theoretical explanation of the phenomenon of career development itself. Moreover, in these studies the very basic questions such as what does development mean to the individual and the organization, why does one person attain higher progress than another, what are the key conditions that integrate the career development of the individual into the effectiveness of the human organization, and the like, have not been explored.

The past occupational studies tend to emphasize deterministic views to explain the phenomenon of career choice and development. One such deterministic approach may be called a cultural-personality view. For this approach, occupational development is assumed to be an extension or variation of the basic personality properties of the individual that have been developed through childhood socialization under the influence of dominant socio-cultural factors connected with each individual. This approach suggests that occupational development is a process of matching between the personality characteristics of the individual and requirements of the occupational role. On the other hand, mismatch between the two is interpreted as an error caused by the incorrect employment selection and/or a part of the trial and error process associated with the occupational choice behaviors. Another view which might be called the "institutional determinism" suggests that development is a process through which the individual is transformed into a kind of person that the institution wants. For this approach, the stages of development are predetermined by the institution, and the individual is only allowed to conform to the socialization pressures at each stage of development within the institution. The failure in development again is interpreted as an error caused by random factors associated with the institutional and organizational environment for career development.

2. Defining Development

Following Hughes (1937), Mansfield suggested that career development can be viewed as a two-sided concept. He pointed out that one side of the concept represents what he called *objective* career development (Mansfield, 1973). For example, Wilensky's (1960) definition of career development may illustrate this dimension: he stated that career development viewed structurally is a succession of related jobs arranged in a hierarchy of prestige through which persons move in an ordered, predictable sequence. The other side of the concept is referred to as *subjective* career development: his career interests and preferences, assessment of career jobs and himself, decisions on career changes, and the like. Mansfield (1973) emphasized that both objective and subjective aspects of career development need to be integrated into a single conceptual framework allowing the interaction between the two. In this way we can avoid deterministic approaches.

The second point to be considered is the nature of relationship between the personal growth and the method of human resource utilization. To consider this relationship, it is assumed that: (1) the individual tries to enhance his personal worth so that his potential can be best utilized from his point of view, and (2) the organization endeavors to develop human resources so that they will be effectively utilized to achieve the needs of the system. The concept of human resource development, as Mills (1975) indicated, requires that there must be a match, or an equilibrium, between the above two principles, at least in the long run. However, since the above two processes are essentially independent of each other, matching between them will not be achieved automatically. Again, assuming a perfect match *a priori* easily leads to determinism of one form or another. There are many turnover studies which suggest a mismatch between the two processes is common rather than unusual (Dunnette, et al., 1973; Porter and Steers, 1973). The concept of "obsolete socialization" may indicate another example of such a mismatch. Caplow (1964) pointed out that it happens quite often that after new members to the organization have acquired certain skills and values, the organization itself has to abandon them due to the change in environment. This phenomenon implies what was once regarded as development now becomes an obstacle to adaptation and progress. Likewise, "oversocialization" (Schein, 1968; Weick, 1969) represents a similar incident in which total conformity to socialization pressures of the organization leads to a loss of innovative capability of the individual in the later stages of career progress.

Equilibrium in development can be defined as a situation in which the individual's endeavors to increase the value of his personal resources matches the organizational practices to develop and utilize them. It is the purpose of our study to explore how this matching situation evolves, and what are the critical incidents that will give rise to the success or failure in organizational career development over time. To explore this research question, the concept of development must be defined by considering the following two critical aspects: (1) the interaction between the objective and the subjective sides of career development, and (2) conditions by which these two independent efforts find mutually reinforcing relationships. Based upon the above considerations, our definition of development can be stated as follows:

> Human resource development is a process of increasing the value of services of the individual by his investing in a given career role position, and by acquiring new skills, abilities, knowledge, motives, and behavioral patterns connected with the role position(s) expected of him as a target(s) for the next move.

For our definition, the process of "acquiring new skills, abilities, knowledge, motives, and behavioral patterns," denoted the subjective aspect of career development. This aspect corresponds to the process in which the individual increases the potential value of his personal resources. This is a process of learning that will take place when the individual is placed in the novel environment associated with his occupational role. On the other hand, the process on "increasing the value of services," implies the objective aspect of career development through which individual performance is evaluated and rewarded by the organization. It is assumed that the above two processes become activated simultaneously when the individual becomes committed to his career role.

3. The Process of Commitment

Studies on vocational choice and development have addressed themselves to the question of how people become committed to their occupational role. Super (1957) viewed a person's vocational preference and career commitment as an attempt to implement a *self-concept*. This term indicates that a person selects an occupation in which the requirements of the work provide a role consistent with his picture of himself. The self-concept reflects a person's history of vocational preferences developed during adolescence and implemented in adult life. Super pointed out that the entire sequence of development can be broken down into the following three different phases in order of the levels of one's vocational maturity: (1) fantasy stages, (2) tentative stages, and (3) realistic stages. For this approach, a person's career is assumed to develop following the vocational image established in the early stages of one's life cycle, and changes in adult life are interpreted as simply an elaboration of, or variation on, an already established theme.

Hall (1971) proposed a similar concept, *career subidentity*, to explain changes and growth in career phenomenon. He defined career subidentity as an aspect of a person's identity that is engaged in working in a given career area. According to Hall, occupational choice is a process of subidentity selection, and career growth is conceived of as differentiation and adjustment of career subidentity. For example, as the person acquires more knowledge, ability, or motivation related to his career role, his career subidentity grows, i.e., creation of new aspects of the self. Hall continued that experience of success in attaining career goals generates feelings of psychological success, increasing self-esteem and reinforcement of needs for a competent identity. These experiences, then, enhance career commitment of the individual and prepare conditions for proceeding to the higher stages of development.

Both the self-concept (Super, 1957) and the career subidentity (Hall, 1971) theory emphasize the integrating function of personality in career-related decisions of the individual. These theories provide a simple framework to relate seemingly random or exogenously induced incidents ocurring in one's career as internally consistent events. However, the framework tends to overdetermine the process of development due to the rigid assumption of personality. In addition, these theories seem too grand and descriptive to be analytical of the important conditions that will facilitate or deter the process of career commitment in the organization and occupational settings.

Contrary to the psychological explanation of career development as discussed above, the sociological approaches tend to emphasize the impact of the organization structure upon the process of career development. Becker (1964) pointed out that the social structure of the organization and its patterned effects upon the individual is the key to explain the phenomena of career development. According to Becker, the process of development can be summarized by two key concepts, the situational adjustment and commitment. The *situational adjustment* is a process of change in which individuals take on the characteristics required by the situations they participate in. Becker stated that the person, as he moves in and out of a variety of social situations, learns the contingency for continuing in each situation and for success in it. If he has a desire strong enough to continue, the ability to assess what is required, and can deliver the required services, the individual turns himself into the kind of man the situation demands. Becker added that sequences and combinations of small units of situational adjustment produce the large units of role learning that make development possible. The concept of *commitment* (Becker, 1960 and 1964) explains the consistency in the pattern of adjustments from one situation to another. According to him, a person is said to be committed when we observe him pursing a consistent line of activity in a sequence of varied situations. The committed action is marked by the actor's rejection of other situationally feasible alternatives in favor of choosing one particular course of action that best suits his goals. Becker suggested that in so doing, a person often ignores the principle of situational adjustment and carries on his consistent line of activities in spite of short run losses. In other words, the process of commitment consists of linking one's past decisions and choice behaviors with his present and/or future course of action to maintain behavioral consistency. This consistency is a critical part of development strategies by which the individual can convert the fruit of his past adjustments into investments for future development. Becker's theory suggests that situational adjustment produces a change—the person shifts his behavior with each shift in the situation. Commitment produces a stability—the person subordinates his immediate situational interests to goals that lie outside the situation.

For the purpose of our study, we may not need to assume either personality constructs or structural determinism in order to explain the process of commitment. The focus of our research is directed toward exploring, within the organizational setting, how the individual chooses a particular course of behavior, what aspects of the individual and the career environment become critical in determining the individual's behavior in the career role, and why. For the purpose of our study, commitment is defined as a process of investing one's time and energy toward attainment of the career goal. A career goal consists of a set of career targets. Career targets can be any aspects of the organizational role equipped with the higher level of organizational resources, and is seen as being accessible from a given career role of the individual after a certain level of investment. By definition, attaining a target changes one's position in the structure of resource allocation within the organization, and thus commitment becomes directed toward acquiring additional organizational resources. It is this resource acquisition that makes career progress possible. The next question becomes, what are resources, and how do they become accessible to the individual?

Development evolves within the career environment. Career environment is defined as a subset of organizational resources connected with a given career role of the individual. The environmental resources can be classified into the following three categories: positional, personal, and interpersonal resources. Positional resources consist of: (1) terms and conditions of employment including pay and benefits, (2) the quality of work itself, (3) legitimate right of access to the material-financial resources of the organization (machinery, equipment, facilities, budget, manpower, etc.), and (4) the formal decision-making authority connected with one's position. Personal resources may consist of personality components of the individual: skills, abilities, knowledge, intelligence, motives, values and beliefs, goal preferences, and so forth. These factors belong to the individual, and their utilization is largely subject to the individual's initiative. But they are a part of the organizational resources as often mentioned: "Our employees are our most important — our most valuable — assets" (Brummet, et, al., 1968). Interpersonal resources may consist of the chances by which one individual can receive from the other valuable services such as support, cooperation, trust, influence, friendship, and the like. These are "properties" of two or more individuals. But, if one of them "uses" up these properties, they no longer become available between the parties to the relationship. However, as long as these properties are properly maintained, they will function as a very important set of resources. Because, parties to the relationship can account for receiving critical services from one another beyond the limit of the formal structure of the organization. Although interpersonal resources are created, owned, and exchanged informally, they are still an important category of resources for the organization. Both the individual and the organization can greatly benefit from the proper management of these resources. One invests his time and energy in a given role position expecting that the greater the investment, the higher will be the chances that he will succeed in making a shift in his resource position within the environment for career development. Next, we will examine what conditions in the career environment make investment feasible for the individual in the process of career progress.

4. Structure of Resource Allocation Within the Organization

Our resource theory of the organization suggests that the organization is conceived of as a system of resources structured to serve as a means (1) to attain goals of collaboration, and (2) satisfy the personal interests of each individual who collaborates. Structuring the pattern of resource allocation, rather than subjecting allocation to a competitive process, becomes a prerequisite for any attempt by organizing, because the structure stabilizes division of labor on the one hand, and induces commitment or investing behaviors on the other. The structure consists of rules and regulations for distributing (transferring and delegating) organizational resources among members of the organization so that the following two basic questions associated with the allocation problems can be solved. (1) What amount of resources should be connected with each functional role of the organization? (2) How, and by whom, should each role position be occupied? "A right person to a right place" is not the answer to these questions, because the questions themselves are asking who is the right person, and what is the right place? Our definition of development suggests that the following two propositions should be the criteria by which a pattern of resource allocation can be designed if the organization is to answer the above distributive questions. (1) Resource distribution to the individual should be made an increasing function of his investment level. (2) The investing behavior of the individual should be accompanied by an increasing value of his personal resources prompted by the process of learning. Figure 1 illustrates how a pattern of resource allocation can be structured in the organization to incorporate the above key propositions.

In Figure 1, career progress is displayed as a combination of two cyclical phenomena. One of the cycles shown on the left side of the diagram illustrates a "performance process": commitment→ investment→evaluation and selection→acquisition of organizational resources→positional change. The other cyclical phenomenon shown on the right side of the diagram (using dotted lines) displays events constituting a "learning process": learning of skills and knowl- edge→acquisition of personal resources→increased value of human capital→acquisition of organizational resources→positional change. The organization for development needs to promote two cyclical processes to an optimal extent so that the limited amount of resources can be utilized to ensure the development of both the individual and the organization. Next, the components of the allocative structure that regulates the cycles of development will be discussed.

(1) *Investment Function.* Investment is conceived of as an accumulation of credit of various kinds (performance, contribution, merit, qualification, innovation, etc.) attained through role activities and recognized by the organization as attributable to a particular individual. Suppose a person wishes to invest in his occupational role for development, he may want to know what combination of his time and energy allocation on his career role activities will lead to the desired investment level. This question may represent a "predictor" problem from the investor's point of view. On the other hand, from the organization's point of view, the question becomes, what behaviors of the individual should be credited (or discredited) as contributing to the profit (or loss of it) of the organization. This may represent a "criterion" problem from the evaluator's point of view. The classical dichotomy, cosmopolitans and locals, or professionals and generalists (Goulder, 1958), may exemplify the problem of investment functions. The theory suggests that the investment function may have a quite different character between the two occupational groups: for the highly professionalized jobs, a set of universalistic and highly specified criteria by which the individual role activities are guided and evaluated can be

Figure 1

The Process of Resource Acquisition and a Pattern of Organizational Resource Allocation

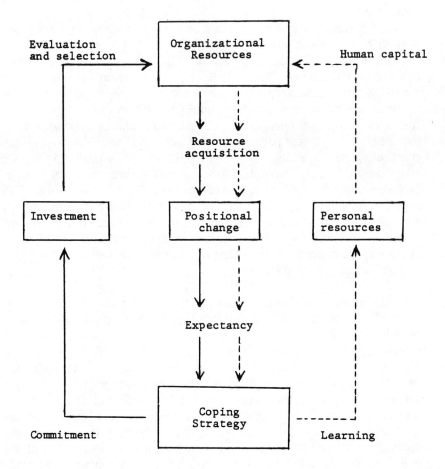

identified, whereas for the generalist's job such criteria may be more particularistic and diffuse. However, the difference between cosmopolitans and locals seems to be a relative matter from our approach of organizational career development. Cosmopolitans working under the bureaucratic organization – doctors in large general hospitals, scientists and engineers in the R & D department, lawyers and accountants employed by large offices and firms, and so forth – have to go through the process of resource acquisition for their career development. Despite differences in occupational categories, it becomes critical for the individual in the process of organizational career development to formulate a strategy for investing in his given occupational role.

Under the process of organizational career development, investing behaviors of the individual are a function of the career targets conceived by the individual and the magnitude of environmental pressures of the organization for task performance. First, the individual may set his career goals and targets by his own choosing. He may want to make his activities on the role most instrumental to the acquisition of skills, knowledge, and expertise for achieving his career targets. On the other hand, regardless of the career expectations of the individual, demands on the given role may require him to commit and invest his time and energy in tasks so that his task behaviors will produce the performance desired by the organization. Simply stated, the individual must face pressures derived from the two different processes for his career progress, the *learning process* and the *performance process*. In Figure 1, it is assumed that each individual formulates his investment function such that the manner in which he copes with the pressures of the environment will produce outcomes at an optimum level between the learning and performance processes. Formulation of such an investment function depends on: (1) the career targets chosen by the individual, and (2) information on the organization's criteria by which his performance in the role is evaluated. Once the investment function is established, it will enable the individual to develop a strategy regarding how to cope with (accepting, rejecting, changing, neglecting, etc.) immediate demands of the environment.

(2)   Selection Schedule and Expectancy.   As Becker (1964) suggested, development is only possible by a committed action – the person must subordinate immediate situational interests to goals that lie outside the situation. However, to make commitment possible a person must be able to estimate the subjective probability or expectancy that commitment pays off. If he is skeptical about the outcome of commitment, it will be very difficult for him to subordinate interests that benefit him immediately to future goals. On the other hand, it becomes

necessary for the organization to establish an unambiguous schedule to make consistent decisions on whom to move, when, how, and at what speed (Schein, 1971). It is the establishment of this kind of schedule that enables the individual to formulate a clear expectancy about the outcomes of his commitment. Therefore, in addition to the condition that the individual knows how to behave for investing, it is necessary that he has unambiguous expectancy that achievement of a career target is a function of the level of investment.

The idea of promotion-from-within is a basis for formulating organizational policies on human resource utilization. A study conducted by Campbell and his associates (1970) reported that out of the organizations they selected, on the basis of their progressive policies on human resource development, almost all of the organizations (96 percent) believed in filling positions from within their own organization. In addition, the most frequent estimate reported by the executives and personnel people in the sample organizations was that at all levels of management, at least 90 to 95 percent of managers had come from either one of the following three internal sources: promotion from non-managerial jobs, promotion from lower level of managerial jobs, and lateral transfers. The authors cited the studies done by Megginson (1963), Pamplin (1959), and Newcomer (1955) which reported similar statistics about the utilization of internal managerial resources. However, the important question is how to administer the system of promotion-from-within. Campbell and his associates discussed three schedules of personnel selection, schedules based upon: (1) experience and seniority, (2) strict performance evaluation, and (3) the assessment center method. These three are not necessarily alternatives, but probably integral parts of the elaborate system for internal manpower selection.

Expectancy on attaining a career target and a goal may be determined by: (1) the degree of stringency in the evaluative and selection criteria of the organization, (2) the time required for reaching each successive stage of development, and (3) an individual's estimate of his potential for development, or "self-esteem" (Korman, 1967). The stringency and time factors will constitute the level of goal difficulty. It is known that the intermediate level of goal difficulty tends to motivate the individual most strongly toward attainment of the goal, while too easy and too difficult goals tend to be avoided as targets of commitment (Locke, 1968). This thesis suggests that the organization's schedule for selection requires a design, which avoids these two extreme situations: stringent selection after a long period of commitment (difficult goals that will be associated with low expectancy of success), and lenient selection within a short time period (easy goals with very high expectancy of success). Instead, the schedule may require a design with moderately stringent selection within a relatively short period of time. These features will produce a stimulating environment for career development in which equal chances of success and failure challenge the individual efforts, and failure for the first trial allows the success for the next. The self-esteem theory of career development (Korman, 1967) suggests that those who estimate their potentials high tend to have a higher expectancy of attaining difficult career targets than those who estimate their potential as low. This theory indicates that the choice of career targets may be a function of an individual's estimate of his career potential. However, an important question is to what extent the individual's estimate is correct. The individual may either underestimate or overestimate his abilities to grow. This question involves a cost of commitment, because it is an error in expectancy that induces a high cost of commitment (or noncommitment) for both the individual and the organization.

(3) Cost of Commitment. Decisions on commitment or noncommitment may depend on the relative costs, economic as well as psychological, involved in each decision. Expectancy that career development may be more prosperous in the organizations elsewhere will make commitment to the given organization more difficult than would otherwise be the case. However, the decision to change the organization, based on the above expectancy, involves costs arising from the type I error, i.e., costs that would be incurred by leaving, when staying with the organization is the right answer. In addition, to the extent one is involved in socio-cultural aspects of the organization, changing the organization incurs psychological costs for losing these aspects and having to adjust to a new social environment elsewhere. On the other hand, the decision to stay committed to career development in the given organization involves costs derived from the type II error: costs that would be incurred by not taking chances of changing the organization when the change actually pays off. Young mobile managers, as Jennings (1967) reported, may be highly sensitive to the type II error in their career decisions. Therefore, they become very active in searching for information on the job market, willing to take chances, and ready to move from one organization to another. Cosmopolitans may be more sensitive to the type II error than locals, probably because of the relatively high transferability of their investment from one organization to another. This indicates that for the highly professionalized people, investment in one organization can be transferred without discount, or with premium perhaps, to another organization, thus minimizing chances of the type I error associated with changes of the organization. On the other hand, the permanent employment system, or the rigid seniority tends to create an expectancy

that encourages an overestimation of the chances of making type I errors (or an underestimation of type II errors) along with the individual's emotional attachment to the system.

One of the most important problems for the organizational career development may be how to evaluate the costs of career decisions incurred by erroneous expectancy of one's development. It is likely that decisions to stay or leave, choice of targets, investments strategies, and commitment may be made based upon incorrect expectancy of chances for future development. The preceding discussion on expectancy suggests that frequent interaction between the individual and the organization is critical for both parties to come to share realistic expectancy on potentials for development. The interaction must be facilitated in such a manner that the individual is challenged by moderately demanding assignments rather frequently, followed by feedback on his peformance. This will enable the individual to formulate a realistic expectancy of his career progress. Since organizational career development requires commitment over a long period of time, it will be critical for the individual and the organization to share a realistic expectancy of the outcomes of commitment. Frequent interactions may enable each party to reach career decisions that will minimize the cost of commitment.

(4) *Individual's Learning and Human Capital Gains of the Organization.* As Mills (1975) emphasized, both the individual and the organization can be better off by accelerating the cyclical processes of career development. The development model displayed in Figure 1 indicates that facilitating an individual's learning at work must be one of the bases for an organization's programs of human resource development. To promote the process of learning, it is necessary that various training methods such as, coaching from supervisors, job rotation, in-company training courses, off-the-job courses and training programs, and so forth, are utilized systematically, in addition to encouraging self-development efforts of the individual. Training will be more effective when opportunities for learning occur in close connection with career progression (Schein, 1971). This implies that training programs need to be developed as an integral part of career design in the organization. Development of a career design buttressed by comprehensive training programs will make it possible for the organization to have flexible planning and utilization of human resources. On the other hand, this system will enable the individual to have a clear expectancy of the outcomes of commitment.

The "manpower chaos" (Campbell, et al., 1970) may imply a situation in which the career development system of the organization is not in equilibrium: one person's personal resources are overqualified while those of another are underqualified. Under this circumstance, the entire system of career development (training, performance evaluation, selection, etc.) may turn into mere lip-service, and the distribution of organizational resources may become a tool for internal politics or a part of the organizational rituals of status giving to reinforce loyalty. To avoid this situation, it is imperative that the organization establish a system-wide manpower development program, in which the various training methods are systematically utilized in order to minimize the gap between resource allocation and gains in human capital, which are valued by the organization.

5. Dynamics of Development: A Research Question

It is the purpose of the present study to explore why some individuals achieve a higher level of progress in the organization, while others do not. For example, a person may see clearly how to invest in his given role. He may have a high expectancy that he is going to achieve a career target by following the investment function he conceived, For this person, the commitment process may involve less cost, and role activities may provide good opportunities for learning. On the other hand, for another person role activities may involve a lot of ambiguity and conflict between what he wants to do, what he is expected to do, and what he is actually doing. He will have a poor expectancy of attaining his career target. Since commitment will be perceived as more and more costly for this person, he will decide to leave the organization, or may choose an easier target available in the organization. This example suggests that the organizational environment for career progress can become significantly different among individuals with respect to its capacity to allow investment, to provide expectancy of achieving a target, and to give opportunities for learning.

Dynamics in development may arise, because different organizational roles are under pressures of the environment, which demand a different set of role activities. For the individual in the process of career progress, his urgent problem is how to cope with pressures from the immediate environment for task performance. As discussed earlier, the environment is conceived of as a subset of the organization's resource system connected with the role of each individual. However, some components of the environment for a given person become a part of the environmental resources for another person, because of interdependent relationships among resources. For example, the personal resources of a person may be treated as a part of "manpower" by another person. Likewise, positional resources of a person may be of interest to another person, especially when the functional role interdependence becomes salient between the two. Therefore, a group of individuals (the *role-set* members; Katz and Kahn, 1964) will have strong interest in how each member in the set utilizes the resources of the common environment. This indicates that the role-set members will send their expectations to the focal person in the set regarding how he should perform tasks that involve utilization of resources of common interest. We call these expectations perceived by the focal person "environmental pressures."

For our career development model, it is critical that environmental pressures of a focal person in the process of progress should have a quality such that his coping behaviors generate outcomes consistent with the conditions for development specified earlier. However, the quality of the environment can be significantly different among individuals, because of the difference in assignment, and the composition of role-set members connected with the career role of each individual. In addition, some individuals may succeed in changing their work environment so that it will provide favorable conditions for their career development, while some others may fail to do so.

For our study, career development of newcomers in the organization is the focus of investigation. Given this unique sample of managers, the general research question stated in the beginning now can be specified as follows: what factors in the interrelationships between newcomers in the organization and their career environment will determine the level of their progress during the early periods for organizational career development? In the following section a set of propositions will be presented in order to explore this research question.

6. Determinants of Career Progress for the Newcomer in the Organizaton

For our study, the career progress of college graduates recruited by one of the large industrial organizations in Japan will be examined based on data collected over the first three years using a method of longitudinal investigation. A unique organizational control imposed by the Japanese organization upon the process of career progress of our newcomers gave us an excellent opportunity to study the career development phenomenon under a quasi-experimental setting. That is: (1) All newcomers sampled for our study were male college graduates fresh from school. They were considerably homogenous with respect to age and educational background. (2) They had no experience of formal employment prior to the recruitment. (3) All subjects were tested and selected as having potentials to fill middle and upper management positions within the sample organization. (4) Employment involved the idea of a lifetime relationship between the recruit and the organization. Therefore, it is assumed that all newcomers had expectations, at least at the point of employment, of pursuing their career goals within the given organization. (5) They went through the same training programs during the probationary period, and subsequently all of them were subject to supervision by the central personnel office with respect to their key career decisions. (6) All recruits started their career at the bottom level of the managerial hierarchy, but with different assignments depending upon differences in their educational background.

The employment conditions discussed above indicate that the initial state for career progress seems pretty well controlled. As Figure 1 illustrates, differences in the degree of career progress may occur because of differences among newcomers regarding how to cope with environmental pressures of the organization. For our study, it is assumed that the following three factors are relevant in explaining the differences in effectiveness of coping behaviors among newcomers: (a) ability factors, or potentials, (b) an attitude change after encountering the organization, especially development of negative attitudes toward a career role, and (c) the quality of leader-member relations. It is the major purpose of our study to evaluate the impact of the above factors upon the process of managerial career progress based upon the empirical data collected from one of the Japanese business organizations and its people. There exists a considerable volume of literature that suggests the possible impact of each factor upon the process of progress.

First, studies conducted using the assessment center method (Bray and Grant, 1966; Dunnette, 1971; Finkle, 1976) provide some evidence concerning the effect of personal resources of the individual upon progress. Bray and his associates (1966 and 1974) conducted a pioneering study in this field. In their study, a group of college graduates recruited by Bell Telephone Company went through a series of test sessions called the assessment center. The recruits' performance on each test was rated by the assessment staff members along the 25 psychological dimensions assumed to be predictive of a newcomer's progress in the organization. In addition, staff members rated the overall potential of each recruit based on all the test results. Then, the predictive validity of the overall ratings was tested using the level of managerial responsibility each recruit attained after eight years in the Bell System as a criterion outcome of managerial progress. It was found that the overall potential rated at the beginning of the recruit's career was predictive of the managerial levels attained after eight years. Moreover, the factor analysis conducted, based upon the 25 development variables, produced the following seven dimensions as responsible for defining the domain of personal resources of the individual: (1) administrative skills, (2) interpersonal skills, (3) control of feeling, (4) intellectual ability, (5) work-oriented motivation, (6) passivity, and (7) dependency. (The last two dimensions were found to have negative contributions to progress.)

Second, studies on organizational assimilation or socialization present an interesting story about the attitude change occurring with some newcomers during the very early stages of their career life. These studies reported that for the newcomers to the organization who are prone to an idealistic image of their job and career, the starting job and its environment are often perceived as too anemic to be creative, and the organization's practices for socialization are felt as pressing for obedience (Berlew and Hall, 1966; Bray, et al., 1974; Dunnette et al., 1973; Graen, et al., 1973; Graen, 1976; Porter and Steers, 1973; Schein, 1964). One of the results of this conflicting experience is the development of negative attitudes among newcomers toward their organization and career. For example, Schein (1964) emphasized that socializing practices of the organization, based upon a stereotyped image of the newcomer, are likely to create *disillusionment* on the part of the newcomer. This feeling depresses the newcomer's initiative toward progress, but solicits conforming or rebelling behaviors against the pressures for socialization (Schein, 1968 and 1971). Dunnette and his associates (1973) suggested that turnover in later phases of career development is more likely to occur among those who experienced severe disillusionment during the first year and resultant motivational withdrawal.

Third, a series of studies conducted by Graen and his associates (Dansereau, et al., 1975; Graen, 1976; Graen, et al., 1973) raised evidence to suggest an impact of leader-member relations upon the process of career progress. Using a longitudinal research method, these studies documented that the newcomer to the organization can start changing the environment for his career progress by acquiring interpersonal resources from his immediate supervisor. The study conducted by Dansereau and his associates (1975) reported that the newcomer may receive critical assistance from his supervisor through a resource-exchange relationship that they called "vertical exchange." The results of their study indicated that the quality of vertical exchange relations each newcomer experienced during early stages of his work life is predictive of the level of role development for the subsequent time periods. They found that the high exchange newcomers also experienced higher level leadership support and attention, lower dyadic problems, more satisfaction with their jobs, and a pattern of role behaviors preferred by the supervisor, compared to those who experienced a low exchange relationship with their supervisors during the period for role making within the organization. This *role making* proposition suggests that the newcomer is allowed to exploit his environment in order to acquire the extra resources necessary to enrich the content of his role. According to the vertical exchange model, the high quality leader-member relation requires an exchange of critical services between the newcomer and his supervisor in such a manner that the newcomer's performance helps the leader achieve the goals of his work unit, and the leader's support in turn gives extra resources to the newcomer to develop his investment and learning of the role.

In summary, predictions of career progress based on three factors discussed above (i.e., potentials, attitude change, and leader-member relations) are called here, the *assessment center hypothesis*, the *disillusionment hypothesis*, and the *role making hypothesis*. Part I of this thesis consists of examinations of each hypothesis in more detail based on the survey of relevant literature. Then, Part II will be devoted to the empirical testing of the three hypotheses and other alternative ones using the data collected for our longitudinal investigation on the process of managerial career progress within one of the Japanese organizations.

Chapter II

The Assessment Center Approach

The assessment center approach is based on the assumption that individuals have different qualities of personal resources with which they grow in the organization. The assessment center approach called this quality of personal resources, "potential," of the individual. This approach also assumes that the effect of environmental factors upon progress is either random or benign to the potential of the individual throughout the course of career development. For this approach, potential of the individual assessed at the start of the career is regarded as the single most reliable predictor of the managerial progress during a given period of time for career development. Therefore, assessing individual potentials accurately using multiple testing methods and multiple assessors becomes the highlight for this approach. In this chapter, the "management progress study" conducted at AT&T (Bray and Grant, 1966; Bray, et. al., 1974) will be discussed first. The AT&T study constitutes a milestone in the area of managerial career development studies. The study not only employed the assessment center method systematically as a model for predicting managerial progress of the newcomer at AT&T, but also proposed a new paradigm of research in the area of managerial progress studies. Following the discussion on the AT&T study, other assessment center studies that followed the AT&T experiment will be discussed with an emphasis upon reliability of the method, its predictive validity, and methodological problems associated with the assessment center approach.

I. The Management Progress Study at AT&T

1. Design of the Research

In 1956, a pioneering study on the process of managerial development was begun at the Bell Telephone Companies at AT&T focusing upon young male employees selected as candidates for middle and upper management. A longitudinal investigation named a Management Progress Study called for monitoring, over the eight-year period, the process of development of the 274 new recruits with college degrees and 174 non-college, lower-level managers who had been employed by the Bell

System. The purpose of the study was to identify critical career events that will determine the success or failure in business careers of young managers during their formative years in the organization. The following four basic research questions were asked (Bray, et al., 1974, 4–5).

1. What significant changes will take place in men as their lives develop in a business context?
2. Conversely, are there changes we might expect or desire that do not occur?
3. What are the causes of these changes or stabilities? More particularly, what are the effects of company climate, policies, and practices?
4. How accurately can progress in management be predicted? What are the important indicators and how are they best measured?

The design of research to explore the above questions consisted of two parts: (1) evaluating managerial potential of the new recruits based upon the assessment center method, and (2) intensive interviews during the research period with personnel of the company, who were in charge of supervising the new recruits at each department. To serve the first part of the research, a list of management progress variables indicating qualities important in managerial success were developed based upon the research materials and information from personnel executives inside the Bell System. The following 25 variables were finally selected as critical dimensions of managerial success and were measured by the assessment center method:

1. Organizing and planning
2. Decision making
3. Creativity
4. Human relations skills
5. Behavioral flexibility
6. Personal impact
7. Tolerance of uncertainty
8. Resistance to stress
9. Scholastic aptitude
10. Range of interest
11. Inner work standards
12. Primacy of work
13. Oral communication skills
14. Perception of social cues
15. Self-objectivity
16. Energy
17. Realism of expectations

18. Bell System value orientation
19. Social objectivity
20. Need for advancement
21. Ability to delay gratification
22. Need for superior approval
23. Need for peer approval
24. Goal flexibility
25. Need for security

The assessment center method involved multiple testing methods for obtaining information to rate each participant on the progress variables listed above. The AT&T assessment center administered the following test batteries with the help of professional assessment staff members. For further details on tests and their administration, see: Bray and Grant, 1966; Bray, et al., 1974; Grant, et al., 1967; Grant and Bray, 1969.

Interview: A two-hour interview was conducted with each recruit. The interview procedures were loosely structured. Discussions commonly involved such topics as the subject's educational background, reasons for joining the Bell System, expectations for the future, religious and political interests, and hobbies. The interviewer summarized his notes and wrote reports for each interviewee.

In-basket: The subject was given three hours in which he reviewed the materials in the "basket" which a telephone company manager might expect to find (letters, notes, telephone messages, reports, etc.). He was asked to take appropriate action on each item. Then, discussions were conducted concerning his approach to the managerial tasks: his evaluation on the general organizational situation as perceived through materials, priorities and inter-relationships among decisions, his reasons for taking particular actions or lack of actions, and his view on supervisors, peers and subordinates inferred from the material.

Manufacturing problems: A small business game in which the participants assumed the roles of partners in an enterprise manufacturing toys was played by a small group of subjects. They were required to buy parts and sell finished products under fluctuating market conditions to make profit and maintain inventories. Group decisions were necessary and participation of each subject was observed and evaluated by two assessment staff members.

Group discussion: Participants were instructed to assume the role of managers each having a foreman, who was qualified for promotion. Participants were given five minutes to speak on behalf of the candidate they endorsed regarding his promotability based upon information on his merit and demerit handed out five minutes before the speech. After the presentation, participants were required to discuss the hypothetical foremen and to reach a group decision regarding their promotions.

Projective tests: Various projective techniques were employed: Rotter Incomplete Sentences Blank, Bell Incomplete Sentences Tests, and Thematic Apperception Test.

Paper and pencil tests: (1) School and College Ability Test, (2) A Test of Critical Thinking in Social Studies, (3) Contemporary Affairs Test, (4) Edwards Personal Preference Schedule, (5) The Guilford-Martin Inventory of Factors, (6) Opinion Questionnaire, Form B, and (7) Survey of Attitudes Toward Life.

Miscellaneous: Personal history questionnaire, and short autobiographical essay.

On the first week of employment, each recruit went through the 3-1/2 day assessment session to respond to all test batteries discussed above. Reports on recruits' performance on each test were prepared by the professional staff members (psychologists) either in a written form or by ratings based on the scoring keys imbedded in each test. On the basis of these reports, staff members rated each subject, using the 25 management progress variables, on a five-point scale. After the subjects had been rated, staff members judged overall potential of each recruit regarding the likelihood of his achieving middle management (District Manager) in ten years or less within the Bell Telephone Company. Staff prediction based upon the potential ratings indicated that 40 percent of the recruits had middle management potential, 48 percent did not, and the remaining 12 percent were questionable.

2. Factor Analysis of the Development Variables

To identify what aspects of personal resources measured by the assessment center contributed to defining the dimensions for predicting managerial progress, the 25 development variables were subjected to factor analysis for a hierarchical solution (Bray and Grant, 1966). The analysis produced seven factors following after one general factor. Table 1 displays a list of factors and their components, together with test batteries that showed significant relationships with each factor in terms of correlation coefficients. Table 1 indicates that there may exist two broad areas in which personal resources of the individual can be evaluated: (1) skills and abilities (administrative skills, interpersonal skills, intellectual ability and control of feeling), and (2) motivation (work-orientation, need for advancement, etc.). In addition, correlation coefficients between the factors and assessment methods suggested that information derived from the various situational tests (In-basket, Group Discussion, and Manufacturing Problem) had the most significant influence upon staff ratings, while the information derived from the paper-and-pencil tests were found to have limited influence upon ratings.

Table 1

Factors for the Development Variables and Their Correlation with the Test Methods

Factor	Content and Correlation with the Method
I. General Effectiveness:	Overall staff prediction, decision making, organizing and planning, creativity, need for advancement, resistance to stress, human relations skill. (Manufacturing Problem .67)
II. Administrative Skills:	Organizing and planning, decision making. (In-basket .76; Group Discussion .48)
III. Interpersonal Skills:	Human relations skills, behavioral flexibility, personal impact. (In-basket .45)
IV. Control of Feelings:	Tolerance of uncertainty, resistance to stress. (Group Discussion .47)
V. Intellectual Ability:	Scholastic aptitude, range of interest. (Mental Ability Test .79).
VI. Work-oriented Motivation:	Primacy of work, inner work standard. (Group Discussion .45; In-basket .44)
VII. Passivity:	Ability to delay gratification, need for security, need for advancement. (Group Discussion -.39; Personality measure on activity level -.43)
VIII. Dependency:	Need for superior approval, need for peer approval, goal flexibility. (Personality measure on achievement -.29)

Adapted from Campbell, J.P., et al. *Managerial Behavior, Performance, and Effectiveness,* pp. 219, 220, and 221. Copyright © 1970 by McGraw-Hill Book Company. Used with the permission of the publisher.

3. Early Careers of New Recruits to the Organization

Bray and his associates (1974) reported the organizational situations for career development of the newcomer to the Bell Telephone Companies as follows.   After the assessment was over, recruits left the assessment center to start their jobs in one of the Bell Companies, which participated in the management progress study (Chesapeake and Potomac, Michigan, Mountain, Northwestern, and Pennsylvania).   Each telephone company was organized functionally into the department (plant, traffic, commercial, engineering, accounting, etc.) with Department Head (the fifth management level) at the top, then down to Division Head (the fourth level), and District Manager (the third level), which is the bottom rung of middle management.   Specific programs of orientation and training varied from location to location.   But in common, the orientation process involved a combination of interview, formal sessions, and on-the-job discussions.   Bray and his associates reported that most of the training programs were extensive: trainees actually worked in a number of non-management assignments, were rotated, and went through lectures and extensive reading assignments.

When a recruit started his job, he became a member of the first level management.   According to the authors the Bell System intent was that the college recruits in the same cohort as the men in the study would reach the third, District level of management within ten years of the time of employment.   This goal was almost in the class of a company dogma, even though much evidence existed that it had been approximated.   By the end of the eight years covered by the management progress study, the original college group of 274 had dropped to 167 due to terminations and deaths.   It was found that nearly all men who were still with the Bell System remained on duty with their original telephone companies.   However, more than half of the recruits (57 percent) had changed departments at least once.   Bray and his associates noted that the shifts of department were seldom made with the purpose of providing developmental opportunities for the recruit through job rotation.   They usually took place because of the needs of the business, or occasionally because of the fact that the recruit was not "making it" in one department and it was thought he might be more successful elsewhere.   Changes of job within a department, however, were made for the purpose of development.   The plan was that a recruit would develop and prove himself in one department before being promoted to the District level; an interdepartmental move for further development was regarded as appropriate after the third level of management was reached.   Survival and progress in middle management after eight years varied not only by company but also by department to which the recruit was originally assigned. Table 2 shows that for college graduates the highest rate of progress occurred in the accounting department. Plant and engineering showed lower rates of progress, but there was a large difference in the termination rates between the two. Of the 12 men who had started with one of the "other" departments, nearly all had left. Bray and his associates suggested that in addition to the company and department differences, the organizational context of the job to which the recruit was assigned also had a strong impact upon the career progress of the recruit. The effect of environmental factors upon progress, documented by the AT&T study, will be discussed later.

4. Determinants of Progress

To identify which factors in the management development variables were most responsible for determining managerial career progress, correlation coefficients were computed between the level of managerial responsibility each recruit attained in eight years and the development variables rated at the assessment center at the point of employment. Table 3 displays a summary of the results. In Table 3, figures shown in the first column indicate correlation coefficients between assessment variables and the overall potential ratings by the staff members (the concurrent study), while those in the second column indicate correlations between the assessment variables and the level of managerial responsibility each recruit attained in eight years at AT&T (the predictive study). Results of the concurrent study suggest that to the extent the recruit is rated highly by the assessment staff members with respect to skills (administrative and interpersonal), abilities (intellectual ability and control of feelings), and motivation to work and advance (including low passivity and dependency), he is more likely to be judged as having a high potential of career success in the organization. Likewise, the predictive study shown on the second column indicates that the outcomes of career development after eight years can be predicted by the same sets of variables as those for the concurrent study. Although the predictive correlations have shown considerable "shrinkage" compared to the concurrent ones, most of the coefficients were found to be statistically significant. In addition, it was noted that the pattern of correlations looked quite similar between the two studies. Bray and his associates tested the similarity of patterns of correlations between the two columns based upon the 25 assessment variables. They transformed 50 correlation coefficients (25 for concurrent and another 25 for predictive studies) into Z scores to calculate a product-moment correlation between the two. The similarity between the two correlation profiles was found to be very high ($r = .94$). In addition to the managerial level, salary data for each recruit was collected as the

Table 2

Termination and Progress of College Graduates
by Department at Original Assignment

Original Department	Number of Recruits Original Group	Remainder Group	Percent Terminated	Percent Promoted Original Group	Remainder Group
Plant	62	32	48	15	28
Commercial	58	32	45	26	47
Traffic	51	32	37	26	41
Engineering	55	46	16	20	24
Accounting	33	24	27	36	50
Other	12	1	92	8	100
Total	271	167	38%	23%	37%

Source: Bray, D.W., et al., *Formative Years in Business: A Long-term AT&T Study of Managerial Lives*, p. 65, Table 9. Copyright © 1974 by John Wiley & Sons. Used with the permission of the publisher.

Table 3

Correlation Between Assessment Variable Ratings and Overall Staff Ratings and Management Level at Reassessment

Factor and its Component	Overall Assessment Rating* (N = 207)	Level at Reassessment** (N = 123)
Administrative Skills		
Organization and Planning	.61	.28
Decision making	.59	.18
Interpersonal Skills		
Human relations skills	.66	.32
Behavioral flexibility	.63	.21
Personal impact	.57	.15
Control of Feelings		
Tolerance of uncertainty	.39	.30
Resistance to stress	.51	.31
Intellectual Ability		
Scholastic aptitude	.46	.19
Range of interest	.45	.23
Work-Oriented Motivation		
Primacy of work	.48	.18
Inner work standard	.46	.21
Passivity		
Ability to delay gratification	-.30	-.19
Need for security	-.32	-.20
Need for advancement	.60	.31
Dependency		
Need for superior approval	-.18	-.14
Need for peer approval	-.16	-.17
Goal flexibility	-.13	-.18
Salary progress***	.48	—

*rs .14 or higher p < .05;   .18 or higher p < .01
**rs .18 or higher p < .05;   .23 or higher p < .01.
***Median value based on correlations within company subgroups.

Adapted from Bray, D.W., et al. *Formative Years in Business: A Long-term AT&T Study of Managerial Lives*, p.77, Table 15. Copyright © 1974 by John Wiley & Sons. Used with the permission of the publisher.

second criterion measure of managerial progress. Correlation coefficients between potential judgment and the salary level at the time of reassessment were calculated for each telephone company separately. A correlation coefficient shown in the last row of Table 3 indicates that the overall staff judgment also predicted the recruit's salary level after eight years of business experience (median correlation, $r = .48$).

Relationship between the overall potential judged at the assessment center and the managerial level attained by the time of reassessment was further examined in terms of differences in the success ratio between the two potential groups. It was found that out of the 61 college recruits who were predicted as having the potential to reach the District manager level in less than ten years, 39 (64 percent) were reported to have actually realized the prediction. On the other hand, the ratio for those who were judged as failing to reach middle management was found to be significantly lower (32 percent, or 20 out of the 62 recruits) compared to the high potential group ($X^2 = 12.36$; $p < .001$). Bray and his associates pointed out that when we consider the fact that this result was obtained in spite of the effects of different rates of progress in different companies and departments (see Table 2), the accuracy of prediction is even more impressive. In addition, the authors emphasized that during the period of research, information on the subject's performance at the assessment center was kept confidential. Therefore, they concluded there was no chance of contamination of criterion outcomes by the assessment results.

The annual interview conducted with superiors of the recruits as a second part of the research provided data to examine the effect of the work environment upon progress. The annual interview protocols were rated along scoring keys developed for assessing environmental conditions each recruit encountered at his work place during the period of research. Table 4 displays correlation coefficients between the environmental conditions evaluated over the eight years and management level each recruit achieved by the time of reassessment. Table 4 indicates that aspects of work environment such as job challenge, responsibility, autonomy in assignments, and leadership contributed significantly to the development of newcomers during early stages of their managerial career. To examine the effect of environmental factors in a more straightforward manner, the four key aspects shown in Table 4, i.e., achievement models of bosses, job stimulation and challenge, supervisory responsibility, and unstructured assignments, were combined into a single composite scale called *job challenge*. Then, the recruits were trichotomized based on this combined scale into high, moderate, and low job challenge groups. It was found that out of the 64 recruits who were classified High on the composite job challenge scale, 59 percent of them (the 38 recruits)

Table 4

Correlations Between Aspects of Work Environment and Management Level at Reassessment

Factor	Correlation Coefficient (N = 155)
Job stimulation and challenge	.44*
Supervisory responsibility	.34*
Structure versus unstructured assignments	.48*
Objective stress of assignments	.30*
Working alone versus working in groups	-.08
Morale of groups	.08
Supervision from bosses	.37*
Achievement models of bosses	.43*

*$p < .01$

Source: Bray, D.W., et al. *Formative Years in Business: A Long-term AT&T Study of Managerial Lives,* p. 71, Table 11. Copyright © 1974 by John Wiley & Sons. Used with the permission of the publisher.

actually attained the District level in eight years, whereas for groups classified as Moderate (64 recruits) and Low (39 recruits), the percentages of attaining the District level were found much lower; 31 and 8 percent respectively.

5. Interaction Between Potential and Job Challenge

The AT&T study disclosed two important dimensions as having significant causal effects upon managerial progress: (1) potential of the individual and (2) job challenge.   The personal resources of the individual and environmental conditions may function independently or interdependently with each other in determining managerial progress, depending upon the pattern of interaction between the two.   For example, it is quite likely that if a person is capable and does well on one job, chances that his next job will become more challenging and important may be much higher than otherwise would be the case. On the other hand, job challenge and potential can be two independent factors in determining the level of managerial progress. To examine the pattern of interaction between the two factors, subjects were classified into a three (High, Moderate, and Low challenge) by two (High and Low potential) crosstabulation table.   Then, success ratios were compared among the subgroups derived from the crosstabulation. Table 5 was developed for the purpose of the present discussion based on the results obtained by Bray and his associates in their crosstabulation study. Table 5 displays the success ratio for the District level of management based upon the four different subgroups: High potential and High challenge (HH Group), High potential and Moderate plus Low challenge (HL Group), Low Potential and High challenge (LH Group), and Low potential and Moderate plus Low challenge (LL Group). Examination of success ratios indicates that both potential and job challenge factors have significant independent effects upon progress. However, job challenge seems to have a stronger effect on progress than potential: out of the 51 subjects who had high job challenge, 71 percent of them actually attained the middle management level regardless of their predicted potentials, but high potential alone could bring only 64 percent of subjects to the same managerial level. This was caused by the fact that the situation for progress becomes much better where the subject may lack potential but is able to experience high job challenge (61 percent of success), than where he has high potential but happens to be in a mediocre job challenge position (50 percent of success). In addition, Table 5 displays a particular pattern of interaction: the promotion ratio into the middle management level becomes the highest for the HH group (76 percent), and in contrast the ratio becomes the lowest for the LL group (20

Table 5

Number and Percentage of Subjects who Achieved Middle Management Level Based upon the Potential and Job Challenge Groups

Potential	Job Challenge		Row Sum
	High	Moderate & Low	
Predicted to reach middle management	76% (25/33)	50% (14/28)	64% (39/61)
Predicted to fail to reach middle management	61% (11/18)	20% (9/44)	32% (20/62)
Column sum	71% (36/51)	32% (23/72)	48% (59/123)

Figures in parentheses indicate number of subjects promoted out of each subgroup entries.

Adapted from Bray, D.W., et al. *Formative Years in Business: A Long-term AT&T Study of Managerial Lives*, p. 75, Table 14. Copyright © 1974 by John Wiley & Sons. Used with the permission of the publisher.

percent).   On the other hand, the probability of success remains at a considerably high level for both the HL and LH groups (61 and 50 percent respectively).   This pattern of group differences may suggest the existence of a *compensatory* relationship between the potential and the job challenge factors.   That is, if either high potential or high job challenge is associated with the recruit, the loss in either one of the factors can be compensated by the positive effect of the other one. Absence of both factors (low potential combined with a less challenging environment) constitutes the worst situation for managerial progress, but as long as either high potential or high challenge (or preferably both) is present, the situation for career development seems to be all right for the newcomer.   A conclusion reached by Bray and his colleagues seems to endorse our interpretation of the combined effect between the potential and the job challenge factors.   They stated that,

> Very broadly, progress in an organization can be conceived of as a product of the characteristics of the employee as these interact with opportunities provided by the organization.   The employee's characteristics include his abilities and knowledge, his motivation, and his impact on others.   Opportunity involves not merely the number of job openings at higher levels, but chances to display ability and to develop, characteristics of supervisors, methods used to determine promotability, and organizational climate (Bray, et al., 1974, 68).

In summary, the AT&T management progress study produced evidence that the multiple assessment methods enable us to identify recruits' potentials for managerial career progress with the organization. Especially, a variety of situational tests (In-basket, Manufacturing Problems, and Group Discussions) provided critical information to estimate the recruit's potential with respect to his skills, abilities, and motivational qualities for progress.   Also, it was found that the staff judgment may have a strong concurrent validity, and a relatively weak but significant predictive validity on the outcomes of management progress.   Bray and Grant (1966) computed a partial correlation coefficient between the staff prediction and the salary level at the time of reassessment holding the effect of the paper-and-pencil tests constant. The result indicated that a substantial portion of criterion variance was left to be explained by the staff judgment.   Based on this evidence, they concluded that the staff judgement did contribute to predicting the level of managerial progress of the new recruit at AT&T during their formative years in business.   In addition, the study produced evidence that the environmental conditions within the organization summarized as "job challenge" are also responsible for predicting the level of management progress.   Environmental factors such as job stimulation and challenge, supervisory responsibilities, unstructured assignments, and achievement models of bosses, were found to be critical when attempting to account for the variance in managerial levels reached by the recruits in their first eight years in the Bell System. Examination of the interaction effect between potential and job challenge factors indicated that the High-challenge and High-potential groups produced the best yield in managerial progress, while the Low-challenge and Low-potential groups yielded the worst. In other situations, the effects were found complementary for progress.

II. The Assessment Center Studies

In response to the AT&T experiment (Bray, et al., 1974), assessment centers were established at Standard Oil of Ohio (Thomson, 1970), IBM (Greenwood and McNamara, 1967; Hinrichs, 1969; Wollowich and McNamara, 1969), Sears (Bentz, 1971), and in many other companies and government agencies. Finkle (1976) reported that over 1,000 organizations were found to be adopting the assessment center method for a number of purposes: promotion decisions, identification of potentials, training and development purposes, developing of assessors and assessment batteries, and so forth. Bender (1973) presented a report of his survey on operational features of the established assessment center method. He found that the companies sampled for his survey were using the following methods as primary evaluation devices: In-basket (91 percent of respondents), Business Games (88 percent), Leaderless Discussions (100 percent), Films (15 percent), Video Tapes (44 percent), and Psychological Tests (61 percent). Also he reported that about 70 percent of the companies had their assessment devices developed locally, while the rest of them were purchased externally. As Finkle (1976) suggested, the major function of operating assessment centers is to provide management with a set of standardized information which helps them make personnel decisions The Worbois study (1975) indicates that one of the typical forms of the "institutionalized" assessment center may look like the following.

1. Purpose: Identification of non-supervisory personnel with potential for supervision.
2. Twelve people participate in eight activities during a one-day workshop (Interview, Management Questionnaire, In-basket, Luncheon, Film Case Discussion, Management Decision Game, Selection-Simulation, Self-Evaluation.)
3. A chairman and four third- and fourth-line supervisors observe the participants' behavior during the day's activities.
4. The chairman and the four management assessors evaluate the performance of the twelve participants during the next two days.

5. Feedback is provided to the participants and the organization.
6. Evaluations include: (a) overall potential, (b) potential level of supervision, and (c) separate evaluations of each of the twelve abilities upon which assessment is made.

As Finkle (1976) and Bender (1973) suggested, despite some common characteristics in methods, differences in the emphasis and the purpose allow a large variation in the operating features of the assessment center programs. Next, we will discuss some basic problems associated with the assessment center method as a model for the managerial progress study.

1. Reliability of the Method

Bray and Grant (1966) stated that the success of assessment depends largely upon the competence of assessors. For the AT&T assessment methods, professionally trained staff members (the psychologists) administered the entire procedure. However, a large volume of evidence exists suggesting that incumbent managers trained by professionals can perform reliable assessment (McConnel and Parker, 1972; Worbois, 1975; Hardesty and Jones, 1968; Thomson, 1970; Hinrichs, 1969; Greenwood and McNamara, 1967; Wollowich and McNamara, 1969; Bray and Campbell, 1968). For example, in the IBM program, Greenwood and McNamara (1967) employed a team of four assessors (combinations of psychologists, sociologists, and line managers who had basic training in assessment techniques) for evaluating 288 participants from six different IBM divisions. The 432 reliability coefficients were calculated based on different tests and different combinations of assessors, with a median reliability coefficient of .74 for overall ratings and .76 for overall rankings on assessee's potential. These coefficients were found slightly higher than those derived from the AT&T study based on all professional assessors (i.e., .75 for both rating and ranking scales). Greenwood and McNamara reported that no systematic differences were observed with respect to the degree of agreeing with potential rating among any combination of assessors. This finding suggests that the reliability of the rating scales will not be affected seriously by non-professional assessors if they are selected and trained properly. Likewise, for the SOHIO program Thomson (1969) reported much higher interrater agreement between managers and psychologists. In his study, coefficients ranges from .73 to .93 with a median coefficient of .85.

In many studies, reliability estimates were calculated for each method separately, e.g., for interview (Grant and Bray, 1969; Glaser, Schwarz, and Flanagan, 1958; Prien, 1962), situational tests (Bray and Grant, 1966; Greenwood and McNamara, 1967), and projective tests

(Grant and Katkovsky, 1967; Hogue, Otis and Prien, 1962). Results of these studies indicate that a large variation in reliability coefficients may be inevitable among the different methods of assessment. For example, Glaser and his associates (1958) obtained satisfactory reliability estimates for the interview and the group discussion problem (.65 and .74 respectively), however, for the role-playing exercise, the estimate was found damagingly low (.34). In the AT&T study, Bray and Grant (1966) obtained the .75 interrater agreement for the group discussion using overall rating scales, but .60 for the manufacturing problems. Based on a more extensive literature review, Dunnette (1971) concluded that in general the internal analysis of data generated from multiple assessment programs tended to show that staff members' ratings were of acceptable reliability.

2. Predictive Validity

An application of the multiple assessment method as a model for the managerial progress study is directed toward establishing the *predictive* validity of the method. Very often, however, reports on the successful assessment center program are made based only upon the *concurrent* validity tests (Laurent, 1970; McConnel and Parker, 1972; Worbois, 1975). Table 6 displays a summary of the assessment center studies which are reported as an attempt to test the predictive validity of the methods. Validity coefficients shown in Table 6 represent correlation coefficients between the staff members' judgments on the potential of the assessees at the assessment center and the success criteria measured after a certain lapse of time for each assessee as outcomes of career progress within the organization. Since all of these studies were oriented toward predicting outcomes, it is reported that no feedback of assessment information was made to either management or to the participants in order to avoid criterion contamination. In Table 6, validity coefficients range from .10 to .64. First, an examination predictive validity for each study seems to indicate that the coefficients may partly be a function of length of time involved in prediction. For example, studies reported by Albrecht (involving 1 year) and Thomson (2-1/4 years), which were compared to other studies that required longer time intervals, tended to indicate that the shorter the time interval, the higher the predictive validity. However, it must be noted, as a second point, that both studies are also characterized by homogeneity of participants with respect to the nature of their jobs, i.e., professionals and technicians (Thomson) and marketing managers (Albrecht). For other studies, job types of participants tend to be diverse. This is particularly true for Dicken and Black's study that produced mixed results. Thus, it may be noted that

Table 6

Summary of Predictive Studies

Author	Sample	Predictor	Criterion	Time	Result
Bray and Grant, 1966	AT&T college recruits N=271	Psychologists' judgment on over-all potential	Salary Level	8 years	r=.48 (median)
Wollowick and McNamara, 1969	94 IBM lower, middle managers	Psychologists' judgment on over-all potential	Level of Management	3 years	r=.37
Thomson, 1970	71 pro's and tech's in SOHIO	Observers' judgment on over-all potential	Supervisor's rating on over-all potential	2-1/4 years	r=.64
Albrecht, et al., 1964	31 newly assigned district marketing managers	1. Forecasting-budgeting 2. Sales 3. Interpersonal 4. Combined	Ranking by managers and peers combined on same four measures	1 year	1. r=.49 2. r=.58 3. r=.43 4. r=.46
Dicken and Black, 1965	31 first level supervisors from mfg. firm & 26 officials from insurance firm	Psychologists' judgment on over-all potential using psychometric data only	1. Ratings 2. Salary 3. Job level	3-1/2 years for mfg. 7 years for ins.	Mfg. / Ins. 1. r=.51 / .31 2. r=.58 / .28 3. r=.20 / .10

predicting relatively short-term career outcomes based on subjects with homogeneous backgrounds tends to produce higher validity coefficients. However, available data are too small to make any conclusive statement as to what causes the variation in validity coefficients for the assessment center method.

3. Methodological Problems as a Model for Managerial Progress

It is important to note that the original research design used for the management progress study at AT&T was built upon the following two considerations: (1) exploring the *process* of development by monitoring the change over time, and (2) validating development variables based upon the assessment center method. However, the richness of the original AT&T themes were unfortunately not fully inherited by the flourishing assessment center studies that followed after the pioneering study. That is, most of the institutionalized assessment centers abandoned the first theme of the AT&T study and concentrated upon the second, to address itself to a very simplified perspective for the study of managerial progress. The simplification was made possible by adopting the following two assumptions on development. The first one is on the idiosyncratic nature of managerial progress. This assumption allows the assessment center approach to interpret progress as a variation of individual traits expressed over a certain period of time. The other assumption for the assessment center approach has to do with the effect of the work environment upon career progress. For this approach the career environment is seen as a sort of "black-box" in which the effects of environmental factors are considered to be either benign or orthogonal to the hypothesized relationship between the potential and the criterion outcomes. Based on these two assumptions, the assessment center approach resorts to undertaking a simple two-variable framework of prediction: predictor traits versus criterion outcomes. Thus, the research and practice based on the assessment center method were given the rationale to pursue as high predictive coefficients as possible as evidence for successful managerial development programs. Wallace expressed a concern about this simplified view of the managerial progress. He stated that:

> [This trend] is forcing us to employ criteria which may be deceptively predictable, dangerously reinforcing of the status quo, and demonstrably inappropriate to some of the broader social issues with which management in government and industry is confronted (Wallace, 1974, 397).

We will have to ask ourselves how high the validity should be. Should it be .10, .50, or .90, and why? What does a high or low validity coefficient mean to the organization and its people? Prediction may face a dilemma: if the predictive coefficient is low, then validity of the method must be questioned, but if it becomes too high, again the "true" predictive validity may be questioned on the ground that a systematic "method bias" might have been involved in the prediction procedures. Moreover, the assessment center method would face the traditional, "criterion problems" (Campbell, et al., 1970; Dunnette and Kirchner, 1958; Ghiselli and Haire, 1960; Guion, 1976, 1965 and 1961; Korman, 1968; Smith, 1976; Thorndike, 1949). For example, Korman (1968) and Dunnette (1963) criticized the nature of criteria used for the assessment center approach. Korman pointed out that the criteria used as measures of career outcomes for the assessment center are often factorially complex in a sense that the concrete behaviors relevant to the attainment of such criterion outcomes are hard to identify. Korman stated that,

> It is apparent that such administrative criteria as ratings, level changes, salary, etc., cannot be considered psychologically meaningful behaviors in and of themselves, but rather must be thought of factorially complex in nature, with their factorial composition varying over time and as a function of variety of variables too numerous to mention here. . . . It would seem to follow, then, that attempting to predict such criteria is a difficult matter since, (a) the behaviors to be predicted are unknown, and (b) the relevant behaviors change over time (Korman, 1968, 316).

Smith (1976) emphasized the multidimensional character of criteria. Instead of quest for the "ultimate criteria" (Thorndike, 1949), she proposed a three-dimensional system to classify and to relate different types of criteria by focusing upon: (1) the time-span to be covered, (2) the specificity desired, and (3) the closeness to organizational goals. This classificatory system indicated a hierarchical relationship among criterion measures, in which the outcome measures can be ordered and related along a "hard-to-soft" continuum (Smith, 1976). The criterion problems associated with the assessment center method can be examined based on the framework proposed by Smith.

(1) *The Time-Span to be Covered and Interpretation of a Time Factor.*   The managerial development study typically involves a longitudinal investigation of the process of the recruits' changes over time. The thrust of a longitudinal study is that information derived from the process enables us to understand what goes on during the period of development. Moreover, knowledge about the process provides us with the practical tools to manage the process of change toward attainment of more desired outcomes, after the initial conditions for development are given.   The assessment center method does involve a time factor. However, it may not be called a longitudinal study in the true sense of

the meaning as discussed above, because the assessment center approach lacks interest in what is involved during the period between the initial assessment and reassessment. Reassessment tends to be a mere "follow-up" study to see the end results, and processes are considered as uneventful passages of time.

A study conducted by Ghiselli and Haire (1960) indicates that the knowledge of processes is critical in predicting the end results. They reported an interesting result in that what they called a "dynamic dimensionality" of the criteria involved in prediction over time. That is, it was possible for them to predict the first three weeks of performance by one battery and the last three weeks by the other, but it was not possible to predict both with the same battery. Ghiselli (1956) reported another dynamic example. He found that different individuals can achieve an end, or a "state," of the same value by different combinations of behaviors. This unique phenomenon can be labelled as an *equifinality* of the developmental processes. Dynamic relationships between predictors and criteria as discussed above can be best studied by longitudinal research designed to document the process of change over time. The question involved here is not how long should be the time period covered by the study – a week, a month, a year, or ten years? But the question is how to interpret the physical length of time, and how to document it as a sequence of meaningful events that give rise to the emergency of criterion outcomes over time.

(2) *Specificity-Generality.* As Table 6 indicates, criteria used for the assessment center method are usually very general with a marked contrast to its specificity in testing methods. One way to introduce more specificity to the criterion measurement will be to apply multiple methods to the evaluation of outcomes of development (Campbell and Fiske, 1959; Lawler, 1967). Worbois (1975) reported results derived from one such attempt. In his study, "external" predictor judgments made by the assessment center method were evaluated against the "internal" criteria rated by the incumbent supervisors at on-the-job situations. Three kinds of internal criterion scales were used: (1) specific behavioral items which had been used in the sample company, (2) the twelve ability scales used in the assessment center but now rated by the immediate supervisor of each assessee, and (3) overall ratings by supervisors. Worbois reported that on a concurrent basis, correlation coefficients between the external and internal ratings ranged from .47 to .07 showing a generally acceptable intercorrelation pattern between the two sets of ratings. Worbois emphasized that potential ratings by the assessment center should be predictive of "whatever" makes up successful performance of the assessee on the job. The Worbois study would be of

much interest if the internal, multiple criterion measurement were repeated over time for the predictive study, together with the evaluation of other behavioral and environmental variables assumed to be predictive of the outcomes of career development.

(3) *Closeness to Organizational Goals.* Guion (1961) proposed the following five steps as critical for the systematic attempt of criterion development. Briefly, these steps are: (1) analyzing job and organizational needs, (2) developing measures of actual behavior relevant to the needs, (3) identifying criterion dimensions by factor analysis, (4) testing reliability and construct validity, and (5) testing predictive validity against each predictor. Steps (1) and (2) specified by Guion may correspond to the criticism made by Wallace (1974): needs of the individual and the organization may change over time, but criteria chosen for the assessment center approach tend to be rigid and abstract. Steps (3) and (4) coincide with the criticism raised by Dunnette (1963) and Korman (1968) with respect to the factorial complexity of the criterion outcomes. The assessment center method tends to choose predictors and criteria that are somewhat remote to the immediate needs of the individual and the organization. For the individual, his immediate problem would be how to cope with the environmental pressures in such a way that progress becomes possible as an outcome of the coping process. Therefore, the individual must face the "predictor" problem regarding the outcomes of his role behavior. On the other hand, for the organization the immediate problem would be what the "criteria" are for evaluating the individual's performance for the attainment of the goals of the organization. We need to consider interrelationships among a broader set of criteria and predictors, ranging from the immediate to the remote ones, for establishing a match between the individual's predictors and the organization's criteria.

Then, how does it become possible for the assessment center to predict the complex outcomes as shown in Table 6, despite the apparent criterion problems discussed above? Korman explained the secret of the assessment center method as follows.

> . . . Judgmental prediction is not as "criterion-oriented" as psychometric prediction. Rather, it may be that the judgmental predictors change the meaning of the criterion they are predicting psychologically so that what they are predicting is the general level of adequacy with which the person will be able to function in a complex environment and the extent to which he will be able to handle the various stresses which exist in the managerial role. Furthermore, since such stresses undoubtedly vary both betwen jobs and within the same job over time, it is also probable that one of the reasons for the relatively positive results found for the "judgmental" predictors is that the judge incorporates such "change" and "re-action to change" as aspects of the behavior he is predicting (Korman, 1968, 316-317).

Korman's explanation can be summarized as follows: in a successful attempt of the assessment center method, (1) assessors can identify critical aspects of environmental pressures (including their change over time) to which the assessee will be exposed in the process of his career development, (2) assessors can evaluate a set of personal traits that are responsive to each aspect of environmental pressure, (3) they have a "theory" or implicit assumptions about the process of interaction between the environment and personal traits, and (4) based on this theory, judgment can be made for each assessee as to the "potential" that the hypothesized course of events might occur in him. The above may be the reason why the assessment ratings are often called "clinical" judgments (Campbell, et al., 1970). The point, however, is that unless the above four steps can be documented by the "actuarial" data, the assessment center method will remain as an *art of prediction*, and nobody, including the judges themselves, can explain the mechanism by which the assessment ratings acquire predictive validity.

4. Selection as a Strategy for Managerial Resource Development

The assessment center method strongly endorses a "selection strategy" as a model for the organizational career development.   The managerial resource development policy known as an "early identification of managerial potential" (Lourent, 1962) may be one of the typical programs based on this selection strategy. This policy insists that the organization's effort to identify potentials of the individual should be made early enough before they become contaminated by the random impact from the career environment of each individual. For the purpose of selection, the assessment center plays two key roles: (1) the method produces a set of standardized information, which aids personnel decisions, and (2) it provides opportunities to demonstrate potentials for those people, who would have been deprived of such opportunities without the assessment center. However, the method also has problems. A study conducted by Kraut and Scott (1972) reported one of the problems associated with the selection strategy of the organization. Kraut and Scott tested validity of the IBM assessment center program based upon the participants who were nominated by their immediate supervisors on the basis of their promotability to a higher managerial level.   In this particular program, information on the individual's performance at the assessment center was fed back to management to help them decide who were to be promoted. Five years later, data on the managerial level of participants were collected, and correlated with ratings by the assessment center. Admittedly, the two measures showed high correlation because of criterion contamination. However, Kraut and

Scott concluded that the correlation coefficients between the assessment ratings and managerial levels after five years seemed moderate enough to attenuate the heavy method biases (what they called the "crown prince" effect and the "kiss of death" effect) involved in the study. It was found that in their study criterion variance consisted of a mixture of two parts: (1) phenomenon variance that represents a true effect of individual potential upon progress, and (2) method variance caused by nomination of assessees for participation and by feedback of assessment ratings for promotion decisions. The above result indicates that for the operating assessment center geared to the selection strategy, it becomes critically important to separate the "true" potential effect from the "method" effect upon managerial progress. Otherwise, it becomes very difficult to defend the method of selection.

The Kraut and Scott study reported another problem connected with the selection decisions. It was found that the outcomes of career development included a considerably high incidence of "negative" progress, i.e., demotion. A considerable number of demotions occurred within five years after the participants had been promoted to first-line managers based on their assessment ratings. For example, out of 40 sales managers who were judged to have potential for first-line management and who were promoted to the position accordingly, 20 percent of them were later demoted from that position. The percentage of demotion was a little lower for managers, who had been rated to have a potential beyond the first-line. Two reasons will be pointed out to explain this adverse result. The first reason may be that wrong men were selected. If we follow this assumption, demotion will be interpreted as a case of "selection error." Therefore, elaborating test batteries so that the selection error can be minimized becomes the prescription to improve the method. However, it is obvious that the pursuit of this line of activity will not necessarily lead to an elaboration in the managerial development system of the organization. For example, suppose the assessment center can predict career outcomes of assessees almost perfectly, i.e., with zero selection errors, then, what else could the individual and the organization do for their development other than maintaining the status quo? The other explanation may require the opposite assumption: right men were selected, but something that happened within the organization after the promotion prevented some managers from realizing their potential on the job. This assumption also raises a question, i.e., what exactly did happen to those who were demoted during the period of their career progress? However, an attempt to answer this question requires a consideration beyond the scope of the selection approach. Thus, even under this assumption, it would be very difficult for the assessment center approach to carry out a systematic effort to explore the problems associated with the process of career development within the organization.

In summary, a strict selection approach based on the assessment center method tends to create a rigid system for the practice of managerial resource development. If the predictive accuracy is low, we will be tempted to elaborate test batteries so that the assessment center can spot correctly a kind of person who best fits the success criteria "given" by the organization. Contrary, if the predictive validity is high, very little would be left for us to do other than maintaining the status quo. The assessment center studies produced evidence that the personal resources of the individual do have a significant impact upon the outcome of organizational career. Nevertheless, the very basic question "how" the person who is judged to have high potential at the assessment center actually achieves a high level of career outcomes is yet to be answered by the assessment center approach. Korman (1968) suggested that the potential judged by the assessment center may imply the "general level of adequacy" with which the person will be able to function in the complex environment of the organization. It is likely that the assessment ratings may be tapping this general adequacy level (as we often say, "He is all right," or "He is a right-type person.") And, this is why the assessment ratings show high predictive validity with such career outcomes as salary, managerial level, overall ratings, etc., which also implies the general level of adequacy for organizational life. One of the questions to be asked for a more advanced career progress study may be whether a person who is judged to have high skills in organizing and planning, for example, could in fact utilize his potential on these skill dimensions effectively to make progress in the organization. Moreover, progress may imply changes over time: change in the subject himself as well as change in the conditions of the work environment. Thus, it will be of much interest to explore the dynamic relationship between potential and these changes over time so that we can understand the "process" of career development. The assessment center approach, however, assumes that all parameters in the model, except criterion, remain stable over time, and the process is essentially predetermined by the individual's potential at the point of employment, rather than being dynamic over time.

Chapter III

Disillusionment or Psychological Success:
An Early Stage Attitude Change

Attitude change approaches assume that progress in later stages within the organization is attributable to the nature and the direction of changes that the newcomer experiences as a result of interaction between him and his organization at very early phases of the managerial career. Past studies identified two modes of such attitude change that the newcomer to the organization may typically go through: (a) development of a negative attitude characterized by *disillusionment* with one's organization and career role (Dunnette, et al., 1973; Graen, 1976; Porter and Steers, 1973; Porter, et al., 1976), and (b) a positive attitude accompanied by the experience of *psychological success* or *success syndrome* (Berlew and Hall, 1966; Hall, 1968; Hall and Nougaim, 1968). The attitude change approaches emphasize that differentiation among newcomers between the negative and positive attitudes occurs during very early phases of their organizational career, i.e., during the first year. Once this differentiation occurs, it tends to be irreversible and begins to have strong influence upon progress in later stages of career development. According to Hall and Nougaim (1968), the first year is critical for learning. This is the period when the newcomer becomes maximally ready to develop and change. If the first-year experiences are left with development of positive attitudes within the newcomer, progress in the subsequent periods becomes somewhat automatic, and vice versa.

I. Direction of Change in Early Phases

Attitude change in the early phase of career progress is considered as a product of the interaction between the newcomer and the organization (Porter, et al., 1975). The newcomer comes to the organization with hopes, goals, preferences, values and beliefs, etc. (i.e., "career expectations") attached to the job and the organization of his choice. Likewise, the organization may have expectations about what the newcomers will do and what they will not do, what kind of managers they are going to be, and the like. Employment decisions may require matching of expectations between the applicant and the organization.

But, matching at this stage may remain only as a "psychological contract" (Levinson, et al., 1962; Schein, 1970). Based on this contract, interaction processes take place involving the reality factors of the organization and the individual.

1. Change Mechanisms

Bennis and his associates (1973) presented a conceptual scheme for analyzing the process of changes in attitudes and values occurring, when an individual faces the coercive forces of the organizational environment. According to them, the process of change under coercive pressures consists of three separate, though overlapping subprocesses termed sequentially as: the unfreezing process, the changing process, and the refreezing process. The *unfreezing* phase involves the process of removal of threats or barriers to change by disconfirming (or by avoiding confirmation of) old values and attitudes, and by inducing guilt anxiety within the individual for resisting change. Once a person becomes unfrozen, the changing phase will follow either through identifying oneself with a novel object in the field, or through scanning the situation. Bennis and his associates pointed out that both identifying and scanning mechanisms are mediated by the process of cognitive redefinition, which makes the ultimate attitudinal changes possible. For example, switching the object of identification, or the object of reference, will cause a change in the balance of psychological forces operating in the "behavioral field." If this happens, a new set of behaviors that are consistent with the redefined field is likely to emerge. In another situation, a new set of behaviors may simply be chosen as a result of a careful evaluation or scanning of alternatives available in the situation. That is, if the environmental pressure of the organization can be introduced in such a way that a person may perceive changing his behavior in a manner congruent with the pressure as being the best available alternative for obtaining a positive result, or reducing pain, then a new set of behaviors implied by the pressure will be acquired by the person. *Refreezing* involves the integration of any new responses into the rest of the person's personality and into its significant ongoing relationships. Probably, once the process of refreezing is completed successfully, the old environmental pressures will fall into a "zone of indifference" (Barnard, 1938), and then he will be moved to the next stage of change with a new set of environmental pressures.

It is an oversimplification to assume that the nature of organizational environment for the progress of the individual is merely a set of coercive forces. Moreover, the process of behavioral change presented by Bennis and his associates seems to be too abstract, and does not clarify the process of interaction between the individual and the organization. The uniqueness of phases of change for the newcomer to the organization was documented by Graen (1976) based on empirical data derived from the studies on the process of organizational assimilation. According to Graen, the assimilation process would include the following three more or less distinct phases through which the newcomer and the environment of the organization interact to bring about changes in the relationship between the two over time.

(1) *Initial Confrontation.* During the initial phase (the first two weeks of the newcomer's tenure in his study), the newcomer had to cope with the discrepancies between his expectations about the situation and his assessment of the actual situation. As a consequence of confrontation with the concrete conditions of his role situation, the newcomer changed his beliefs about his role and the organization. "Disillusionment" of the newcomer with his role situation was one of the most conspicuous outcomes of this phase. Disillusionment, then, depending upon the magnitude of the expectation gap, affected the role readiness of the newcomer. Newcomer who had to face the most severe disillusionment rejected the role given by the organization ("role rejection"), while those who had expectation discrepancies under a tolerable range accepted their role ("role acceptance").

(2) *Working Through.* Graen reported that during the second phase, from about the second week to the twelfth week of the newcomer's tenure, the newcomer was allowed to cope with the role situation and make an adequate adjustment to the situation (a "time out" period). At this period, the newcomer had a fair grasp of his role, began polishing the required skills, and developed acquaintances with his role set members. Now, he was ready to change, and to establish working relationships with his role set members, especially with his supervisor. During this period, a negotiating process between the newcomer and his supervisor, or some of his peers, began to establish mutually favorable sets of understandings regarding roles and working relationships between them. Graen pointed out that the overlapping of the "subjective organization" between the newcomer and his supervisor is one of the outcomes of this phase. He reported that the degree of overlapping of the perceived role situations between the newcomer and his supervisor differed depending upon the newcomer's readiness to accept or reject his role.

(3) *Integrating.* The final phase, after about the twelfth week in his study, was the period for integration of the newcomer into the ongoing role set. This phase was characterized by increased feedback from the supervisor in terms of role demand and corrective action for monitored

role behavior of the newcomer. The outcome from this process was the role differentiation among newcomers. Those who established successful integration with the role set members (the role accepting group) reduced the level of role ambiguity, and increased the level of involvement in their role markedly. Whereas, those who failed to establish integrative relationships with role set members (the role rejection group) showed a considerably higher level of role ambiguity, and a discrepancy between the supervisor's demand and the newcomer's involvement in role activities. Moreover, it was found that role differentiation at this phase of career development is responsible for the turnover rates that showed significant differences between the two role readiness groups: after one year, only 27 percent of the role rejecting newcomers were still on the job, while among the role accepting newcomers, the rate of staying on the job was found to be 55 percent.

2. Disillusionment
Disillusionment may develop among newcomers through a period of initial adaptation phases as a result of confronting the organization's strong disconfirmation of unrealistically high career expectations commonly held by the newcomer. As Graen (1976) reported, the process of initial confrontation tends to create not only severe disillusionment on the part of the newcomer, but also a considerable waste of human resources for the organization due to: (1) the high incidence of turnover, and (2) the underutilization of managerial potentials for those who were disillusioned but decided to stay on as mediocre performers. Schein (1964) stressed that the lack of a proper mechanism to adjust these expectation discrepancies (i.e., "unrealistic" expectations of the newcomer versus "stereotype" views on the new recruits maintained by the organization) often causes feelings of disillusionment for the newcomer. Based on interviews, Schein (1964) identified the following five issues as major concerns among new college graduates. (1) Will the job provide an opportunity to test myself, to find out whether I can really do the job? (2) Will I be considered worthwhile? Will my contribution be appreciated? Will I be given any real responsibility? (3) Will I be able to maintain my integrity and individuality? (4) Will I learn and grow? (5) Will the organization in which I work meet my ideals of the rational business organization described in the economics and business courses? On the other hand, Schein pointed out that an organization's stereotype of the new college graduate tends to develop based on the sporadic contact with the graduate; The college graduate is (1) overambitious and unrealistic in his expectations, (2) too theoretical, idealistic, and naive to begin an important initial assignment, (3) too immature and

inexperienced to be given much responsibility, (4) too security-conscious, (5) unwilling to recognize the difference between having a good idea and selling it for implementation, and (6) must be "broken in" before his resources become available to the organization.

Schein (1964) pointed out the difficult position of the lower-level managers who are usually asked to be an agent of socialization for the newcomer. He stated that in many companies the first- or second-level supervisors do not have enough job security. Hence, they tend to generate a climate of conservatism based on the stereotyped images as a defense for their feeble positions, when they deal with newcomers having a higher degree of ₊ducational qualifications. Schein proposed that for the purpose of overcoming a manager's conservatism and the problem of disillusionment on the part of the newcomer, (a) the selection of supervisors for the new college graduates should be niade carefully, and (b) the supervisor should be trained as an agent of socialization with respect to the following three points:

(1) To heighten the supervisors' awareness of the difficult problems, which they and the new man will face.
(2) To provide an opportunity for supervisors to share with one another their insecurities, concerns, and problems in dealing with college graduates.
(3) To create relationships among supervisors, which would make it possible for them to consult with one another as a means of obtaining help in dealing with new and unusual problems as they arise.

The above discussion suggests that the magnitude of experiencing disenchantment with the organizational career may be a function of the discrepancy between the expectations that the newcomer brings into the organization and the company's counterpart expectations based upon the organization's reality. A study conducted by Dunnette and his associates (1973) exemplified a mechanism of disillusionment. They conducted a survey to explore what makes the college graduate newcomer decide to leave the company. For this survey, one large employer of college graduates was selected, and about 1,000 college graduates who either were currently employed by the firm or had left the firm during a two-year period with a tenure of four years or less, were asked to respond to questionnaires about motivation, job expectations, and job experiences. The usable sample consisted of 525 currently employed and 495 terminated graduates (who were on new jobs in other firms). It was found that both terminees and employees almost equally agreed (using JDI scales) on the job features they considered as important for their current job satisfaction and overall fulfillment on the job. Job features endorsed as important were: (1) feelings of accomplishment, (2) interesting work, (3) opportunity to use abilities, (4) opportunity to get ahead, and (5) good salary. Conversely, such features as company policies, security, and working conditions were reported relatively less important. Next, the subjects were asked how many of these job features they wanted to have upon graduation from college. The results indicated that the subject's emphasis on job features was almost the same between the "current" and "graduation" points. The above finding suggests that the job features the subjects wanted did not change during the period between graduation and thereafter, or between terminees and current employees. Basically, the same pattern of responses was reported on expectations. Subjects were asked to rate the expectations that they had before joining the company concerning the occurrence of job features presented earlier. Both the terminees and current employees were found to share highly optimistic views about the occurrence of job features for their forthcoming jobs, especially with respect to good salary, interesting work, opportunity to get ahead, fair company policies, opportunity to use one's abilities and job security.

The above two instruments, the importance ratings and the expectations on job features measured what college graduates *wanted* to have. In this regard, no systematic differences were observed among employees who stayed on and those who left the company. However, the difference became salient when considering how well these high hopes and expectations were *fulfilled.* The quality of experiences on the job was examined for the terminees using the same job-feature check list with respect to the following three points: (1) their first job, (2) the job held at the time they decided to leave the company, and (3) their present job with the new company. Current employees also described their first job assignment in addition to their present job with the company. The comparison between the "wanted" and the "fulfilled" dimensions suggested the following results.

(1) In general, the first job assignment in the company brought rather sharp disenchantment, both to the college graduates who were still with the firm and to those who left later. In every respect, actual experiences were found to be below what they had expected. Particularly, the first job with the company was seen as the one that severely frustrated their high hopes and expectations on such aspects as using one's abilities, accomplishment, opportunity to advance, and interesting work.

(2) Discrepancies between expectations and actual experiences in the first assignments were found to be more severe for those who left later, compared to those who stayed in the company. Especially,

terminees experienced higher disenchantment in responsibility, recognition, interesting work, and opportunity to advance.

(3) For those who stayed, the "current" experiences were described as exceeding expectations held at the time of graduation regarding such job features as responsibility, being in charge of others, and variety of tasks.   In other aspects, current experiences were described as falling below what they expected, but showing considerable improvement from the first assignment.   In contrast, for those who left, experiences in the company were seen as totally frustrating.   Experiences they had at the time they decided to leave the company were described either basically the same as, or worse than, those experienced on their first assignments. They could improve the quality of work experience only by changing the company.

(4) Differences in job experiences between terminees and employees were also documented in motivational terms.   Dunnette and his associates (1973) developed a composite Motivation Index (MI) based on subject's perception of expectancy, valence, and instrumentality associated with both their first and their current jobs (for terminees, the last job in the company).   The results indicated that the MI scores derived by summing the products of three motivational components over 15 JDI items, tended to discriminate between terminees and current employees not only for their first jobs, but also for the current job (for employees) and the last job (for terminees).

The above findings help us understand the mechanism of disillusionment and the outcomes from it.   (1) The college graduate employees, regardless of the probability of their leaving or staying after employment, tend to emphasize the importance of having opportunity to use their own abilities, interesting work, opportunity to get ahead, and feeling of accomplishment.   (2) They tend to be optimistic in their expectations about the occurrence of these job features on their forthcoming job after graduation.   (3) But, these job features are usually hard to obtain on their first job, and relatively so even after the two-to-four year company experiences.   Thus, the newcomer's frustration begins to mount.   (4) To the extent that the discrepancy between expectations and actual experiences on the job fails to be narrowed, motivation to make progress on the job becomes deteriorated, and (5) a separation from the company starts to take place among those who were most disillusioned.

However, it must be noted that the above findings reported by Dunnette and his associates were derived from the analysis of data based on a "recall" study.   It is likely that in their study the subjects might have been tempted to recall, when they answered the questionnaire, only such past experiences that were consistent with their present situation, or such experiences that enhanced the *social desirability* of their past decisions on whether or not to stay with the company. That is, the current employees may be tempted to describe their present jobs relatively better than the first ones, and the terminees to describe their present jobs in the new company far better than their first and last jobs in the old company. Because, recalling their past experiences otherwise would probably make it difficult for both groups of subjects to accept their present positions. To avoid the contamination that might be caused by the social desirability factors, the design of research may require monitoring the process of change on a "real" time basis.

3. Psychological Success and Career Commitment

Disillusionment is an attitude change toward the negative direction. On the other hand, an experience of "psychological success" may represent a change toward the opposite, positive direction. Hall (1968) conducted a study to explore the mechanism of the psychological success experience. A process of transition from one career role (a student) to another (a professor) was investigated based on a group of Ph.D. students at MIT, who went through one of the critical transition rites occurring in their program, the general qualification examination. Hall postulated three major phases which would be involved in the transition process: (1) separation of the person from his customary environment, (2) initiation from the old role to the new one, and (3) incorporation or reintegration into the original environment. Using a 29-item semantic differential scale, the perceived "professor" role and the student's "self-identity" were measured before and after the examination. A factor analysis on the semantic differentials produced three independent dimensions: (1) supportiveness, (2) personal potency, and (3) intellectual competence.

It was found that students who passed the examination increased their self-identity ratings significantly on potency and competency dimensions on the after-exam measure compared to the same measure before the exam. This increase in self-identity indicated that for the successful students, the perceived distance between the professor role and the student's self-image was reduced significantly after the examination. Hall emphasized that this reduction was facilitated by the growth in "subidentity" for the students who could successfully meet the challenge, because the ratings on the professor role remained almost identical between the before- and after-measures. He concluded that the subidentity growth occurred for the successful students as a result of overcoming strong, personally meaningful challenges, which led them to the experience of a psychological success and an increased self-esteem.

Hall and Nougaim (1968) reported an interesting result in the psychological process of career commitment. They examined changes in need patterns of the new managerial recruits over their first five years in a large business organization (at AT&T). Hall and Nougaim assumed that the strength of needs, and the degree of need fulfillment will show systematic difference in accordance with the progress in career commitment of the recruits over time. Need strength and need fulfillment were measured based on Maslow's need categories for the two different groups of recruits, those who achieved a successful level of managerial progress and those who failed to do so. Hall and Nougaim reported that the pattern of need change of the recruits over five years involved a shift in the recruit's concern between the two broad need areas, i.e., the concern for safety and the concern for promotion and achievement, rather than involving the five need areas postulated by Maslow (1954 and 1962). They pointed out that the changes in need patterns during the five-year research period had typically reflected the shift in what they called "developing career concern" of young managers. The authors explained this finding as follows. During the early stages of recruits' careers in which their status and role situations in the organization are unstable and unpredictable, a safety need tends to be predominant among all young managers. However, for a group of successful managers, satisfaction with safety need increased by the end of the fifth year, whereas for the less successful managers, the safety need still remained at a high level and satisfaction with it did not increase significantly throughout the research period. Concern for promotion and achievement characterized the next stage of progress. Both high and low success groups showed a significant increase in the strength of achievement and esteem needs over time. However, again only the successful group reported high satisfaction with these needs by the end of the fifth year.

Hall and Nougaim (1968) summarized the above findings using the term, *success syndrome*. This concept denotes a set of mutually reinforcing incidents that arise in the course of developmental phases. According to the authors, a sequence of events that constitute the success syndrome can be summarized as follows. (1) For all managers, the need for achievement and esteem increases over the years that they are with the company. (2) Managers who have met high standards of performance will be rewarded with promotion and pay increases, thus decreasing their need for safety. (3) Those successful managers have achieved a great deal and have been given additional responsibilities. Therefore, their satisfaction with achievement and esteem increases and becomes significantly greater than their less successful colleagues by the fifth year. (4) Possibly, as a result of their greater satisfaction with higher order needs, they become more involved in their jobs. By the fifth year, their work is significantly more central to their need satisfaction than is the work of the less successful group. (5) With increased job involvement, they are more likely to be successful in future assignments than other managers who are not allowed to fulfill their higher-order needs. Thus, the successful managers become caught in an upward spiral of progress.

Based on the above findings, Hall (1971) proposed a theory on the *career subidentity growth.* With additional support from theories on "self-esteem" (Korman, 1967) and "achievement motivation" (Atkinson and Feather, 1966; McClelland, et al., 1953), Hall advanced the following propositions as key components of his theory on career success.

I. Over time, the career subidentity grows as (a) the individual incorporates additional career-relevant dimensions into his identity, and (b) the individual increases his sense of competence on all dimensions of career subidentity.

II. Over time, the congruence between the career subidentity and the perceived career role increases.

III. Increases in career subidentity, career commitment, self-esteem, and probability of future career goal-setting will result from success in attaining a goal which satisfies the following criteria: (a) the goal was set by the person, (b) the path to the goal was defined by the person, (c) the goal was perceived as challenging or difficult but attainable, (d) the goal was central to his self-identity, and (e) the goal was perceived as being relevant to the career role.

IV. The extent to which a man's initial job assignment provides the conditions for psychological success (job challenge and autonomy) will continue to be positively related to his career commitment, performance, and success in subsequent years.

4. Adaptive Behaviors

Along the continuum characterized by the two extreme experiences (i.e., disillusionment and psychological success), there may exist a variety of adaptive behaviors as the "modes" of attitude change. The compliance behavior known as "conformity" (Merton, 1957; Schein, 1968 and 1971) may represent one of the types of adaptation. Past studies identified this pattern of behavior using various terms: "defensive identification (Hall, et al., 1970), "over-socialization" (Ziller, 1964, Weick, 1969), a "visitor's attitude" (Graen, 1976), and total conformity known as the "organization man" (Whyte, 1956), or as the "other-directed" person (Riesman, 1950).

For example, the thesis presented by Riesman and Whyte indicates that the picture of successful qualities in business has changed dramatically. The traditional belief that the way to success in American business corporations is to follow in the footsteps of great individuals like

Henry Ford or John Rockefeller has given way to a view that success now comes to the individual who is adaptable, socially attuned, and sensitive to the thinking and desires of other individuals. In effect, it may be true that the entire system of mangerial development in today's large business organizations is strongly oriented toward producing a "pool" of human resources for middle and upper management through systematic moulding efforts. However, Porter and Lawler (1968) pointed out that in contrast to the general acceptance of Riesman's and Whyte's views, data derived from the empirical research tend to support the view that the "inner-directed" person characterized as forceful, imaginative, and independent, still has a place in contemporary organizations. For example, Fleishman and Peters (1962) found a significant negative correlation ($r = -.44$) between conformity (a measure for the "other-directedness") and job performance. Roadman (1964) studied 56 middle managers in a large industrial organization. Peer ratings were obtained for each manger on factors describing the character of inner-directedness. The promotion rates of those managers were obtained over the next two years. The results showed that the majority of promotions went to those managers who were described relatively high on originality, independence of thought, aggressiveness, and self-expression. Likewise, Porter and Lawler (1968) demonstrated that those managers who see their jobs as demanding a set of inner-directed behaviors (forceful, imaginative, independent, self-confident, and decisive) are more effective in performing their jobs than those managers who see their jobs as demanding relatively fewer such behaviors. Also, they found that the higher the level of management, the more the manager was inner-directed.

Evidence raised by Porter and Henry (1964) indicates that the propositions advanced by Riesman and Whyte, and empirical data that seem contradictory to their theses, may represent different strata of the same structure of the managerial resource development system of the organization. They reported that at the lower levels of management, a manager is required to exhibit more aspects of other-directed behavior to be successful in his position: that is, he is required to behave like an organization man more frequently than those who were established as members of middle management and who enjoy the autonomy connected with their positions. It is likely that the conflicting view of the nature of men working in the contemporary organization may be a reflection of conflicting organizational pressures that men have to cope with through-out their business career within large complex organizations.

Based on the study of the Forest Service organization, Hall and his associates (1970) reported that the reasons (sources) upon which people base identification with the organization changed over time. Among a cross-section sample of the Forest Service personnel, it was found that identification with the Forest Service (as an organization and as an occupation) and the importance attached to the value of "public service" increased monotonically as a function of the number of years spent in the organization. However, it was found that this trend was supported by two qualitatively different types of identification for Forest Service people. That is, after about 11 to 15 years in a Forest Service career, the type of identification shifted from "positive" to "defensive" areas, although manifested levels of identifying with the organization and occupation of the Forest Service did not change due to the shift in the internal source of identification. Hall and his associates found that in the early stages of the Forest Service career, the foresters showed a higher and increasing importance for autonomy needs, esteem needs, professionalism, and land management. But after about 15 years of tenure, all these positive values disappeared; instead security needs started to increase to replace a loss in higher-order needs. Hall and his associates concluded that the positive identification and the individual's higher-order needs (esteem, autonomy, and self-actualization) are in accordance with the goals of the organization, i.e., growth-oriented, or higher-order need identification. But for the defensive identification, the indivdual's lower-order needs (security, dependency, avoidance of threat and challenge) are in accordance with the organization's need to control its members, i.e., deficiency-oriented, or lower-order need identification.

Many studies suggest that defensive identification may develop in the very early stages of a new recruit's career (Berlew and Hall, 1968; Bray, et al., 1974; Schein, 1964 and 1975), with differential behavioral patterns and career outcomes resulting from this defensive identification. If this happens, the recruit may decide to stay with the organization as a "hired-hand" or a "visitor" (Graen, 1976; Graen, et al., 1973). The above finding suggests that the organization's effort to redevelop or rechannel its people may need to be implemented much earlier than might normally be expected.

II. Job Challenge and the Experience of Psychological Success

The preceding discussion indicates ' that the newcomer's attitudinal position on the "disillusionment-conformity-psychological success" continuum is a result of the interaction among complex factors (individual as well as organizational) that become salient upon the newcomer's encounter with the reality of the organization. However, the study conducted by Berlew and Hall (1966) suggests that the quality of environmental pressures each newcomer experienced during the first year in the organization is critical in predicting the direction of change of the newcomer for the subsequent time periods. Based on the data derived from AT&T's management progress study, Berlew and Hall (1966) tested the hypothesis that the quality of the recruit's first-year experience with the environmental pressures of the organization will have a critical impact upon the career progress of the recruit. To test this hypothesis, the "company expectations," defined as type and quality of contributions expected for a recruit by the company (by immediate supervisors and bosses), were evaluated as a measure of the quality of the environmental pressures. The underlying assumption for this hypothesis was that high company expectations will challenge the recruit's capability: men would feel most challenged and try to meet the challenge in jobs where the company's expectations are high, and less so in jobs where the company's expectations are low.

The interview protocols derived from annual meetings with the superiors of each recruit were rated as to the extent that the recruit received challenging expectations by the company each year. Ratings were made, using a 3-point scale, along the 18 aspects consisting of: technical competence, learning capacity, imagination, persuasiveness, group membership skills, communication skills, supervisory skills, decision making, organizing ability, time-energy commitment, sacrifice of autonomy, sociability, acceptance of company norms, self-development, maintenance of public image, loyalty, and initiative. Then, a composite expectation score was computed for each recruit by adding all 18 expectation items on an annual basis. The two criterion measures were developed to be correlated with the composite expectation scores. The *success index* was constructed by combining the company appraisals on recruits' overall performance and potential evaluated after four or five years of the recruits' career, with salary information (corrected for the starting salary level) corresponding to each period of the above company appraisals. The other criterion variable was called a *performance index*. This measure was basically a composite of annual performance ratings conducted by the Bell Telephone Companies. Table 7 displays correlation coefficients between the composite score of company expectations evaluated annually, and the performance and success indicies measured during the fifth (company B) and the fourth (company D) year in the recruit's career at AT&T.

Table 7 indicates that the company expectation scale shows high correlations with the performance and success indices. Especially, for Company B the strength of association between the expectation and outcome variables seems very consistent over time: the correlation co-

Table 7

Correlations of Company Expectations for
First Four and Five Years with Success Measures

Year	Performance Index	Success Index
Company B (N = 44)		
First	.54**	.32*
Second	.42**	.28*
Third	.58**	.37**
Fourth	.56**	.25*
Fifth	.36**	.33*
Company D (N = 18)		
First	.29	.37
Second	.21	-.07
Third	.35	.33
Fourth	.56**	.68**

*p < .05
**p < .01
One-tailed test
Adapted from Berlew, D.E., and Hall, D.T. "The Socialization of Manager: Effects of Expectation on Performance," *Administrative Science Quarterly*, 1966, 11, 207-23, pp. 215-16 (Tables 1 and 2). Copyright © 1966 by *Administrative Science Quarterly*. Used with the permission of the publisher and authors.

efficients ranged from .36 (fifth year) to .58 (third year) for the performance index, and .25 (fourth year) to .37 (third year) for the success index. In Company D, the expectation scale showed significant correlations with the criterion indices only at the final year. In general, Table 7 implies that: (1) the recruit who had an experience working under high company expectations at one time period, tends to receive similarly high expectations for the next time period, and (2) as the authors hypothesized, the experience of high company expectations (i.e., high job challenge) during the very early stages of the recruits' career predicts the criterion outcomes consistently over time.

To explain *how* the above two sequences of events came into being throughout the process of career development at AT&T, Berlew and Hall (1966) advanced two hypotheses. One of them stated that personal attributes, typically potentials of the recruits, are responsible for the observed consistency between company expectations and development criteria. The other hypothesis indicated that the consistency may represent an outcropping of the organizational socialization process triggered, and facilitated, by high company expectations. A phenomenon corresponding to the first hypothesis may look like the following. The company somehow identifies the most talented men and assigns them to the most demanding jobs in the first year of the recruits' career. If these talented men perform well on their initial assignments, the chances that they will have more challenging jobs and relatively high performance for the next year increases. If this sequence of events is repeated over time, then company expectations and progress measures will become highly correlated both within and between the two measures. In other words, the first hypothesis indicates that the observed high correlations are the outcome derived from the company's practice for early identification of managerial talents and their selective development. On the other hand, the second hypothesis that Berlew and Hall (1966) called the "organizational socialization hypothesis" indicates that the initial assignments must have been done at random, disregarding individual differences in potential ratings. But, the quality of assigned jobs differed significantly in terms of company expectations about how high his performance should be. According to the second hypothesis, it is this difference that caused the differential career outcomes in later years. Berlew and Hall pointed out that if the first hypothesis holds true, the observed high correlation between job challenge and career outcomes would have little to do with the organizational socialization. On the other hand, if the second hypothesis holds true, the observed results can be interpreted as outcroppings of the dynamic processes of management career progress.

To examine the validity of each hypothesis, the first year expectation scores were correlated with a variety of data concerning the recruits' personal characteristics collected for the management progress study (Bray and Grant, 1966) using the assessment center method at the start of recruits' career. It was found that only 4 out of the 45 assessment variables examined turned out to have significant correlations with the first year expectations. This result indicated that the initial job assignments were made almost at random with respect to the potential of each recruit. Based on this result, the authors hinted that what happened to the new recruits during the first five years of their managerial career might be the process of organizational socialization facilitated by company expectations. Berlew and Hall described the process of organizational socialization as follows. (1) For the new recruit, meeting high company expectations in the critical first year was accompanied by the internalization of positive job attitudes and high standards of performance. (2) These attitudes and standards contributed to the attainment of high performance and success, which in turn reinforced learned values and attitudes. (3) And thus, a new recruit who had met the challege of one high demanding job was subsequently given a more demanding job, and the level of his contribution rose even more as he responded to the company's growing expectations for him. The authors emphasized that the key feature of the organizational socialization is in the concept of the first year as a *critical period of learning*. According to them, this is the period when the trainee becomes maximally ready to develop and change in the direction of the company's expectation. Therefore, probably never again will he be so "unfrozen" and ready to learn as he is in his first year. This is why the experience with high job challenge in the first year becomes so critical for success in the future. The authors concluded that for the benefit of the individual and of the investment in him, "no organization can afford to treat this critical period lightly" (Berlew and Hall, 1966, 223).

Studies reviewed for this chapter suggest that the newcomer's encounter with the organization is accompanied by changes in his attitude. If the change occurs in a positive direction (e.g., an experience of psychological success), he will be "channeled" into a process of steady career progress. If the change takes place in a negative direction (e.g., an experience of disillusionment), he will be doomed to the process of failure or separation from the organization during the subsequent periods for career progress.   For the present study, the newcomer's attitude toward his career role and his organization in the first year will be measured using out "disillusionment" instrument. For the purpose of our study, the disillusionment hypothesis does not ask why this negative feeling exists among some of our sample newcomers.   Instead, the hypothesis is directed toward exploring what will be the effects of forming negative attitude at the start of a career (regardless of the reasons for attitude change) upon his progress within the organization during the subsequent time periods.

Chapter IV

The Role Making Model

The role making approach of managerial progress addresses itself to the exploration of mechanisms of interpersonal role development based on the resource exchange relation between the newcomer and his supervisor. This model suggests that for the newcomer, role development is a process of establishing a high level of interdependent role activities with significant others in his role set, especially the supervisor. Graen (1976) pointed out that for facilitating the role interdependence with the supervisor, the newcomer will engage in what he called the "vertical exchange" process through which the critical resources desired by each party are exchanged. For example, the newcomer may receive from his supervisor assistance, support, job autonomy, and attention, which constitute vital resources to the development of his own role position, in exchange for his contribution to the attainment of group goals for which the supervisor is responsible. Under this model, the supervisor plays an important motivation function for his subordinates. He will provide them with a clear picture regarding his preferred pattern of role activities, outcomes associated with each of the role activities, and his willingness to help them achieve outcomes. Also, he will send feedback to his subordinates as to the discrepancy between the preferred and actual pattern of role activities based on his monitoring of their behaviors.

In this chapter, the two key aspects of the role making model, a motivation function of the supervisor and a mechanism of interpersonal resource acquisition, will be discussed first. Then, empirical evidence of the process of role making derived from the study of *organizational assimilation* (Dansereau, et al., 1975; Graen, 1976) will be examined with an emphasis on the effect of exchange relations upon outcomes of the assimilation process.

I. Interpersonal Resources with the Supervisor

Studies on organizational socialization reported difficult positions of the supervisor as an agent of socialization vis-à-vis his new subordinate to the organization (Berlew and Hall, 1966; Bray, et al., 1974; Campbell, et al., 1970; Schein, 1964; Schein and Lippit, 1966). Results of such studies indicated that various interpersonal barriers existing between the supervisor and his new subordinate tend to prohibit development of a resource-exchange relationship that would help facilitate the process of role development for the newcomer. However, despite these difficulties in establishing interpersonal relations for newcomers, they must work with the supervisor because "the supervisor is the organization itself." "If he is good, the organization is usually viewed favorably. If he is ineffective in working with the newcomer, the organization itself is seen negatively" (Porter, et al., 1975, 184).

1. Supervisor as a Facilitator of Progress

The importance of the supervisor as a contributor of resources to the newcomer's progress was stressed by Bray and his associates in their study of managerial progress at AT&T. They illustrated two contrasting experiences that the newcomers to the Bell Companies went through with their supervisors (Bray, et al., 1974, 72-73). The authors reported that for one of the recruits who achieved a higher level of progress, his work career involved being supervised by a series of very demanding bosses, who were creative and decisive for the most part, and who believed firmly in developing subordinates through participating in problem solving. On the contrary, for another recruit who ended up with poor achievement in the period of his career development, his first boss did everything himself, giving his men very little latitude to avoid "overloading" them. The authors continued that the boss did nothing to stimulate creativity: meeting a deadline was his conception of a challenging assignment and he frequently did things for his men rather than forcing them to develop. In connection with the study of job challenge, Hall conceptualized the role of a supervisor for the subordinate's progress as the one for creating job challenge for his subordinates. Hall stated that:

> In particular the assistance, support, and confrontation provided by the man's superior, plays an important role in a person's career development. The supervisor can push the person to set meaningful, challenging work goals and to define ways of achieving them; he can provide assistance or coaching in the process of attaining them; he can help evaluate success or failure on particular goals; and he can help the person problem-solve (for) future improvement: In short, the supervisor can facilitate both the process of success and effective coping with failure (Hall, 1971, 72).

Locke summarized the function of a supervisor vis-à-vis his subordinate's progress as an "agent of value facilitator" (Locke, 1976). He emphasized that the supervisor as an agent can act as a value facilitator for his subordinate to help him attain desired values associated with his organizational roles, i.e., (a) *task-related values:* interesting and challenging work, help in attaining work goals, freedom from interruptions, good equipment, etc., and (b) *rewards for task performance:* promotion, pay raises or high earnings, verbal recognition (Locke, 1976, 1326). Oldham (1976) reported that the supervisor can be in a position to exercise various "strategies" to influence the subordinate's performance and work attitudes. According to Oldham, a leader's behaviors can be conceived of as strategies to the extent that they are consciously directed toward manipulating physical-psychological conditions of the subordinate's work environment to stimulate his motivation to work. Oldham reported that motivational strategies used by supervisors consisted of: (1) personally rewarding, (2) personally punishing, (3) setting goals, (4) designing a feedback system, (5) placing personnel, and (6) designing a job system. In his study, managers who reported frequent use of these strategies, except punishing strategy, were rated by subordinates as being highly effective in motivating members. In addition, it was found that the frequency by which managers exercised job design strategy correlated highly with the effectiveness of subordinates: .45 with performance effectiveness and also .45 with motivational effectiveness of the subordinates.

Research results like the above suggest that the supervisor can help facilitate the process of career progress of his subordinate in the organization by: (a) creating additional resources (support, assistance, task redesign, etc.) for his subordinate, and (b) providing environmental conditions that stimulate the subordinate toward attainment of various career targets. Conversely, traditional studies on leadership style (Katz, et al., 1950 and 1951; Stogdill and Coons, 1957; Stogdill, et al., 1956; Fiedler, 1967; Blake and Mouton, 1964) suggest very little regarding how leadership effectiveness, viewed from the supervisor's or organization's point of view, can influence the *subordinate effectiveness* in terms of his developmental point of view. For traditional studies that Graen and Cashman (1975) called "average" leadership studies, subordinate effectiveness has been considered, by definition, as a subset of leadership effectiveness. Therefore, research efforts to explore membership effectiveness in terms of leader's behavior toward his member tend to be neglected under the traditional leadership studies.

2. Motivational Function of the Leader
In contrast to the traditional "structural" approaches to the leadership phenomenon (Hollander and Julian, 1969), recent developments in the area of leadership "processes" give us insight into how different leader

behaviors can differentially influence subordinate motivation and work attitudes. House conducted a series of studies on the influence process of leader behaviors in terms of "consideration" and "initiating structure" upon performance and satisfaction of subordinates based on the theory that he called a path-goal theory of leadership (House, 1971; House and Dessler, 1974; House and Mitchell, 1974). According to House, the path-goal leadership theory is based upon the path-goal hypothesis advanced by Georgopoulous and his associates (1957) and previous research supporting the broad class of expectancy theory of motivation (Atkinson, 1964; Graen, 1969; Lawler, 1971; Vroom, 1964). The central proposition of a path-goal theory of leadership states that, "the motivation functions of a leader are to increase the net positive valences associated with the path-behavior-to-work-goal attainment, and increase the subordinate's path instrumentally with respect to work-goal attainment for personal outcomes and the behavior required for work-goal attainment" (House, 1971). Simply stated, the proposition suggests that the leader can affect subordinates' behavior by influencing either one, or both, of the following motivational components of work behavior: (1) valence associated with goals, path to the goals, and goal-attaining behaviors, and (2) instrumentality of path to the goals.

Among a set of hypotheses developed by House to test the relationships between leader behaviors, subordinate motivation, and work outcomes, the following two hypotheses may be particularly interesting in that inquiries are directed toward exploring a long discussed controversy in the area of leadership studies concerning "consideration" and "initiating a structure" (Korman, 1966).

(1) Leader initiating structure increases the path instrumentality for subordinates, whose roles have nonroutine task demands by decreasing role ambiguity. The more ambiguous the task, the more positive the relationship between leader initiating structure and subordinate satisfaction and performance.

(2) Where tasks and/or environment are frustrating and stress inducing, consideration will result in increased social support for followers and thus reduce the negative valence associated with task-oriented behavior.

The above hypotheses state that the influence of leader behaviors in terms of consideration and initiating structure upon subordinates' satisfaction and performance is moderated by the nature of the subordinate's task. Initiating structure may help eliminate ambiguity associated with the task and increase the value of the path instrumentality, while consideration is expected to attenuate conflict and frustration on the job and thus, to increase the valence associated with the work-goals and goal-attaining efforts. To test the above hypotheses, House (1971) considered the degree of *task autonomy* as a summary index for motivating potential (or motivational deficiency) of the subordinate tasks. Then subjects were trichotomized based on this index (Low, Medium, and High autonomy). The underlying assumption for this classification was that being Low in autonomy tends to create frustration and stress on the job, while being High in autonomy tends to induce task ambiguity, with Medium being situated between the two extreme situations. Then, House made predictions on the interaction effects between task autonomy and leader behaviors upon the subordinate's responses as illustrated in Table 8. He explained each prediction as follows.

(1) *Structure-Performance Relationship.* This relationship will become stronger (+) for Low autonomy tasks than for High autonomy tasks (-). Because, for the former, role demands are more likely to be dissatisfying, so that initiating structure will control behavior and ensure higher performance. On the other hand, for the latter situation, initiating structure will be irrelevant to performance, since the subordinate is less dependent upon the leader for resources, assistance, or guidance.

(2) *Structure-Satisfaction Relationship.* Task autonomy will have a positive moderating effect upon this relationship. That is, the relationship will be stronger (+) under High task autonomy than under Low task autonomy (-). This hypothesis was based upon the expectation that for autonomous tasks, the role demands are likely to be more ambiguous than for less autonomous tasks. Therefore, under High autonomy a leader's structuring behavior will serve to reduce role ambiguity, increase clarity of path-goal relationships, and thereby increase satisfaction.

(3) *Consideration-Performance Relationship.* This relationship will become stronger (+) for Low autonomy tasks than for High autonomy ones (-). Because it is assumed that for Low autonomy tasks, the role demands are more likely to be dissatisfying and consequently leader consideration will become more relevant to motivating subordinates toward higher performance, than for High autonomy tasks in which role demands tend to be satisfying by themselves.

(4) *Consideration-Satisfaction Relationship.* For the same reason as stated in (3), the relationship will be stronger (+) for Low autonomy tasks than for High autonomy ones (-).

Table 8 displays the observed strength of association between leader behavior and subordinate response based on correlation coefficients reported by House. The magnitude and the direction of correlation coefficients obtained tend to give support to the predicted relationships.

Table 8

Predicted and Observed Relationships Between Leader Behaviors (Consideration and Initiating Structure) and Subordinate Responses (Performance and Satisfaction) Based Upon the Level of Task Autonomy

| Autonomy | Initiating Structure | | | Consideration | | |
	Performance	Satisfaction	N	Performance	Satisfaction	N
Low	+ (.47**)	− (.19)	61	+ (.42**)	+ (.37**)	59
Medium	± (.18)	± (.21)	68	± (.11)	± (.30*)	74
High	− (.18)	+ (.33**)	62	− (.08)	− (.23)	59

+, ±, and − signs denote strong, medium, and weak relationships predicted, respectively
*p < .05
**p < .01
Figures in parentheses denote observed correlations averaged over six performance and satisfaction scales.
Adapted from House, R. J. "A Path-goal Theory of Leadership Effectiveness," *Administrative Science Quarterly,* 1971, 16, 321-38, (Tables 2 and 4 from pp. 331 and 334). Copyright © 1971 by *Administrative Science Quarterly.* Used with the permission of the publisher and the author.

The examination of the strength of association suggests that the task autonomy tends to moderate, as predicted, the relationship between leader-member relationships. As House intended, his study contributed to reconciling and integrating the conflicting results of previous studies on consideration and initiating structure by focusing upon the process of leadership influence in terms of its motivational functions for subordinates. However, in his study it is not quite clear as to how leader behaviors actually create the hypothesized motivational effects for the subordinate. For example, no direct evidence is presented in his study that suggests the extent to which leader behaviors, in terms of consideration and initiating structure, were actually effective for increasing or decreasing the instrumentality values and valences perceived by the subordinate in each task situation. That is, we are not sure whether the obtained results were actually "caused" by the changes in motivational components in each situation (Sheridan, et al., 1975), or by some other variables that were not controlled for in House's studies. Secondly, Table 8 suggests that the motivational function of the leader, in terms of both initiating structure and consideration, tends to have a stronger impact upon subordinates' performance and satisfaction in a situation where the subordinates lack task autonomy, than in a situation where they have higher autonomy. As Porter's (1961 and 1962) study suggested, low autonomy may indicate a situation characterized by a general lack of resources, or the lower levels in organizational hierarchy. If this is true, the results shown in Table 8 may indicate that the lower the subordinate's autonomy and the hierarchical level in the organization, the greater is the leader's influence (especially leader's consideration) upon the subordinate's performance and satisfaction. Because leader's influence has greater resource values for the subordinate in such a situation. Conversely, Table 8 displays that in higher autonomy tasks, and probably in higher levels of the organization, the supervisor completely lacks a path-goal means to influence the subordinate's performance.

3. A Process of Motivating the Newcomer Toward Progress

Graen (1969) conducted a study to explore how the supervisor can motivate his subordinates by inducing them to behave in accordance with components of the *effective performer model* for role behaviors. He stated that under the effective performer model, job performance of the subordinate is a monotonically increasing function of the sum of the products between attraction of the role of effective performer and the perceived expectancy that increased effort will lead to more effective performance. To test this propostion, three different reward systems were experimentally created within the real work situation of the company. In his study, these reward systems represented three different inducement procedures available for the supervisor to motivate his subordinates for effective performance.

The first reward system consisted of merely monitoring individual performance and providing feedback to participants ("control" group). The second reward system included the first and emphasized effective performance by giving a pay increase as an incentive for future continued effectiveness ("obligation" group). The rationale for this second reward system was that participants might be grateful for the pay increase and feel obligated to continue to earn pay increases. The third reward system included the first and emphasized effective performance by giving achievement feedback and offering future achievement feedback contingent upon future effective performance ("contingency" group). The rationale for this third reward system was that it yielded a predictable system for the participants. If the contingencies between performance and rewards are established and maintained by the organization in an unambiguous manner, participants can predict rather accurately the consequences of their performance and in a sense achieve more control over their payoffs.

The participants (169 women) worked at computer-related clerical tasks for two days. The task involved extracting specified bits of information from a huge matrix of numbers on computer tape. A single best method for performing each task was emphasized during the skill acquisition activities. This was considered the role behavior the organization preferred. After working under either one of the reward systems, participants were asked to rate *attraction* or *preference* of various outcomes associated with their role performance. These outcomes were categorized into the following eight groups: accomplishment, achievement feedback, recognition, responsibility, human relations, policies and practice, salary, and working conditions. Also, the participants were asked to report the perceived *instrumentality* of their work role for the attainment of eight different outcomes listed above, in addition to *expectancy* regarding the extent to which their increased work effort would result in more effective job performance.

Table 9 displays that the reactions of the participants were quite different although they were working at the same tasks, at the same time, in the same room, and under the same conditions. The participants who worked under the "Obligation" reward system showed higher satisfaction with their salary than participants working under either the "Contingency" reward system or the "Control" reward system. Those persons working under the Contingency system demonstrated higher

Table 9
Reactions of Participants to the
Different Organizational Reward Systems

Organizational Reward Systems	Satisfaction with Role Outcomes	Instrumentality of Role Performance	Value of Role Performance
Contingency System	*Achievement feedback **Recognition Salary	**Achievement feedback **Recognition **Human Relations Salary	*Achievement feedback *Recognition *Policies and practices *Working conditions Salary
Obligation System	Achievement feedback Recognition **Salary	Achievement feedback Recognition Human relations *Salary	Achievement feedback Recognition Policies and practices Working conditions Salary
Control System	Achievement feedback Recognition Salary	Achievement feedback Recognition Human relations Salary	Achievement feedback Recognition Policies and practices Working conditions Salary

*p < .05 (Significantly higher than other reward groups)
**p < .01 (Significantly higher than other reward groups)
Source: Graen, G. "Role-making Processes within Complex Organizations," in M.D. Dunnette (ed.), *Handbook of Industrial and Organizational Psychology*, p. 1216. Table 4. Copyright © 1976 by Rand McNally College Publishing Company. Used with the permission of the publisher.

satisfaction with the achievement feedback and the recognition they received than those working under the other two systems. Table 9 also shows that the participants working under the three reward systems also differed regarding their estimates of the instrumentality of their organizational roles. Those working under the Contingency system felt their organizational role was more instrumentally related to the attainment of achievement feedback, recognition, and personal treatment than persons working under either of the other two systems. Those working under the Obligation system saw their role as having higher instrumentality for the attainment of pay increases than did those under the other two systems.

Graen emphasized that under the Contingency system, (1) the relationship between the performance and rewards became more predictable for the participants. As a consequence, participants viewed role performance as more instrumental in gaining preferred outcomes than those under the other systems. (2) They endorsed significantly higher value or role performance than those working under the Control and Obligation reward systems with respect to achievement feedback, recognition, policies and practices, and working conditions. (3) They also expressed higher satisfaction with the outcomes of their role performance in terms of achievement and recognition. The above findings indicate that a different set of leader behaviors in terms of reward administration does create consistent changes in the motivational components of the subordinate. Especially, the Contingency treatment produced significant increases in perceived instrumentality value of the participant's role position for attaining achievement and recognition, both of which incidentally carried significantly high valences as desired outcomes of role performance.

For the next step, examinations were made as to how these changes in motivational components affect the subordinate's satisfaction and performance of his role. Graen tested the effect of motivational change by formulating predictions of subordinate satisfaction and performance based upon the effective performer model of motivation discussed earlier. According to this model, role incumbents were expected to perform well and feel satisfied to the extent that they believe high performance would lead to highly desired payoffs, whereas poor performance would not. An important factor in this model is the link between performance and the payoff (expectancy). Unless this link can be established and maintained, the effective performer model simply does not apply. Based on this assumption, motivational components were transformed using a mathematical formula of the model into a single estimate of what Graen called the *Expected Utility* (EU) of role performance. Then, the EU scores were correlated with the observed satisfaction and performance ratings. Table 10 shows the result.

Table 10

Correlations Between the Predictions of the Effective Performer Model and the Actual Outcomes

Organizational Reward System	Overall Actual	Satisfaction Improvement	Improvement in Role Performance	
			Task A	Task B
Contingency System	.61**	.46**	.35**	.43**
Obligation System	.22*	.02*	−.12	.05
Control System	.43**	.23*	.08	.04

Improvement (residual gains) scores are the post-treatment scores with the pretreatment scores partialed out.
*p < .05
**p < .01
Source: Graen, G. "Role-making Processes within Complex Organizations," M.D. Dunnette (ed.), *Handbook of Industrial and Organizational Psychology*, p. 1217, Table 5. Copyright © 1976 by Rand McNally College Publishing Company. Used with the permission of the publisher.

Table 10 shows that estimates derived from the model correlate significantly with the "actual" overall satisfaction of the participants under all three systems. Graen pointed out, however, that actual overall satisfaction can be influenced by a large number of variables from outside of the situation, such as those things that participants may bring into the role. Thus, an attempt was made to partial out the impact of these outside influences and thereby focus more directly on the "net" impact of the reward system. Figures that appear on the second column in Table 10 display correlation coefficients between the EU estimate and the "improvement" in satisfaction, i.e., the net changes in satisfaction after outside influences were partialed out. The result indicates that although correlations between predicted and actual overall satisfaction showed significant relationships for only those under the Contingency

(.46) and the Control (.23) systems, and not for those under the Obligation (.02) system.

Table 10 also shows that the improvements in role performance on two different tasks were predicted by the effective performer model with differential accuracy for the three reward systems. Only under the Contingency system were the relationships significant between the estimates of the model and the actual improvements in performance. Neither the Control nor the Obligation system produced other than near-zero relationships.

The findings summarized in Tables 9 and 10 tell us more about the process of leadership effect upon subordinates' motivation and role behaviors. Under the Contingency reward system, or under the leader who emphasizes effective performance and reinforces the subordinate with "intrinsic" rewards contingent upon his performance, (1) the subordinate became attracted by such role outcomes as achievement and recognition (valence of these outcomes increased), (2) his perceived instrumentality of role performance for attaining these outcomes increased, and (3) his expectancy that increased effort will result in more effective job performance also increased. Moreover, Graen's study documented that, (4) these increases in motivational components lead to "improvements" in role performance and satisfaction of the subordinate, because of the increased expected utility of his role behavior.

The studies conducted by House (1971) and Graen (1969) are quite similar in that both researchers emphasized the importance of the motivational functions of the leader's behavior vis-à-vis his subordinates. However, leader's approaches to the function may show a contrast between the two studies. For the path-goal approach, motivational functions of the leader can be conceived of as those of "diagnosis." For this approach, the leader's function is to identify motivational deficiencies (the sources of ambiguity, conflict, and frustration) associated with the subordinate's tasks. Then, he is expected to cure these motivational defects by either eliminating (by initiating structure) or attenuating (by consideration) these deficiencies through his therapeutic actions. The results displayed in Table 8 may support this interpretation. That is, in Low autonomy tasks where a variety of motivational defects are expected to exist, leader behaviors of initiating structure and consideration are found most effective, and tend to enhance performance and satisfaction of subordinates. On the other hand, in High and Medium autonomy tasks where motivational deficiencies are expected to be less severe, leader behaviors exerted little influence over subordinate motivation. Especially, the leader seemed to lack the means of influencing the subordinate performance under these situations.

In Graen's contingency approach, the functions of the leader are conceived of as a motivational "guide" for the subordinate's behavior. His functions seem to be presenting a map, to draw paths (contingencies) to arouse and guide the motivational forces of the subordinate toward the attainment of desired outcomes, to give feedback as to whether he stands on the right paths or not, and finally to reward him for achievement and recognition. Results presented in Table 9 indicate that this contingency guidance of the leader does influence the subordinate's motivation. Also, in Table 10, it was displayed that under the Contingency reward system, improvements in satisfaction and performance are the function of the increased instrumentality of role performance and the increased expectancy that the effort on the task would lead to more effective job performance.

The other difference between House's and Graen's approach may involve a discussion on "leadership motivation." In traditional leadership studies, why a leader takes, or is suggested to take, on a particular leadership style has not been examined at all. Instead, a selection of criteria that satisfy a common-sense view of leadership effectiveness has provided rationale for motivation of the leader, together with the empirical correlations between such criteria and a particular leadership style. As we have seen already, in House's study the leader is interested in diagnosis of the subordinate's task. But, his real motivation seems to be in establishing a link between the subordinate's behavior and his performance and satisfaction based on the leader's prescription derived from his task analysis (behavior-performance link). On the other hand, in Graen's study the leader is interested in motivational guidance and feedback to the subordinate. His motive seems to be in establishing a link between the subordinate's behavior and reward outcomes with the emphasis that the reward outcomes should be contingent upon the role performance of the subordinate (behavior-performance-outcome link). Under the Contingency situation the supervisor is regarded as a critical resource in the environment for the subordinate's motivation, satisfaction, and performance. The interpersonal relations for the managerial progress based on this system may require that the subordinate's motivation for effective performance and progress be reinforced by the proper feedback from the supervisor (e.g., achievement and recognition). This feedback links role behaviors between the two persons into a reciprocal process of "vertical exchange."

II. Vertical Exchange and Its Outcomes

Katz and Kahn (1966) proposed a role theory of the organization in which the role-sending and role-receiving, based on the exchange of *role episodes,* constitutes the basic structure and processes of the organization. According to their theory, the behavior of a new person to the organization develops as he responds to role pressures exerted by other persons within the role system of the organization. For the newcomer, role establishment denotes developing interdependent role relationships with the established members of the organization by responding to the sent-role. Katz and Kahn called a group of role senders, the *role-set* members. The role-set members may attempt to shape the focal person's behavior by sending role episodes. A role-set member sends information about how he prefers the focal person to perform the role and attempts to gain compliance by implying the consequences of acceptance and rejection of this request. The focal person's ensuring behavior indicates compliance or non-compliance, and this feedback to the role sender indicates the impact of his message. A sequence of sending-receiving-feedback completes a a role-sending episode. If the feedback behavior is not acceptable to the role sender, he may initiate another episode.

As previous discussions indicated, the immediate supervisor represents the single most important person among role-set members for the newcomers to the organization. To him, the immediate supervisor may represent the organization itself (Porter, et al., 1975). In Max Weber's terms, the supervisor controls the "office." French and Raven (1959) suggested that the supervisory position is equipped with multiple "power bases": reward power, coercive power, legitimate power, referent power, and expert power. In addition, the supervisor can enjoy "idiosyncrasy credit" (Hollander, 1958). Kahn and his associates (1964) stated that theoretically the population of role senders for a given focal person includes all members, whose expectations are relevant to the performance of the focal person. In an empirical study of organizational stress, Kahn and his associates looked for role senders based upon the authority structure and the work-flow structure in the organization, but the immediate supervisor was always chosen as the most significant role-set member, a person with the greatest potentiality of resources for his role development.

The role episode model describing the process of leader-member exchange may look like the following (Graen, 1976). The leader holds a set of expectations regarding the appropriate role behavior of the member (Role Expectation). The leader communicates his expectation to the member through a number of different channels. Although these expectations may be misinterpreted due to noise in the communication process, the member receives and interprets these sent expectations (Received Role). Based upon these perceived roles, the member may modify his role behavior. The feedback to the leader concerning the impact of his sent role is transmitted by the member's role behavior

(Monitored Behavior). If the leader interprets the role behavior of the member as sufficiently discrepant from his role expectations, he may decide to communicate this to the member and thus initiate another cycle of events.

Schiemann (1977) stated that discrepancies in expectations and behaviors are unavoidable products associated with the process of vertical exchange, because of the various "noises" involved in the communication process: *system noise* associated with the communication system itself (channel, network, task-flow, etc.) and *semantic noise* associated with the cognitive processes. According to Graen (1976) discrepancies in expectation and behaviors can be classified into the following four categories corresponding to the different phases of vertical communication. However, discrepancies and noise may not be recognized as such by the parties in the exchange. The *expectation discrepancy* is the difference between the role expectation held by the leader and that received by the member. Only an outside observer with access to both sources of information would be in a position to evaluate this factor. This expectation discrepancy is an index of the noise in the role sending system. The *role discrepancy* is the difference between what the member perceives to be his leader's role expectation and the member's current role behavior. Only the member and an outside observer usually would have information on this discrepancy. In role terminology, this role discrepancy would be an index of the member's perceived conflict between his and his leader's definition of the role. The *feedback discrepancy* is the difference between the member's role behavior and the leader's perception of that behavior. Only an outside observer could have access to this factor. This feedback discrepancy is an index of noise in the feedback system. Finally, the *performance discrepancy* is the difference between the leader's role expectations and his perception of the member's current role behavior. Usually, only the leader and an outside observer would have information on this discrepancy. In role terminology, this discrepancy is an index of perceived conflict between the leader's expectations and his member's role behavior.

1. Reciprocity in Exchange

The vertical exchange model applied to the study of role making of the newcomer stresses the reciprocal relationship (Gouldner, 1960; Homans, 1958) between the newcomer and his supervisor. The role episode model advanced by Katz and Kahn (1966) may imply the one-way influence process. For the role episode model, the emphasis is placed upon the process by which the newcomer to the organization *takes* his role presented by the established members of the organization in compliance with their role pressures and expectations (the *role taking* process). For this approach, role episodes sent to the newcomer may imply a "take-it-or-leave-it" situation, because the newcomer's input into the role-sending processes is not expected to modify the expectations maintained by his role-set members. The role taking process is based on the concept of *partial inclusion;* the organization neither requires nor wants the whole person, but only a "psychological slice" of the person (Katz and Kahn, 1966, 50). Therefore, this approach tends to put emphasis upon analysis of how the established role system functions and is maintained over time against the constant disturbances in the system caused by new human inputs. According to Weick's terminology (1969), the role taking approach may correspond to the organization's exigency of "stability."

On the contrary, the vertical exchange approach emphasizes the process of *role making.* This approach assumes that the role situation of the newcomer usually is only partially defined by the organization, mostly in terms of the formal prescriptions. But, this does not necessarily imply partial inclusion of the individual, rather quite the contrary the individual is encouraged to fill the unwritten half of the scenario so that his role behavior becomes an active part of the on-going organizational processes. From the newcomer's point of view, the role making process implies that he is responsible for establishing his role interdependently with others. To do this, he must be allowed to influence his role-set members (especially his supervisor) for letting them (him or her) respond to what he needs, even amidst the overwhelming role pressures. Graen (1976) emphasized that the process of vertical exchange for role making is characterized as a process of a *negotiated role definition.* Negotiation between a newcomer and his supervisor may take place soon after the introduction of the newcomer into his role situation to modify a depersonalized and partly fictitious new role into a workable, interdependent one. The approach to the negotiation may be the following. The immediate supervisor is ready to trade his legitimate resources (of which the organization has a monopoly) for behaviors of the new incumbent over and above that specified by the formal job description. On the other hand, the new incumbent may try to exchange his contribution to his work unit with the supervisor's influence. This exchange implies an acquisition of extra resources for his role development for the newcomer. His contribution may consist of: (a) expending an unusual amount of time and energy at critical periods, (b) producing exceptionally high quality work on certain vital projects, (c) intervening in interpersonal conflicts to cool emotionally disruptive situations within the unit, (d) doing things designed to make the supervisor look good in the eyes of his supervisors, and (e) performing various protective acts to keep the unit from looking bad (Graen, 1976, 1224–1225). These behaviors and many more are not required as a condition of employment, but they could prove to be the difference between success and failure for the unit.

In summary, the vertical exchange model of the role making addresses itself toward exploring the expanding "influence pie" situation (Tannenbaum, 1962) where the simultaneous "optimum solution" (Campbell, et al., 1970) in exchange may be sought between the supervisor and his subordinates. In this way, the role making model offers propositions for growth (change) of the organization and the individual over their long-range relationships. Again, going back to Weick (1969), it may be pointed out that the role making model corresponds to the organization's exigency of "flexibility."

2. Outcomes of Exchanges

The second point that may overlap the first one has more to do with the application of the model. The role episode approach has attracted researchers, because the model has often been found to be inconsistent with empirical evidence depending upon the situation. For example, Kahn and his associates (1964) demonstrated that within a unit for leader-member exchange, the role episodes were only ambiguously recognized among the subordinates, and many of them reported that they did not know what role should be taken because what the supervisors expected them to do was not communicated clearly. Kahn and his associates (1964) reported that the role stress caused by, (a) organizational, (b) interpersonal, and (c) personality reasons tended to make the subordinate role situation ambiguous and conflict ridden. In addition, role ambiguity and conflict were found predictive of dysfunctional emotional reactions among the subordinates: i.e., tension, anxiety, fear, anger and hostility, sense of futility, loss of self-confidence.

Katz and Kahn's (1966) model opened the way to studies of role perceptions. These studies usually focused their attention on role ambiguity and conflict with an assumption that they will have negative impacts upon the subordinate's job satisfaction and performance (Kahn, et al., 1964; House, 1971; House and Rizzo, 1972). Hamner and Tosi (1974), and Schuler (1975) indicated, however, that recent research has produced mixed results as to the effect of role conflict and ambiguity. Some researchers found a negative relationship between role conflict and satisfaction, but no relationship between role ambiguity and satisfaction (Tosi and Tosi, 1970; Tosi, 1971), while others found a negative relationship between satisfaction and role ambiguity, but no relationship between role conflict and satisfaction (Hamner and Tosi, 1974; House and Rizzo, 1972). Some other researchers suggested that ability (Schuler, 1977), or the organizational level of the employee (Hamner and Tosi, 1974), may be considered as a moderating variable to reconcile these discrepant findings.

The role making model is also interested in exploring role conflict and ambiguity, but for different reasons. For this approach, the perceived ambiguity and conflict are regarded as a part of the immediate outcomes derived from the vertical exchange processes. In other words, the role making model assumes that the process of exchange produces various "interpersonal outcomes" in addition to conflict and ambiguity. Studies on role making processes produced evidence that job challenge, dyadic trust, leadership support and attention, job problems, role conflict and ambiguity, and the like can be conceived of as immediate outcomes from the vertical exchange processes. In addition, a series of studies conducted by Graen and his associates revealed that the quality of exchange relationships characterized by these immediate outcomes (i.e., satisfaction, performance, turnover) of the assimilation process. These outcomes then, may prepare the resource conditions for the subordinate to achieve higher-order outcomes indicative of his career progress within the organization. In the following section, we will examine empirical evidence derived from the organizational assimilation studies designed to explore the mechanism of interpersonal resource acquisition and its effect upon role development based on the method of longitudinal investigation.

III. Organizational Assimilation:
A Longitudinal Study of Role Making

A longitudinal investigation was conducted (Dansereau, et al., 1975; Graen, et al., 1973; Johnson and Graen, 1973; Haga, et al., 1974) to explore the process of organizational assimilation of administrators into a service organization of a large public university. The study was designed to investigate through what processes leader-member relationship affected the process of organizational assimilation. The organizational situation for the research looked like the following. Within the organization, 88 percent of the dyadic relationships involving a supervisor and his members were new due to the organizational change designed to transform its image by de-emphasizing its "bricks and mortar" function while emphasizing its "professional service" function. Thus, almost everybody in the organization had to face the problem of assimilating to the new organizational environment, and in addition to developing his role through interpersonal role making processes. Data collection was divided into four interview waves over the nine-month period (Dansereau, et al., 1975): the initial wave began immediately after the first month of the academic year, the second wave after the third month, the third wave after the sixth month, and the fourth wave after the eighth month. The following four sets of instruments were administered in each interview session: (a) negotiating latitude, (b) the supervisor's contribution to vertical exchange in terms of his activities toward the member, (c) the member's contribution to vertical exchange in terms of his role behavior, and (d) various outcomes of the exchange processes.

1. Negotiating Latitude

To measure the quality and the level of leader-member exchange relations, Dansereau and his associates (1975) proposed the concept of "negotiating latitude." This concept was defined by the participant's perception of his supervisor's willingness to use formal authority to help solve problems on the member's job (Dansereau, et al., 1975; Graen, 1976). Two questions were employed to assess each member's perception on this aspect of leader-member relations. (1) "How flexible do you believe your supervisor is about changes in your job activity structure?" (2) "Regardless of how much formal authority your supervisor has built into his position, what are the chances that he would be personally inclined to use his power to help you solve problems in your work?" Given relatively strong correlations between the two measures (.62, .71, .66, and .72 at two, four, seven, and nine months, respectively), these were summed to form a measure of the member's negotiating latitude. Examination of the distribution of this composite score at the second month suggested that the sample could be divided into two groups: the 31 high negotiating and the 29 low negotiating groups. Based on this classification, a repeated-measure of analysis of variance was applied to examine the effect of vertical exchange upon the process of organizational assimilation.

The validity of dividing the sample into the high and low negotiating latitude groups (which were labelled the "IN" and the "OUT" groups respectively) was tested by examining the discriminant power of this dichotomy over time. The result produced a significant repeated-measure group effect, indicating that those who scored high on negotiating latitude at two months after reorganization (the In-group) are significantly higher in negotiating latitude at four, seven, and nine months, compared to other group members who were low on negotiating latitude (the Out-group). Moreover, this dichotomy based on the second month negotiating latitude was found predictive of immediate as well as role outcomes during the period of organizational assimilation. That is, Dansereau and his associates reported that across the second and seventh time periods, the In-group memebers expressed higher overall satisfaction (using Hoppock Satisfaction Blank) with their jobs than that expressed by the Out-group members (p < .03). In terms of more specific outcomes measured using a Role Orientation Index (Graen, et al., 1972), the In-group members reported a more positive work attitude on intrinsic outcomes of work (p < .01), interpersonal relations with their supervisor (p < .001), supervisor's technical competence (p < .01), and the value of their job performance rewards (p < .001), compared to the Out-group members.

Examination of the focal person's role behavior indicated that the In-group members tended to spend more time and energy for various role-related activities, especially for communicating (p < .01) and administration (p < .01) activities than the Out-group members. In addition, it was found that the supervisor tends to evaluate his In-group member's role behavior as corresponding more to his preference. That is, the discrepancy between what the supervisor expected his subordinate to do and what he perceived his subordinate is actually doing on the job (performance discrepancy) was found significantly lower over time for those with In-group relationships compared to those with Out-group relationships (p < .04). Moreover, it was found that the In-group subordinates evaluated their own role behavior as more congruent with their preferences. In other words, for the In-group subordinate, the discrepancy between what he is doing and what he prefers to do (role discrepancy) was significantly lower across all periods than that reported by the Out-group members (p < .01).

The negotiating latitude scale gave order not only to role outcomes (satisfaction and performance), but also to many other outcomes derived from the exchange process. Briefly, (a) the In-group members reported receiving significantly higher *leadership attention* from the supervisor across all time periods than that reported by the Out-group members (p < .001). In contrast, the Out-group expressed significantly higher needs for such leadership attention compared to the In-group members (p < .001). Also, (b) the In-group subordinate was found to be receiving higher *leadership support* from the supervisor compared to the Out-group subordinate. This finding indicated that the significantly higher needs of the Out-group members for leadership support (p < .001) were not reflected by the supervisor's behavior. Furthermore, (c) the Out-group members reported that the supervisor is more of the source of *job problems* (p < .001). The supervisor in turn replied that he experienced more problems with his subordinate in terms of knowing what the subordinate wants (expectation discrepancy). Finally, (d) in comparison to the Out-group members, the In-group members perceived the supervisor behaviors as highly *sensitive* to their job needs and behaviors with respect to letting them know what he expected and where they stood with him, and helping them with their problems and role development (p < .001). This suggested the In-group members had significantly lower feedback discrepancy than their Out-group colleagues.

The research results discussed above suggested that the degree of latitude that the supervisor granted to his member to negotiate his role was predictive of subsequent behavior of the subordinate and the supervisor's reaction to it. Graen summarized the characteristics of negotiating latitude as follows (Graen, 1976, 1240–1241).

1. It was formed relatively early in the development of the relationship between the supervisor and his member (before the second month) and remained relatively stable (.60) over at least nine months.

2. It was indicated by a member's perception of his supervisor's willingness to help the member cope with his job during the second month after reorganization.

3. It was not related to professional orientation, job type, level in the organization, employment history, education, age, tenure, sex, race, or life cycle.

4. It was not related to leadership style (in fact, 85 percent of all units of two or more members contained both negotiating and constrained focals).

5. It did not interact with either professional orientation or job type on any of the variables below.

6. It was related to correspondence between what the supervisor expected a focal to do and what that superior saw the focal doing (job performance). Negotiating focals were seen as conforming to expectations; whereas constrained focals were seen as deviating progressively from expectations over time.

7. It was related to the level of involvement the supervisor expected and to that which the member reported (with negotiating showing higher involvement than that shown by constrained).

8. It was related consistently over time to the supervisor's treatment of his members. Negotiating members reported receiving higher job latitude, more information, greater influence in decisions, more support of their actions, and greater consideration of their feelings and needs than that reported by constrained members. Supervisors indicated that negotiating members required higher amounts of these outcomes than those required by constrained members to perform their jobs adequately and without undue dissatisfaction.

9. It was related to the severity of job problems involving immediate supervision. Both supervisor and member reports indicated that constrained members experienced more severe problems with supervision than that experienced by negotiating members.

10. It was related to work attitudes consistently over time. Negotiating members

indicated more positive attitudes toward the overall job situation, work itself, supervision, and outcomes received than constrained members.

11. The above relationships between negotiating latitude and involvement, supervisory treatment, job problems, and attitudes were in predictive as opposed to concurrent or postdictive time sequences. The dichotomy between negotiating and constrained members was based upon data taken during the second month after reorganization, whereas the dependent variables were assessed at later times, for example, four, seven, and nine months after reorganization.

2. Leadership Versus Supervision: The Quality of Exchange

The preceding discussion suggests that the quality of vertical exchange summarized by the negotiating latitude scale is predictive of critical outcomes during the period of organizational assimilation. Following Jacobs (1970), Dansereau and his associates (1975) suggested that the differential qualities of vertical exchange experiences between the In- and Out-group members can be attributable to two different sets of leader behaviors characterized by *leadership* versus *supervision*. According to Jacobs (1970) leadership consists of leader's behavior techniques, which are successful in influencing subordinates without recourse to authority, whereas supervision consists of techniques based upon authority as a means of influence. Dansereau and his associates (1975) assumed that the vertical exchange under supervision techniques will rely almost exclusively upon the formal employment contract, and the subordinate in turn agrees to fulfill all prescriptions and proscriptions of the formal organization regarding his position as conditions of his continued employment. In contrast, the vertical exchange leadership techniques will rely on a different basis for influencing subordinate behaviors. The result of their study indicated that the key outcropping of emerging "leadership" techniques lies in the extent to which the supervisor allows the subordinate to negotiate job-related matters. The leadership techniques documented by their study were found consisting of a set of leader's behaviors for providing support, attention, and sensitivity to the subordinate. The subordinate in turn reacted to the leadership techniques with greater than required expenditures of time and effort along the pattern preferred by his supervisor. Moreover, it was found that the leadership techniques have led over time to more positive work attitudes of the subordinate. Based on the above knowledge, Dansereau and his associates concluded that:

> The greater the latitude given to the member to negotiate job-related matters, the higher is the probability that the supervisor is employing leadership and lower the probability that he is using supervision with his member (Dansereau, et al., 1975, 76).

The basis of leadership influence was further explored by Graen and Cashman (1975), and Cashman and Graen (in press). They developed a hypothesis based upon French and Raven's thesis (1959) regarding the bases of power. Their hypothesis states that "leadership" exchanges will involve *expert* and *referent* power of the leader, whereas, "supervision" exchange will involve more *bureaucratic* and *coercive* power, but less expert and referent power (Graen and Cashman, 1975). This hypothesis was derived on the assumption that if the reciprocal, interdependent relationships are characteristic of leadership exchange, then the usage of coercion and bureaucracy would undermine the proposed relationships; but, the usage of referent and expert power would probably enhance these relationships. The results of their study supported the hypothesis. The In-group (leadership exchange) members endorsed the referent and expert bases of leader influence upon their acceptance of the leader's suggestion significantly more often in comparison to the Out-group (supervision exchange) members ($p < .001$ for both referent and expert factor). Likewise, the In-group supervisor reported that the reference and expertise factors were more instrumental for him in influencing the subordinate compared to the Out-group supervisor ($p < .007$ and $p < .020$ for reference and expertise, respectively). In contrast, the Out-group members displayed a significantly higher endorsement of coercive influence than the In-group members ($p < .003$), although their supervisors denied such difference. The Out-group supervisors reported a significantly higher endorsement of bureaucratic influence instead ($p < .040$).

3. Conflict, Ambiguity, and Agreement

One clear motivational function of a high-level exchange relationship is the reduction of job problems perceived by the subordinate associated with his tasks. Examination of the content of the job problems scales employed by Dansereau and his associates (1975) indicated that the question items overlap with what other authors called role ambiguity and conflict (Kahn, et al., 1964; House and Rizzo, 1972). The difference between the two instruments lies in the way the questions were presented: the job problem measure asked the subordinate to report to what extent he perceives ambiguity and conflict as *severe* problems for him to attain outcomes, while the conventional measure asked the subordinate to report his role situations in terms of perceived role ambiguity and conflict. Therefore, being free from severe job problems indicated reduction or nonexistence of role ambiguity and role conflict. More precisely, even under "leadership" exchange, a relatively high level of ambiguity and conflict may exist, but they may no longer be severe problems for the subordinate in his central role activities compared to the situation under "supervision" exchange.

As discussed earlier, the analysis on job problems indicated that both the supervisor and his subordinate in the High exchange group reported less severe conflict and ambiguity problems between the two, compared to those in the Low exchange group. Dansereau and his associates (1975) suggested that the motivational effects of reducing job problems can be seen in developing *contingency* of role behaviors between the supervisor and his subordinate. That is, for those in the High negotiating group, the pattern of behaviors perceived and reported by each party showed a significant convergence, suggesting that the direction and the magnitude of time and energy allocation of the subordinate to his role are guided by clearer "map" presented by his supervisor. The mechanism of convergence looked iike the following. First, for the High exchange group, discrepancies between the preferred and the actual pattern of time-and-energy allocation for the subordinate's role activities became narrowed *within* both subordinate's perception (narrowing role discrepancy) and his supervisor's perception (narrowing performance discrepancy). As a result, reports on the time-and-energy allocation pattern showed a convergence *between* the supervisor and his subordinate, indicating that both the expectation discrepancy and the feedback discrepancy between the supervisor and his subordinate narrowed as a result of high negotiating latitude. The above result indicates that the "congruence" within each party to the exchange is systematically related to the "agreement" between the two parties upon the interdependent nature of their role activities. In the previous section, we have suggested that the contingency system represents a clarity in behavior-performance-outcomes linkage as a structure for motivating a person toward the high performer model (Graen, 1969). The results reported by Dansereau and his associates (1975) indicated that the contingency structure, as defined above, can also be summarized by the congruence within and the agreement between the subordinate and his supervisor on patterns of role activities and the outcomes from them. The above discussion suggests that the high quality of exchange produces a high level of clarity in contingency. This proposition can find further support from the study conducted by Graen and Schiemann (1977 and 1978). They examined the degree of "similarity" between the focal subordinate and his supervisor in terms of their perceptions of the focal's role situation. It was hypothesized that a dyadic relationship with high quality exchange should demonstrate high agreement on a number of dyadically relevant variables, while dyads with low quality exchanges should show poor agreement on these variables. To test this hypothesis, two measures of agreement were developed (Graen and Schiemann, 1977). One is a "profile similarity" defined as D^2/N (sum of the squared distances between leader and member ratings on each of the 53 corresponding items, divided by the number of items). The alternative measure called "pattern agreement" was derived by computing the person-to-person (P) correlations using the same 53 corresponding items within each dyad. For the purpose of statistical analysis, the P values were converted into Z scores using Fisher's transformation. A composite leader-member exchange measure developed by Dansereau and his associates (1975) was employed to categorize the subjects into three different exchange groups (In, Medium, and Out exchange groups), and then this trichotomized scale was utilized as a factor for the one-way analysis of variance with measures of profile similarity and pattern agreement (transformed) as dependent variables. Table 11 displays the results of this analysis.

Table 11

Profile Similarity, Pattern Agreement, and Leader-Member Exchange at Three Time Periods

Index	Out (n = 23)	Mean Medium (n = 60)	In (n = 26)	P
Profile Similarity[a]				
Time One	2.45	1.76	1.89	.0001
Time Two	2.04	1.39	1.17	.0001
Time Three	2.20	1.71	1.72	.0030
Pattern Agreement[b]				
Time One	.32	.60	.64	.0001
Time Two	.27	.56	.79	.0001
Time Three	.34	.63	.73	.0001

[a]A higher score indicates greater disagreement.
[b]A higher score indicates greater agreement.
Source: Graen and Schiemann, 1977, p. 22.

Table 11 clearly shows that the pattern of mean differences for the two agreement measures are consistent, as hypothesized for all three time periods. Especially, on the pattern agreement measure a striking contrast was displayed between the In- and Out- groups at all time periods: that is, in general, a high level of agreement is established for dyads under high vertical exchange (In-group) on the nature of their role relations, whereas under low vertical exchange (Out-group) the agreement is consistently low over time. It must be noted that for the In-group, a very high agreement (the maximum .66 correlation for $Z = .79$ at time two) was reached between the subordinate and his supervisor regarding dimensions critical to the contingency relationships, i.e., leadership attention, leadership support, sensitivity, job problems, feedback, and so forth. But the same relationships remained very low (the minimum .26 P correlation for $Z = .27$ at time two) for the Out-group. Graen and Schiemann concluded that the literature on leader-member agreement shows agreement is not common, but this lack of agreement in the past may be attributable to failure in recognizing the fact that the level of agreement varies as a function of the quality of exchange within the vertical dyad linkage.

4. Organizational Consequences of the Role Making: Beyond an Exchange
The organizational assimilation study conducted by Dansereau and his associates (1975), and the other studies that followed (Cashman, et al., 1975; Graen and Cashman, 1975; Graen, 1976; Graen et al., 1978, Graen and Schiemann, 1978) have consistently produced evidence to support the following propositions. First, managerial units routinely become differentiated into at least two groups in terms of the quality of vertical exchange (In and Out groups). Second, this differentiation occurs rather quickly and can be detected in the variation of negotiating latitude perceived by unit members. Third, different levels of negotiating latitude lead over time to the development of different types of leader-member exchanges, "leadership" versus "supervision." Finally, these two types of exchanges lead to very different outcomes for the unit members.

The above propositions suggest that basically managerial development is the process of achieving "dyadic effectiveness" within a given unit of vertical exchange. This effectiveness may, or may not, depending upon other conditions, lead to the effectiveness of the team or the organization. Thus, the role making model applied to managerial development will involve two critical questions. First, the question is how to develop the dyadic effectiveness of the vertical dyad linkages involving the new recruits to the organization and their managers? Second, how to integrate the dyadic effectiveness with effectiveness of the team and the organization as a whole? For the first question, we have seen that propositions on the "leadership" technique may provide part of the answer. Practically, however, questions regarding who are to be selected as supervisors for the newcomers and how they should be trained for the leadership technique remain to be solved (Schein, 1964).

For the second question, additional considerations may be required, because this question involves discussions about the effectiveness of the supervisor *as a subordinate of his superior.* That is, the second question poses an inquiry about the conditions by which a manager can both be a leader of an effective dyad vis-à-vis his subordinate (lower-dyad effectiveness), and at the same time be a subordinate of an equally effective dyad vis-à-vis his superior (upper dyad effectiveness). When the lower-dyad effectiveness contributes to the effectiveness of the upper-dyad, activities within each successive dyadic unit can be integrated more efficiently into the overall effectiveness of the work organization. Past studies on the influence processes provide some information helpful in exploring this question. Pelz (1952) reported that the amount of influence the manager (as a subordinate) claimed with his superior moderates the correlations between the manager's behavior (as a supervisor) toward his subordinates and the subordinates' reactions to his treatment. According to Pelz, a leader's behavior has significant influence upon his subordinates only when he has influence with his superior, otherwise the leader's influence is not reacted to by his subordinates effectively. A linking-pin function of the leader advanced by Likert (1961) also suggests that the capacities of a leader to exert an upward influence may be critical for the leader in order to link himself to the next highest unit in the organization by overlapping group membership. Wager (1965) documented the Likert thesis by an empirical study. He reported that the leader who has influence with his superior was found more effective in using a supportive leadership style toward his subordinates than the leader who has little influence with his superior.

Cashman and his associates (1975) conducted a study to explore the impact of the quality of the *upper* vertical dyad linkage (supervisor-boss exchange) upon the quality of the *lower* vertical dyad linkage (subordinate-supervisor exchange). In their study, the lower and upper dyadic units were interlocked for an analysis of variance design using two negotiating latitude measures as factors for the analysis, i.e., the subordinate negotiating latitude perceived vis-à-vis his supervisor (dichotomized into In and Out groups) and the supervisor's negotiating latitude perceived vis-à-vis his boss (also dichotomized into In and Out groups). Combining these two factors produced a factorial design for the two-way analysis of variance: (a) the 14 In-subordinates reporting to the In-supervisors (the In-In dyads), (b) likewise, the 15 In-Out dyads, (c) the 14 Out-In dyads, and (d) the 17 Out-Out dyads. The subordinate responses on job problems, work attitudes and perceived leader behaviors, and supervisor responses on subordinate's role behaviors were subject to the analysis as dependent variables for the ANOVA design. Figure 2 displays one of the results from this analysis.

Figure 2 indicates that, first of all, the subordinate's satisfaction with his supervisor's technical competence differs depending upon his exchange position with his supervisor. Generally, the In-group members express higher satisfaction than the Out-group members. Second, this group difference of subordinate's satisfaction becomes widened depending upon whether his supervisor is in the In- or Out-exchange group vis-a-vis his boss. That is, the Out-group subordinates reporting to the Out-group supervisor displayed an exacerbation in satisfaction relative to other subgroups, indicating a significant interaction effect ($p <$ .05) between the two exchange dimensions. The same interaction pattern was observed for subordinate satisfaction with psychological rewards ($p <$ .01). For the other dependent variables, it was found that the upper vertical exchange tends to govern the quality of the lower vertical exchange. For example, the subordinate's report on leadership attention, leadership sensitivity, job problem, and frequency of reporting were found much higher among those working under the In-supervisor than among those working under the Out-supervisor. For these variables, the group difference in the upper-dyad was not moderated by the subordinate exchange position with his immediate supervisor. Exploration on functions of the interlocking vertical dyad linkages was replicated by Graen and his associates (1977). In addition to the previous findings, the results of their study further indicated that: (a) the behavior of the supervisor in terms of level of involvement in role activities was differentiated based on the quality of supervisor exchange with his boss, (b) the behavioral expectations of the supervisor regarding level of his subordinate involvement were also found to be differentiated based on the supervisor-boss relations, and (c) the bases of influence ("leadership" versus "supervision") employed by the supervisor toward his subordinate differed depending upon his exchange position with his boss.

The results reported above suggest that: (1) exchange mechanisms found in the lower dyads are operating even in the upper Vertical Dyad Linkage, and (2) the quality of the upper VDL tends to affect the quality of the lower VDL. The causal direction of influence within the inerlocked vertical dyad linkages may be predominantly downward. Those supervisors who develop high-level exchange relationships with their bosses may receive a greater share of positional resources of their bosses than the other supervisors who failed to do so. Then, the high

Figure 2

Interaction Pattern on Perceived Competence of Supervisor

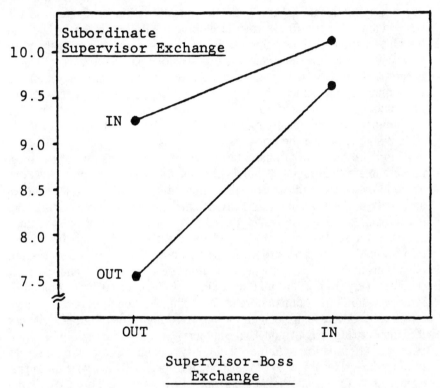

Satisfaction with
Supervisor's Competence

Source:from Cashman, J., et al. Organizational Understructure and Leadership: A Longitudinal Investigation of the
Managerial Role Making Process. Organizational Behavior
and Human Performance, 1976, 15, p.282, Fig. 2.
Copyright © 1976 by Academic Press, Inc. Used with the
permission of the publisher and the authors.

exchange supervisors developed a better position to initiate "leadership" exchange with their subordinates, in comparison to the low exchange supervisors. From the focal subordinate's point of view, this indicates that opportunities for his role development depend partly upon a relationship to which he is not an active party. However, the contribution of the upper VDL to the lower should not be overemphasized. In Figure 2, the In-In role position may represent a best situation for the focal's role development. But, both the In-Out and the Out-In show positions close to the In-In, and far better than the Out-Out position which indicates the worst situation for the focal's role progress. It may be that given a situation where *ceteris paribus* either the focal himself can achieve high quality exchange with his supervisor, or his supervisor can achieve it (for him) with the boss, then role development of the focal subordinate may follow a relatively favorable path, if not the best or the worst.

For the focal subordinate, the supervisor represents one of the most important environmental resources for his role development. However, as we have seen already, potentials of immediate environmental resources are partly a function of the quality of the upper exchange. Graen and his associates (1977) suggested that the quality of an upper dyad may represent an "organizational climate" for the focal person at the bottom of a lower dyad, because from the focal's point of view, it is a constraint, or a "given," to his activities for role development. Therefore, it becomes very important that a linking-pin function of the supervisor intersects the "environmental" and the "climate" boundaries to facilitate effective resource management for his overlapping work units. Under the interlocking VDL model, the supervisor in a linking-pin position performs a function of the "boundary spanner" for the resource transaction. He may try to exploit the potential *external* resources (upper-unit) to enrich the *internal* ones (lower-unit). This part of the function will provide the supervisor with additional resources to meet the demands of his unit members. On the other hand, the same supervisor may endeavor to utilize the given, internal resources to an optimal extent for achieving his (or group's) goals that impinge on him because of his subordinate position in the upper-dyad. This boundary function of the supervisor channels members' performance at the lower level into effectiveness for the upper structure.

The above discussion suggests that if we look at a chain of vertical relationships developing along the organizational hierarchy, we may find a structure of resources allocation within the organization as illustrated in Figure 3. Figure 3 implies that: (a) in each level of organizational hierarchy the focal subordinates can be differentiated into either an In-

Figure 3

Hierarchical Structure of Resources Allocation
for Role Development Within the Organization

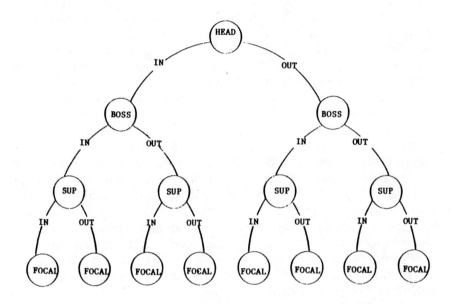

Source: from Cashman, J., et al., Organizational Understructure and Leadership:
A Longitudinal Investigation of the Managerial Role Making Process.
Organizational Behavior and Human Performance, 1976, 15, p.288, Fig. 1.
Copyright ©1976 by Academic Press, Inc. Used with the permission of the
publisher and the authors.

or an Out-exchange group in terms of their relationships with their immediate supervisors (*intraunit differentiation*), and (b) a linking-pin function of the supervisor at each level of the hierarchy produces a chain of vertical dyad linkages that integrates intraunit differentiation into *interunit differentiation*. The development of these two differentiations constitutes a tree-structure for resource allocation within the organization. This kind of structure may not be "visible" from the outsider's perspective and probably even from that of the insider's, but it prepares the *understructure* for role development as against the overt organizational structure for the division of labor.

Going back to the question posed at the beginning, it will be suggested that the contribution of a given dyad to team or organizational effectiveness depends first upon the effectiveness of a linking-pin function of the supervisor in a chain of the vertical linkage structure. Figure 3 implies that role development is conceived of as a process of "increasing centrality" (Schein, 1971) by moving into the In-group exchange relationship within a given unit (short-run development), and then by moving along a chain of vertical dyads (long-run development). A long-run outcome will emerge as a result of an accumulation of short-run outcomes. In this regard, the organization building should start from developing dyadic effectiveness at all levels of the organization followed by an effort to integrate each dyadic unit into a system of effective role performance and development.

Part II

A Longitudinal Study in a
Japanese Business Organization

Chapter V

Managerial Career Progress: Design of the Study

In 1972, a longitudinal study was started in one of the large Japanese business organizations to investigate the process of management progress of newly hired college graduates. The design of research required repeated monitorings on the process of newcomers' process within the organization at seven different points in time over a three-year period. The purpose of the study was directed toward answering the very basic question concerning the process of managerial resources development; why do some people achieve a higher level of management progress during their early period of career development, while some others may fail to do so? More precisely, what are the important indicators of management progress during the formative years in business? How accurately can progress in management be predicted? What are the organizational and personal consequences of managerial progress?

I. Hypotheses Development and the Context of Research

As discussed in previous chapters, three hypotheses were developed to explore the above questions. The *assessment center* hypothesis suggested that the newcomer's potential identified at the start of career development explains the variation in outcomes of career progress at later stages. On the other hand, the *disillusionment* hypothesis indicated that the level of early-stage disillusionment with the career role is predictive of differentiation in later career outcomes. Third, the *role-making* hypothesis suggested that it is the quality of the leader-member relation called vertical exchange that determines outcomes from the process of career development. The present research was designed to test the predictive validity of each hypothesis, with outcome variables measured at seven different monitoring points in time during three years. The outcome measures consisted of three sets of variables with different levels of "complexity" (Smith, 1976): (a) exchange outcomes, (b) role outcomes, and (c) career outcomes. Predictors corresponding to the role making hypothesis (the "vertical exchange" scale) and the disillusionment hypothesis (the "role disillusionment" scale) were measured during the first year of the newcomer's career. On the other hand, the "potential" scale corresponding to the assessment center hypothesis was evaluated in conjunction with the company's employment decisions before the start of the newcomer's career.

1. Hypotheses
In order to test predictive validity, each hypothesis was stated as follows.

(1) *The Role-Making Hypothesis.* The quality of dyadic relations experienced by the focal newcomer during the first year of his organizational career determines the level of outcomes derived from the subsequent periods of career progress in three years. That is, the higher the level of first-year vertical exchange for the newcomer, the higher the level of exchange outcomes, role outcomes, and career outcomes for subsequent time periods.

(2) *The Disillusionment Hypothesis.* The first year role disillusionment is responsible for predicting subsequent outcomes of the career development process, i.e., the greater the disillusionment, the lower the outcome levels achieved by the focal newcomer during three years.

(3) *The Assessment Center Hypothesis.* The newcomer's potential assessed by using multiple testing methods at the time of employment determines the career progress of the newcomer after employment. The higher the potential, the higher the level of outcomes the newcomer will achieve in three years.

The statistical analysis for the present study is based on procedures of "strong inference" (Platt, 1964). This strategy suggests the following procedures as steps for "saving" the hypothesis: (1) test the competing hypotheses, (2) if the result is significant, retain the hypothesis and forward alternative hypotheses to explain the result, (3) test the retained hypothesis against these alternatives, (4) to see whether or not the original hypothesis still can be maintained, (5) if it can be maintained, ask alternative hypotheses again, and so on. For the present analysis, the three competing hypotheses will be tested first (Chapter 6). Then, alternative ways to explain the obtained results will be discussed and tested in Chapters 7, 8, and 9 to examine which hypotheses can survive the test of strong inference.

2. A Paradigm of Research
Figure 4 displays a conceptual system designed for our study to integrate key factors relating to managerial progress into a single, comprehensive diagram for empirical testing. The diagram shown in Figure 4 can be divided into three parts: input, throughput, and output. Personal and organizational factors represent an *input* category. Personal factors may

Figure 4

A Diagram for the Research

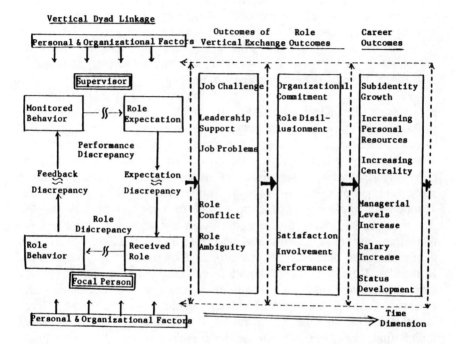

consist of skills and abilities, attitudes and values, needs, interests, preferences, and the like in addition to the personal background data that the individual brings into the organization. The organizational factors can be defined as structural elements of the organization that set a limit upon role behaviors of the individual: functional division of labor, rules and regulations, size, budgetary and administrative controls, hierarchical positions, employment and working conditions, "climate" of the organization, etc. These factors are constraints for the short-run role activities, but can be subject to change in the long-run.

Throughput represents a set of factors that regulate behavior processes. Behavioral processes relevant to the phenomenon of managerial progress are represented in out study by the leader-member exchange process called "vertical exchange." It is important to note that given a set of input factors, outcomes from the career development process can still show a significant difference depending upon how these inputs are "processed" through the vertical exchange relation. Throughput implies processes in which the interaction between the supervisor and his subordinate establishes a discretional environment for their role behaviors. Dansereau and his associates (1975) called this discretional area between the supervisor and his subordinate, "negotiating latitude." Research results reported by Graen and Cashman (1975) indicate that even under the constraint of basically similar structural and personal factors, the leader-member relations still displayed large variation in the amount of discretion shared between the two. They found that for some of the leader-member units, the subordinate reported a higher level of job latitude granted by the supervisor and the supervisor's behavior in turn showed characteristics of a "leadership" technique. Conversely, for the other group the leader-member relations were constrained, and the leader took "supervision" as a method of controlling the interaction processes. Moreover, the leader-member relations were found to be predictive of various role outcomes in later phases of the organizational assimilation process.

Output from the process can be classified into three groups along the time dimension. The first and immediate outcomes from the leader-member interaction consist of leadership support, job challenge, job problems, role ambiguity, role conflict, and the like. They are micro, short-run outcomes for parties to the exchange ("exchange outcomes") in a sense that these outcomes constitute important items in a bargaining list, when each party tries to negotiate the nature of mutual relations. The quality of these outcomes then prepares conditions for the next stage of outcomes which we call "role outcomes." Outcomes at this level may include *attitudinal* measures such as organizational commitment, role disillusionment and satisfaction, and organizational measures like job performance and productivity. Then, following these role outcomes, the last, most complex, "career outcomes" will emerge as final products of a career development process. These outcomes may include a managerial level increase in responsibility, salary increase, and status development. Personal changes that will occur in association with career development, such as increased personal resources or potentials, career "subidentity growth" (Hall, 1971), "vocational maturity" (Super, 1957), and the like may also be included as *subjective* outcomes of career progress.

In Figure 4, three sets of criterion outcomes are related to each other along a "specific-general" or "soft-hard" continuum (Smith, 1976). It is not the purpose of our study to test the nature of the relationship between a particular combination of variables as shown in the research diagram. But, it is the purpose of our study to evaluate the entire diagram as a sytem in which a sequence of events relevant to managerial career progress are related and explained based on a set of key concepts. Figure 4 was drawn based on two assumptions. First, in Figure 4 the leader-member relation is assumed to be the factor that produces behavioral processes most relevant to the phenomenon of career progress within the organization. Other factors (personal as well as organizational) are considered as "exogenous" to the leader-member relation, and still relevant to the process of organizational career development. Second, the diagram shown in Figure 4 assumes that outcomes should be explained in conjunction with individual's behaviors relevant to them. Thus, it is expected that for our study, predictors of career progress explain individual behaviors and outcomes of progress as a set.

In Figure 4, three hypotheses for our career progress study can be explained as follows.

(1) *The Role-Making Hypothesis* is directed toward evaluating the effect of a leader-member exchange upon sets of outcomes. The key to this hypothesis is that the high quality exchange would lead to an acquisition of greater amount of interpersonal resources (i.e., exchange outcomes) for the newcomer. These outcomes, especially job challenge, job enrichment, and leadership support, would provide resources for the newcomer to achieve a more complex set of outcomes: high job performance, more positive attitudes toward the organization and the job, and high levels of career outcomes.

(2) *Disillusionment Hypothesis* will be tested using a measure of "role disillusionment." Past studies emphasized that disillusionment is caused by unrealistically high role expectations maintained by the newcomer "before" employment (Dunnette, et al., 1973; Schein, 1964; Porter, et al., 1975). In our diagram, it is assumed that disillusionment is

an attitudinal change of the newcomer "after" employment occurred as a result of his experience with the organization. A variety of causes may contribute to the formation of this negative attitude: personality types, career expectation and orientation, organizational structure and climate, leader-member relationship, and so forth. However, the main thrust of this hypothesis in our study is that once the newcomer experiences severe feelings of disillusionment, whatever the cause of it, during early phases in his organizational life, he may "turn off" from his career role for the subsequent periods of progress. Past studies suggest that the more severely the newcomer experiences this disenchanted feeling during the early stages in his organizational career, the more likely he will be to leave the organization (Dunnette, et al., 1973; Porter and Steers, 1973; Porter, et al., 1976) Moreover, studies conducted by Graen (1976), Graen and his associates (1973), and Hall and Nougaim (1968) reported that behavioral patterns and job performance for the subsequent time periods will also be affected by this early-stage disillusionment. For our diagram displayed in Figure 4, it is hypothesized that disillusionment will be closely associated with newcomer's commitment to the organization and his satisfaction on the job. The negative attitudes toward the organization and the job may also impact upon his performance in the career role. Then, the formation of this negative "syndrome" (Hall and Nougaim, 1968) during early phases of his career may exacerbate the leader-member relation for the subsequent phases of role development. Or simply, the supervisor's effort to change his subordinate's attitude may have little influence after the subordinate has "rejected" (Johnson and Graen, 1973) his role. In this way, the disillusionment syndrome may doom all the outcomes of the developmental process for the new-comer during the first three years of his managerial career.

(3) *The Assessment Center Hypothesis* can be examined based on a measure of newcomer's "potential" assessed at the point of employment. Past attempts of the assessment center method indicated that potential ratings by the assessment staff based on information derived from various test batteries have predictive validity for the career outcomes of the assessee (Dunnette, 1971; Finkle, 1976). However, very little research has been done to explore how this potential factor affects the newcomer's behavior on the job and the outcomes from it. Korman suggested what "potentials" actually predict may be "the general level of adequacy with which the person will be able to function in a complex environment and the extent to which he will be able to handle the various stresses . . . " (Korman, 1968, 316–317). In our study, this "general adequacy" hypothesis will be tested by examining the relationship between potentials of the newcomers and various outcomes of the developmental

process. If potential implies general effectiveness of the newcomer in coping with the environmental pressures as Korman suggested, then in our diagram, the potential factor will show significant relationships with vertical exchange, exchange outcomes, and role outcomes as well as the most complex, career outcomes.

3. Setting of the Research

The design of research for the Japan management progress study was administered following strategies of the open system method (Graen, 1976). This method suggested in brief the following six steps. (1) The study should seek to understand phenomena of interest, their context and boundary conditions. (2) The research questions in the study should contain a minimum of unproven assumptions. (3) The setting and sample are selected for the study based on the expected operation of the phenomena of interest. (4) The study begins with a broad scope in order that the complete setting and time cycle of the phenomena may be observed. This procedure allows for the testing and refinement of the instrument thereby increasing the quality of the data collected. (5) The major goal in the study is increasing predictive validity by the reduction of sources of bias and error. (6) The analysis must not only show significant results but also consistent patterns of logically integrated and substantially significant results. Further, our research called for a setting for investigation in which: (a) a considerably large number of newly recruited managerial candidates would be available in their employment organization where, (b) systematic organizational efforts for managerial progress (selection, training, assessment, rotation, etc.) have been practiced. Originally, five large Japanese business organizations were selected to meet the above criteria, but two of them were dropped after the second wave monitoring to allow us to concentrate our research efforts on a limited sample of organizations. The research program started in 1972 and was successfully completed in 1975 for the three sample organizations; two department stores and one auto manufacturing organization. For the present study, results derived from one of the department store organizations (hereafter called the DEPART organization) will be presented.

(1) *Sample.* A unit of observation sampled for the DEPART study consists of a male, college graduate newcomer and his immediate supervisor. In April, 1972, 85 male college graduates started their career in the DEPART organization. For Japanese universities, the academic calendar closes its one year term in March of every year. Thus, it has been in common practice for most companies to call in their new college recruits on the first day of April. For the large corporation like

DEPART, new college recruits constitute the strategically most important category of the labor force for their internal, long-range manpower planning, because employing managerial people from the outside open market at their mid-career has been a rather exceptional practice. Instead, middle and upper management positions have been filled by training college graduates extensively and promoting them from within, based on the idea of lifetime commitment. Every year large Japanese organizations try hard to reap the cream of the crop from the new graduate labor market each year, whenever the internal manpower plan demands new resources.

The 85 new recruits employed by the DEPART company showed quite homogeneous characteristics. They were all male college graduates with no prior experience of formal employment. They all passed the company's employment examination. The average age among the newcomers was 23.6 with more than 80 percent distributed between the ages of 23 and 24. The age difference did not indicate the difference in prior work experience, but is indicated whether or not the newcomer had a *rōnin* experience when passing the entrance examination to the college after graduating from high school. In our study 88 percent of the recruits came from private universities, while the remaining graduated from public universities. In total, 87 percent of the recruits earned their degree in LAS and 13 percent of them had degrees in engineering, or in industrial arts and design fields. The DEPART organization offered a slightly higher starting salary to those with engineering as their major field compared to those with LAS backgrounds but within each category no further individual differences were observed in initial employment conditions. In addition, all newcomers started their job at the same level within the managerial hierarchy of the organization.

(2) *Recruitment, Training, and Placement.* New recruits were selected carefully. First, the DEPART company sent a notice of vacancy to the placement service office of several universities for posting. Applicants filed their resumes and usually visited the company's recruitment office to get more information about the company, employment conditions, and a schedule for employment selection tests. The company announced an examination date, and all applicants were assembled on that day to take written examinations consisting of a test on English, essay tests, and paper-and-pencil psychological tests. Applicants who passed the initial selection tests successfully were called back to have an interview for final screening.

The recruits' new life in the DEPART organization started with a ceremony of joining the company held on the first day of April, 1972. This ceremony meant a prelude to the following two-month training program specially designed for new recruits to smooth out their transition from students to company men. This training program is called *"shinyū shain kenshū"* (Literally, a newcomer's studying and learning). During the *kenshū* period, all newcomers moved to the company's training center to live together and go through various training programs consisting of a combination of lectures, readings, discussions, and on-the-job training. As soon as this "live-in" training was over, the new recruits were sent to their first formal assignment. Table 12 displays the newcomers' first assignment classified by a job type and a location of work.

Table 12 indicates that about 80 percent of the recruits were assigned to one of the branch department stores where sales and management constituted their central role activities. Recruits with engineering backgrounds had their initial assignments either at the System Department in the Main Office where they worked mostly as programmers, or at the Merchandising Department where they worked as specialists for promoting particular merchandise. After initial assignments, the newcomers were rotated and transferred for both developmental purposes and for the company's business needs, but these movements occurred mainly within the department of initial assignment. Table 12 indicates that the interdepartmental move (or the interbranch move) of the newcomer during their first three years in the DEPART organization was very low. Also, Table 12 indicates that only one person left the company during that period.

(3) *The Organization for Assimilating.* The DEPART organization sampled for our study is one of the largest department stores in Japan. The organization had about 10,000 employees in 1972 working at a number of branch stores and Main Offices located mostly in Tokyo and Osaka areas. The company's basic personnel policy for new recruits was that they would be developed gradually by various formal and informal in-house training programs, job rotations, transfers, and promotions from within, throughout their lifelong corporate career. The newcomer's employment status becomes very secure, once he passes the six month probation period. Regardless of job security and expectations of long-range development, an awareness of competition among the new cadet members becomes salient because newcomers realize sooner or later that they are in the process of differentiation and it is very difficult to catch up once they are left behind in the process. Therefore, the newcomers are ready to allow themselves to become more flexible in order to meet the company's needs and policies. They are eager to prove that they are not only capable of performing given jobs, but also willing to assume additional responsibilities to help the company.

Figure 5 displays an organization chart for the branch store of the

Table 12

Distribution of New Recruits by Work Location and Job Type in the
DEPART Company at the Initial and Last Periods of Monitorings

Job Type	Branch Store						Main Office	Other Office	Total
	A	B	C	D	E	F			
Sales	18(17)	11(10)	9(7)	16(15)	3(2)	2(2)	0	0	59(53)
Import/Export	0	0	0	0	0	0	0	4(4)	4(4)
Interior Design	1(1)	0	0	0	0	0	0	4(4)	5(5)
Advertisement	1(1)	1(1)	0	1(1)	0	0	0	0	3(3)
Personnel	0(1)	1(0)	2(2)	0(1)	0	0	0(1)	0	3(5)
Accounting	0	1(1)	1(1)	1(1)	0	0	0	0	3(3)
System Design	0	0	0	0	0	0	4(6)	0	4(6)
Merchandising	0	0	0	0	0	0	4(5)	0	4(5)
Total	20(20)	14(12)	12(10)	18(18)	3(2)	2(2)	8(12)	8(8)	85(84)

Figures in parentheses indicate number of new recruits for the last monitoring period.

The 80 recruits are available as complete sample for the final analysis.

Figure 5

The DEPART Organization and a Unit of Investigation

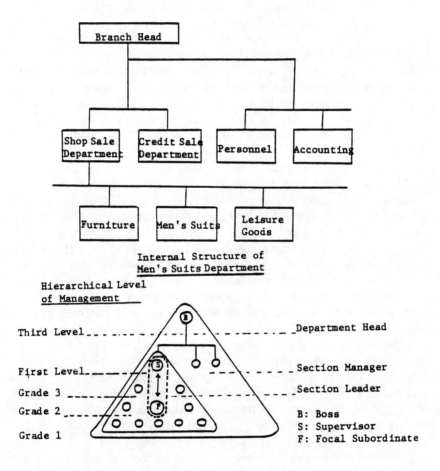

Internal Structure of
Men's Suits Department

DEPART company and an internal structure of the work unit (the Men's Suit Department) to which one of the focal newcomers was assigned. The Men's Suit Department was composed of nine sections. Each section headed by the section manager was segmented based on the commodity differentiation. Within the work unit shown in Figure 5, the section manager was in charge of 16 people composed of two section leaders (Grade 3 level), three Grade 2, and two Grade 1 employees, in addition to eight part-timers. The Department Head with the Third Level or above constituted middle and upper middle management, while section managers with the First Level positions formed the bottom line of the management hierarchy. Then, Grade employees followed after the First Level and were categorized as the General class as opposed to the management people.

Our sample newcomers were all assigned to the Grade 2 positions in different branches and departments. The company had an expectation that the college graduate recruit would reach Grade 3, the section-leader position in three years and the First Level management position in a minimum of three years after being promoted to the Grade 3 level. Then, it is expected to take them a minimum five years after the First Level to be promoted to the Third, middle management position. Since promotion to the Grade 3 was almost automatically granted to all college recruits after three years of experience, the major career concern for them was to reach the first management position in the shortest possible time, i.e., in six years.

For our study, a pair composed of a Focal (F) newcomer and his immediated supervisor (S) was chosen as the unit of observation (see a F-S pair circled by a dotted line in Figure 5). This newcomer-supervisor unit called a "vertical dyad linkage" was monitored using a questionnaire method at seven different points in time during the first three years of the recruit's career. During this period, all newcomers changed their supervisors at least once due to the moves which occurred to either the supervisor or the newcomer himself. Whenever these changes took place, new vertical dyads were identified for further monitoring.

II. Research Procedure

For our longitudinal study, it became critically important to find a way to meet the following procedural requirements: (1) to maintain our respondents committed to the study during the three-year research period, and (2) to keep up with important changes that may happen to newcomers during the research period. To solve these problems, a series of meetings were held with directors, managers, and staff members of the personnel department of the company. At the meeting, the purpose and procedural requirements of the study were explained. Company's support and cooperation provided the investigators with the conditions that made the difficult longitudinal study possible.

1. Questionnaire Development and Administration

The questionnaire used for the present study was developed based on the following four steps. First, staff members of a Japanese research team who were familiar with the concept and theory of organizational behavior studies translated the original English version of the questionnaire into Japanese. Then, for the second step, a *committee* approach (Brislin, et al., 1973) was adopted to check the quality of translation. In the committee, translators and personnel staff members from the company discussed the appropriateness of the wording, merits of each item, clarity of the question, and the context in which the question was asked. As a result, the original translation was modified to a considerable extent: (a) redundancy caused by the word-to-word translation was eliminated, (b) technical terms that would sound unfamiliar to the respondents were either reworded into a more colloquial expression or maintained as they were with a comment for paraphrasing, (c) new question items that would better appeal to newcomers in the Japanese organization were added, and (d) to maintain the context in which the original question was asked, the translation was prompted or was followed, whenever it was necessary, by comments paraphrasing the context of the inquiry. The committee approach was found helpful in checking shared misconceptions among investigators, to avoid professional reluctance to criticize partners, and to induce input and contribution from the company's personnel staff members to the process of investigation.

Third, a Japanese version of the questionnaire developed by the committee was pretested based on the pilot sample. Respondents were encouraged to give comments as to the wording and the clarity of the question items. Based on the feedback obtained from the pilot study, a semi-final form of the questionnaire was constructed to be used for the first wave of the survey. The final stage of questionnaire development involved more changes. The modification primarily involved adding new items and dropping inappropriate ones based on the feedback obtained from interviews with the newcomer who had responded to the questionnaire during the first monitoring wave. The revised questionnaire was administered for the second wave survey and was kept unchanged until the end of the research (see Appendix A for the English version of the questionnaire "retranslated" from Japanese).

The first wave monitoring was conducted in June, 1972 with the following procedures. First, a list of names of the newcomers and their supervisors were provided by the DEPART company. The appropriate supervisor for each newcomer was identified by the personnel office in such a way that: (a) he should have a direct working relationship with the newcomer, and (b) he should have the formal responsibility of performance evaluation for the newcomer. As illustrated in Figure 5, the first Level managers were always chosen as the appropriate supervisors to form vertical dyad linkages with the newcomers.

A list of names matched this way made it possible to "individualize" the questionnaire. The individualization of the questionnaire was devised so that each part in the dyadic relationship received his "own" questionnaire that showed the name of his opposite party on the front page of the questionnaire. For the newcomer's questionnaire, an instruction was given on the front saying that, "In this questionnaire, whenever you find questions asking your opinion about *Your Supervisor*, please answer these questions regarding *Mr. (his supervisor's name)."* Likewise, the questionnaire for his supervisor carried an instruction saying, "In this questionnaire, whenever you find questions asking your opinion about *Your subordinate*, please answer these questions regarding *Mr. (the subordinate's name)."*   Since the questionnaire was made so personal, confidentiality of individual responses was emphasized after the instructions.

The individual questionnaire was put in an envelope together with a self-addressed return envelope and a letter prepared by the company to the respondents.   The letter carried a company message announcing support of the research project and asking respondent's cooperation with it. In the letter, it was made clear that the project was strictly of research interest and the company had no intention of reviewing responses of a particular individual.   The questionnaires prepared this way were distributed through the company's mailing system. The respondents were asked to return the questionnaire within about two weeks either by ordinary mail or by using the company's mailing system. Basically the same procedures were repeated for the rest of the monitoring waves.

For our study, research procedures were established using a formal structure of the organization. This formalization of procedures helped the process of research administration to a great extent. First, it was expected that the respondents' knowledge that their company was helping the research project by using its formal line of authority would have a significant influence for inducing respondents' cooperation with the research. Second, the procedures established for data collection served as a channel of communication between researchers and respondents. Reminders, letters, leaflets or booklets, and the like prepared in order to ask for cooperation were distributed through this channel to the respondents. In turn, comments, questions, and sometimes complaints on the research were sent back from the respondents along the same channel. Third, in the DEPART organization, some of the personnel staff members took care of the internal administration of the research procedure as a part of his or her formal responsibilities during the research period. This indicated a stability of the data-collection method: these personnel people became specialized in handling the complicated procedures for data collection, and the researchers were allowed to continue contact with these same personnel people for trouble shooting and planning for the time period of the next stage of monitoring. Without the patience and contribution of these people, the present study would simply not have been made possible.

2. Interview

For the purpose of enhancing rapport with the respondents, a series of interviews with the newcomer and his supervisor were conducted. Between the monitoring periods, researchers made a trip to see the respondents to personally discuss for an hour the various topics relating to the research and the newcomer's company life. The interview had two purposes. First, the investigators wanted to educate themselves with respect to what the newcomer's tasks in the DEPART company looked like, and what exactly they were doing on the job. This part of the interview helped investigators fill their theoretical concepts with practical terms and knowledge specific to the newcomer's job and his organization: i.e., jargon, customs and practices, an organization chart, the system of personnel administration, etc. This knowledge was, in fact, essential simply for the purpose of effective communication with the respondents. Moreover, verbal descriptions of the job and the role situation given by the newcomers supplied us with the critical information to examine whether the question items listed in our questionnaire were actually tapping most of the important boundary conditions for the role behaviors. As discussed earlier, our knowledge of the "context" of the newcomer's role and role development helped us improve the quality of the questionnaire.

The second purpose of the interview was to convert the investigator-respondent relationship that might be characterized typically by confrontation, suspicion, or indifference between the outsider and the insider, into one buttressed by honesty and trust. For this purpose, the interviewers spent most of their time listening to the interviewee, helping him analyze his role situation, answering questions about the content of the questionnaire, and explaining the purpose and the meaning of our study. In other words, the interview was very unstructured and served entirely for promoting communication between the researcher and the respondents. All newcomers were interviewed at least once at the early stage of the research period, and the majority of them two or three times, depending upon the geographical location of their work place.

Some of the respondents who had not returned the questionnaire were asked to fill it out during the interview session. This follow up method enabled us to maintain a very high response rate in each wave, and across all waves, for the questionnaire survey.

The research procedures described above only represent a highlight of the entire effort made by the investigators and staff members of the company to keep the research project running. Investigators spent much time in preparing a booklet they called a "feedback paper" (reports on the state of research, short essays on men and the organization, etc.) to go with the questionnaire in each wave of monitoring, sending reminders or making telephone calls to collect delayed questionnaires, and writing letters to answer the questions which appeared in the "opinion column" of the questionnaire. It is apparent that the key to the longitudinal investigation is how to keep an original set of sample newcomers responsive all through the successive waves of research intervention. For our research, if either the newcomer or his supervisor happened to fail to return the questionnaire even once, this failure meant that all other information involving this particular focal subordinate could not be utilized for the full scale repeated measured analysis, due to the lack of information for that particular time period. This is why our research procedure required formal commitment of the company and close contact between the investigators and respondents.

The procedures described above can be criticized as involving "obtrusive" measures on the ground that they might have induced reactivity bias by getting so close to the participants and their organization (Webb, et al., 1966). However, our experience also tells us that a series of potentially "interactive" procedures, such as explaining our research and researchers' position to the respondents, asking formal commitment from the organization, and influencing respondents so that they will understand that cooperating with the research project is a meaningful task both for themselves and their organization, must be the very basis to carry out a longitudinal research. It is our belief that the fear of using potentially reactive procedures should not be used as an excuse to violate the relationship of trust between the researcher and participant, or to avoid complicated tasks of the long-range study altogether.

3. Instruments

The conceptual system displayed in Figure 4 was operationalized into a set of researchable components that can be evaluated either by a questionnaire method or by data derived from the company record. The variable sets used for our study will be classified into the following five categories in accordance with research diagram: (1) person variables, (2) organizational structure variables, (3) instruments for vertical exchange and exchange outcomes, (4) instruments for role outcomes, and (5) for career outcomes.

(1) *Person Variables.* Information was collected from company's personnel records for the following sets of variables. (a) *Demographic Variables:* age, name of the university, and major field. (b) *Selection Variables:* The DEPART company conducted a series of selection tests at the time of recruitment for the purpose of screening applicants. The assessment procedures for selection consisted of the following two stages. First, all applicants attended a one-day session of: paper-and-pencil tests, an Incomplete Sentences Blank, an Essay test, and a test of English Proficiency. The last two tests were prepared by the company, but the first one was tailor-made. Personnel staff members of the company read tests and evaluated them along the following scoring keys: The Incomplete Sentences Blank was rated in terms of *Intelligence* using a 4-point scale, and of a *Personality Type* along three prescribed categories for classification; *The Essay* was rated using a 4-point scale, while a test of *English Proficiency* was rated using a 100-point scale. About two weeks later, a group of applicants who passed the first-stage screening based on the evaluation of the above paper-and-pencil tests and other information that was not rated mechanically (academic achievement, a personal history blank, reference, etc.), were called back to have an *Interview* for the final selection. The interview was conducted by a team of five company executives. Interviewers reviewed test scores and the background information of each applicant. Based on this knowledge and performance evaluation of an applicant at interview, they rated each applicant in collaboration using a 4-point scale.

It is known that hiring decisions in the DEPART company were partly influenced by whether or not the applicant had special connections with the company: i.e., if he could exercise outside intervention for hiring on his behalf. For example, the outside influence for hiring a particular applicant may be expected in a situation where a son or a daughter of a company's important customer wants employment with the company, and his or her parents who are regarded as influential, because of business connections with the company, ask a special favor for hiring. this phenomenon is known as *Conne* ("connection" abbreviated for

Japanese). In the DEPART organization, selection records indicated that out of the 85 college graduates who were eventually hired through procedures described above, 15 of them had a *Conne* with a differential degree of influence. However, the impact of *Conne* is subject to statistical analysis regarding the extent to which this outside influence actually affects the company's hiring decisions. This particular variable was rated using a 3-point scale: "0" for none, "1" for weak, and "2" for strong influence.

The researchers were told by the DEPART people that in principle, personnel data on their employees are not disclosed to others. Especially, they said records on performance ratings, potential ratings, appraisals of various kinds, reference, pay, etc., are kept confidential. The assessment record upon recruitment belongs to the same category. This indicates that none of our respondents could have access to ihe assessment data during the research period. Therefore, we believe that contamination of questionnaire responses due to respondent's knowledge of assessment ratings was prevented.

(2) *Organizational Structure Variables.* Information on structural aspects of the newcomer's role situation was collected from company records. The data included information on: (a) focal's work location, (b) job type, (c) size and composition of his work unit, (d) managerial level of the supervisor, (e) demographic characteristics of his supervisor (age, sex, tenure, and educational level), and (f) environmental changes which occurred for the focal person regarding his work location, work unit, and supervisor. The organizational structure variables were assessed systematically at the second, third, and fourth waves of monitoring.

(3) *Vertical Exchange and Exchange Outcome Variables.* Using a questionnaire method, information on the process of vertical exchange between the focal newcomer and his supervisor was collected at seven different points in time between 1972 and 1975. The questionnaire was partly modified after the first wave of monitoring based on the information derived from interviews with the newcomers, but thereafter from the second up to the seventh wave, a standard set of instruments and question items were maintained. In the following, the Vertical Exchange represents an instrument designed to assess the quality of exchange relation itself, while the other three instruments, Job Problem, Job Need, and Job Challenge represent measures on the outcomes of the exchange process.

Vertical Exchange: The vertical exchange scale was developed based on the idea of "negotiating latitude" advanced by American organizational assimilation studies (Dansereau, et al., 1975; Graen, 1976). The original negotiating latitude scale consisted of two items designed to tap the approachability and flexibility of the supervisor as perceived by the focal newcomer. For our study, however, twelve questions were asked to examine a broader range of topics associated with the leader-member exchange. Our vertical exchange instrument included question items regarding: approachability and flexibility of the supervisor, his willingness to use his authority to help the focal solve problems, clarity of expectations and feedback, the focal's latitude to influence the supervisor to change his role situation, and chances to share "afterhours" social and leisure activities. Both focal newcomers and their supervisors were asked to respond from their own point of view as to the extent they experienced the exchange of these role episodes using a 4-point scale. This arrangement was required in order to check the convergent validity of the vertical exchange measure between the focal and his supervisor. For our study, the vertical exchange perceived by the focal subordinate will be treated as a predictor variable representing the role making hypothesis discussed earlier.

Job Problem: The job problem scale was originally devised by Dansereau and his associates (1975). The problem scale developed for our study employed 33 items that represent obstacles to the focal person. The question was asked from two different angles using a 5-point scale. The focal person was asked first, how *frequently* he experiences each of the problems on his job, and second, how *severely* he sees the problem as affecting his endeavor to attain his personal goals. This instrument was designed to evaluate conflict and ambiguity perceived by the focal person arising from: (a) "dyadic problems" (Dansereau, et al., 1975) characterized by lack of trust, unclear responsibility, insufficient information to get the job done, supervisor's reluctance to delegate a part of his authority, poor vertical communication, the lack of performance feedback, etc., and (b) structural/climatic problems such as, unfair company treatment, bureaucratic procedures, company policies, lack of horizontal communication, work overload, unchallenging assignment, improper training programs, distasteful organizational climate, and so forth.

Job Need Receiving and Preferred: Question items used for this instrument were partly derived from the original Leadership Support scale used by Dansereau and his associates (1975) for their American role making study. Our job need scale consisted of the 17 leadership activities relating to the "consideration" and "initiating structure" dimensions of leader behaviors (Stodgill and Coons, 1957). However, for our study these 17 items were designed to measure focal's role situation in terms of the "need-fulfillment" scheme advanced by Porter (1961 and 1962). That is, the focal person was asked to report using a 5-point scale: (a) how much opportunity he sees he is now *Receiving,* and (b) how much opportunity he *Prefers* to be connected with his role position. The receiving dimension corresponds to what Porter called "now" and the preferring dimension to "should." For our analysis, the receiving dimension will be treated as a measure of the outcome from vertical exchange, and the discrepancy between the preferred and the receiving as a measure of deficiency in need fulfillment. Besides the focal persons, each supervisor was also asked to report how much opportunity he was *Providing* to his subordinate, and next, how much opportunity he perceived his focal *Wants* to have.

Job Challenge: The job challenge scale was administered only at the final, seventh wave. The 20 episodes indicating the challenging task characteristics were presented to the focal person using a 5-point rating scale to evaluate how frequently he experienced each of the episodes connected with his role activities. This instrument was developed based on a list of "critical incidents" collected through a series of interviews with focal newcomers and their supervisors. These episodes consisted of critical incidents characterized as: requiring more technical knowledge and expertise, more planning and independent decision making, more chances of contribution and recognition, more coordinating and leadership activities, and so forth. In order to check the convergent validity, the supervisor was also asked to respond to the same questions regarding the degree his focal is provided with each of the challenge episodes.

(4) *Role Outcomes.* Using a questionnaire, the following set of variables, what we called role outcomes, was measured at seven different points in time during the research period: Organizational Commitment, Role Disillusionment, Need Fulfillment, Job Performance, and Success Potential. These variables were separated from other outcome sets, because they were assumed to be more "soft" than general career outcomes, but casually more "complex" than specific exchange outcomes.

Organizational Commitment: Organizational commitment has been studied by many authors regarding its dimensions as well as the causes and outcomes of the commitment phenomenon (Brager, 1969; Gouldner, 1960; Grusky, 1966; Hall and Schneider, 1972; Hrebiniak and Alutto, 1972; Porter, et al., 1976; Sheldon, 1971). Following Porter and his associates (1976), organizational commitment was defined in our study as referring to the nature of an individual's relationship to his organization such that a high commitment to the organization denotes: (a) a strong desire to remain a part of the organization, (b) a willingness to exert high levels of effort on behalf of the organization, and (c) a definite belief in and acceptance of, the values and goals of the organization. Based on this conceptualization, 16 questions were asked of the focal using a 7-point rating scale with respect to: loyalty to the organization, identification with the values and policies of the organization, willingness to put forth extra effort for the success of the organization, concern about the fate of the organization, willingness to recommend the organization as a place to work, and so on.

Role Disillusionment: This instrument consists of question items concerning the environmental and structural impact of the organization upon the level of the focal's determination to remain committed to his organizational role. In past studies, the disillusionment phenomenon has been defined as a discrepancy between focal's expectation before joining the organization and his actual experiences on the job after employment (Dunnette, et al., 1973; Schein, 1964). This approach emphasizes the comparison of focal's responses at two different points in time (before and after employment) and tries to predict the newcomer's subsequent behavior (dissatisfaction, motivational deficiency, and eventual turnover) as a function of divergence between the expected and actual experiences. However, under this approach, what experiences of the focal newcomer on his role actually make him *feel* disillusioned have not been documented. Moreover, past studies do not necessarily indicate clearly that it is this disenchanted feeling that is responsible for explaining differential outcomes from the career development process. In contrast, for our study the direct impact of the environmental and structural aspects of the organization upon the focal's feeling of role disillusionment was assessed using a 7-point rating scale. The organizational characteristics (company policies, reputation, future prospect, etc.), work itself, leadership, and a reward system, of the company constituted sources of impact represented by the 19 question items. The focal subordinate was asked to respond to the degree of impact each aspect has upon his attitude toward the organization using seven response alternatives ranging from, "Strong impact to make me feel like quitting the company" (the lowest, −3 points) to "Strong impact to make me feel like staying with the company" (the highest, +3 points), with a neutral point (0) that states, "No impact at all." The predictor scale derived from this instrument will be used to test the second disillusionment hypothesis.

Need Deficiency: As discussed in the Job Needs section, the discrepancy score between the Job Needs Preferred (JNP) and the Job Needs Receiving (JNR) was defined in our study as a measure of job satisfaction. For this operational definition, the discrepancy score, $D^2 = \Sigma(JNP\text{-}JNR)^2/N$, indicated the deficiency in job need fulfillment. Thus, the smaller the D^2, the higher the job satisfaction, and vice versa

(Lawler, 1973; Porter, 1961 and 1962). To check this assumed relationship, a direct measure of overall satisfaction was administered in each wave of monitoring: using a single-item scale, the focal newcomer was asked to report the level of his overall job satisfaction. (At the final wave, seven satisfaction items were included.)

Job Performance: The supervisor was asked to rate, using a 5-point scale, his focal's behavior on the job with respect to accountability, alertness, interpersonal skill, planning, technical skills and know-how, the level of contribution, interpersonal attraction, and willingness to contribute. Each evaluative dimension was accompanied by a statement that paraphrases specific behaviors relevant to the dimension. In addition to the "external" ratings based on our questionnaire, the "internal" performance ratings were also available from the DEPART organization's annual performance appraisal.

Success Potentials: In addition to the rating of focal's "present" job behaviors, the supervisor was also asked to predict focal's "future" success in the company using a 5-point scale along the following three dimensions: (1) general promotability, (2) success as a line manager, and (3) success as a staff specialist.

(5) *Career Outcomes:* Information on career outcomes corresponding to the period of our search was collected from company records. Available information included: (a) the amount of basic salary, (b) the amount of bonus, (c) the level of managerial responsibility, and (d) company's performance appraisals. Unfortunately, however, it was found that for the DEPART newcomers, both the salary and managerial level of responsibility yet did not show any meaningful variance by the end of the research period. Thus, out of the information collected from the company's records, only bonus information and company's performance appraisals were utilized as measures of career outcomes for the newcomers during their first three years in business. In addition to the above outcome criteria, our career outcome measure also included information on: (1) the company's reappraisal of newcomer's potential conducted at the last research period, and (2) ratings by the immediate supervisor regarding the extent his focal subordinate seems to be a "right-type" person for the company.

Performance Index: Using Company's performance appraisals corresponding to our fourth, fifth, sixth, and seventh wave of research, one of the composite career-outcome scales named a *performance index* was constructed. Since the company's rating scales were not consistent across appraisal points, original scores were standardized within each appraisal point and were distributed with a mean 50 and a standard deviation 20. Then, all standardized scores were summed for each individual and divided by a number of appraisal points. Thus, the performance index developed this way implied a rank-order performance scale averaged over four different appraisal points.

Potential Index: During the period between wave 6 and wave 7 monitorings, the DEPART company conducted reappraisal of new recruit's potential based on what they called a "multiple rater" method. This method required that multiple raters who are in a position to observe different "facets" on the focal's activities on the job evaluate his potential based on their knowledge from day-to-day observations. A team of raters for one newcomer included six to seven persons consisting of superiors (the immediate supervisor and his bosses), peers (Grade 2 and 3 levels), the focal himself as a self-observer, and a staff member of the personnel department. They evaluated focal person's potential using a 6-point scale with respect to the following five dimensions: (1) technical skill, (2) administrative skill, (3) interpersonal skill, (4) energy, and (5) intelligence. Question items relevant to each dimension were summed and an average score was computed for each dimension and each rater. For our analysis, the potential ratings developed by the above method, were transformed into a single *potential index* by aggregating these ratings across both the dimensions and the raters.

Bonus: The amount of bonus awarded during the last research period was found to be the only piece of pecuniary data that showed any meaningful variance to be analyzed. The straight yen value was used as an outcome criterion without adjustment.

Right Type: The last measure of career outcomes was derived by asking the supervisor, at the final wave of the questionnaire survey, how he perceived his subordinate as being a *right-type* person for the company. Each supervisor rated the extent to which he perceived his focal subordinate as: (1) attracted to the company, (2) a right-type person for the company, and (3) likely to make progress in the organization. The same questions were asked of the focal.

Table 13 displays a summary of instruments administered during our longitudinal investigation of management progress in the DEPART organization. The timing of the monitorings was carefully selected by consulting with personnel staff members of the company so that the research activities would not coincide with peak business periods. Table 13 indicates that a set of scales derived from Organizational Commitment, Role Disillusionment, Job Need, Job Problem, Vertical Exchange, Job Performance, and Success Potential can be available for the repeated-measure analysis covering the periods between the second and the seventh monitoring waves.

The period up to Wave 3 covers the first-year experience of our

Table 13

Instrument and Its Administration

Instrument	Number of Items	W-1 (6/72)	W-2 (11/72)	W-3 (3/73)	W-4 (7/73)	W-5 (11/73)	W-6 (3/74)	W-7 (2/75)
Focal Person								
Organizational Commitment	(16)	X	X	X	X	X	X	X
Role Disillusionment	(19)	X	X	X	X	X	X	X
Job Need Receiving	(17)	X	X	X	X	X	X	X
Job Need Preferred	(17)	X	X	X	X	X	X	X
Job Problem Frequency	(33)	-	X	X	X	X	X	X
Job Problem Severity	(33)	X	X	X	X	X	X	X
Vertical Exchange	(12)	-	X	X	X	X	X	X
Satisfaction	(1)	-	X	X	X	X	X	X*
Job Challenge	(20)	-	-	-	-	-	-	X
Supervisor								
Job Performance Success	(9)	X	X	X	X	X	X	X
Potential	(3)	-	X	X	X	X	X	X
Job Need Provided	(17)	X	X	X	X	X	X	X
Job Need Wanted	(17)	X	X	X	X	X	X	X
Vertical Exchange	(12)	-	X	X	X	X	X	X
Satisfaction Perceived	(1)	-	X	X	X	X	X	X
Job Challenge	(20)	-	-	-	-	-	-	X
Interview		X	X	X	X	X	-	-
Company Record		X	X	X	X	-	-	X

X - Instrument was administered.   *Including 7 items sample newcomers in the DEPART organization, while Waves 4 and 5, and Waves 6 and 7 correspond to their second and third year career respectively. The first three years were selected for the intensive monitorings to document the "process of role establishment" of the newcomer within the organization. The DEPART company had an expectation that all college recruits who started their career at the Grade 2 position would reach the section-leader position (Grade 3) by the end of the third year. This is the first formal change that occurs to the college recruits, although the company practice made it a rule to award the first promotion to almost all of them. However, DEPART people emphasized that the first three years are critical in order to predict progress during the next three years in which promotion into the First management level begins to take place. The present study is designed to document "how" each recruit establishes his first position as a springboard to First line management. The follow-up monitorings that started after the present study for the purpose of collecting information on pay, bonus, promotion, performance evaluation, and so forth, will make it possible for us to explore the "process of differentiation" based on the findings of the present study.

Chapter VI

Testing of Three Hypotheses

In this chapter, three hypotheses advanced in Chapter 5 to explain the process of managerial progress will be examined based on the empirical data collected by our longitudinal research. The total 229 questionnaire items were factored into 26 analytical dimensions based on the results of factor analyses. Then, these factored scales were analyzed using a repeated-measure analysis of variance method or a simple correlation method.

I. Scale Development

In order to reduce a large number of questionnaire items into a manageable set of variables for analysis, each instrument was factor analyzed using principal components with varimax rotation. A series of factor analyses was performed at each time period based on total sample ($N = 190$) derived from the three sample organizations for our research. Both the factor structure and content of each factor showed a basic similarity across all time periods. Appendix B displays summary results of the factor analyses based on the final wave of research. Each dimension identified by the factor analysis was given a label as follows:

(1) *Vertical Exchange (VE)* produced two factors. The first factor labeled *Dyadic Contingency* was characterized by supervisor's recognition of newcomer's potential, his understanding of subordinate's expectations and problems, his willingness and latitude to help the subordinate, etc. The second factor named *Job Latitude* indicated focal's latitude to get the job done, his contribution and influence, and autonomy on the job.

(2) *The Job Problem (JP)* instrument yielded three factors. The first factor labeled *Dyadic Problems and Constraints* denoted poor vertical communication, lack of proper instructions, no chance of participation, lack of authority, budget constraints, etc. The second, *Climate* factor represented such problems as backbiting, university clique, invasion of privacy, favoritism, the rigid seniority system, and so forth. The third factor called *Resource* problems was loaded with items indicating disadvantageous work location, lack of mobility, poor facilities, low salary, and understaffing.

(3) *Job Need (JN):* Two factors were derived from this instrument. *Leadership Support* was contributed by such items as supervisor's consideration, his attention, trust with the supervisor, feedback, chances of being heard, confidence in supervisor, etc. The second factor labeled *Job Enrichment* denoted opportunities for participation, chances to put one's own ideas into work, doing what one really wants to do, more authority, opportunities for learning expertise and know-how, inside information, etc.

(4) *Job Challenge (JC)* also produced two factors. The first factor indicated an experience of *Increased Centrality.* This dimension was characterized by opportunities for visible contribution and recognition, learning supervisory skills, being consulted by the supervisor with important decisions, and demonstrating one's beliefs and abilities. The second factor named *Task Demand* represented a list of items concerned with doing tasks that challenge one's ability, planning and coordinating tasks, making a formal report, participating in innovative tasks and problem solving, speaking for the supervisor and the company, etc.

(5) *Role Disillusionment (RD):* Disillusionment with the *Role Content* constituted the first factor. This dimension was characterized by disenchanted feelings associated with poor chances for participation and decision making, authority given, work itself, supervisor's treatment, opportunities for learning, and so forth. The second factor indicated the newcomer's disillusionment with *Profitability* of the organization, featured by disillusionment with company reputation, company's future prospects, chances of salary increase, working conditions, company policies and practices, and the like.

(6) *Organizational Commitment (OC)* yielded two factors. The first factor, *Psychological Value of the Company,* was contributed by focal's responses as to the degree which he feels the company to be the best place to work, pride in being a member of the company, choice of the organization being right, he can tell his friends this is a good place to work, he has a willingness to work harder, company climate and policies encourage work effort, and he hopes the organization grows. The second factor, called *Risk of Committing,* was negatively contributed by such items as, willingness to move for better pay and jobs, willingness to quit if conditions become exacerbated, and the degree of feeling questionable about the company's treatment.

Based on the results of factor analyses discussed above, a composite scale was constructed for each factoral dimension by summing up all question items relevant to the dimension. Tables 14 and 15 display reliability estimates (Cronbach's alpha) of factor-analytically derived scales computed for newcomer's and supervisor's scales respectively. In

Table 14

Reliability Coefficients (Cronbach's alpha) of the
Factor Scale Computed for Newcomer's Reports
(N = 80)

Factor Scale	Monitoring Period					
	W2	W3	W4	W5	W6	W6
Vertical Exchange (12)	.87	.90	.92	.90	.91	.91
Job Problem: Frequency						
Dydadic Problems (11)	.79	.79	.72	.69	.79	.78
Climate Problems (8)	.69	.67	.75	.71	.80	.71
Job Problem: Severity						
Dydadic Problems (11)	.79	.88	.85.	.78	.85	.88
Climate Problems (8)	.81	.82	.81	.78	.84	.81
Job Need: Receiving						
Leadership Support (7)	.85	.90	.91	.91	.90	.88
Job Enrichment (7)	.88	.89	.92	.90	.93	.91
Job Need: Preferred						
Leadership Support (7)	.77	.84	.86	.86	.92	.87
Job Enrichment (7)	.80	.80	.86	.86	.93	.89
Job Challenge						
Centrality (8)	–	–	–	–	–	.92
Task Demand (7)	–	–	–	–	–	.86
Satisfaction (7)	–	–	–	–	–	.80
Role Disillusionment						
Role Content (9)	.91	.90	.91	.91	.92	.85
Profitability (7)	.83	.81	.82	.81	.85	.80
Organizational Commitment						
Value of the Org. (9)	.81	.78	.78	.79	.76	.77
Risk of Committing (4)	.73	.79	.71	.79	.69	.78

Figures in parentheses denote number of items included in each scale.

Table 15

Reliability Coefficients (Cronbach's alpha)
of the Factor Scale Computed for Supervisor's Reports
(N = 80)

Factor Scale	Monitoring Period					
	W2	W3	W4	W5	W6	W7
Vertical Exchange (12)	.77	.76	.91	.73	.81	.73
Job Need: Providing						
Leadership Support (7)	.71	.72	.86	.78	.77	.76
Job Enrichment (7)	.81	.83	.90	.82	.83	.76
Job Need: Wanting						
Leadership Support (7)	.80	.84	.92	.81	.82	.85
Job Enrichment (7)	.82	.84	.92	.86	.84	.86
Job Challenge						
Centrality (8)	–	–	–	–	–	.87
Task Demand (7)	–	–	–	–	–	.84
Job Performance (9)	.88	.92	.94	.92	.90	.93

Figures in parentheses denote number of items included in each scale.

each table a reliability coefficient for the vertical exchange scale was computed based on the overall VE scale constructed by combining two vertical factors. Because of the high intercorrelation between the two factors, the combined vertical exchange scale also produced high internal consistency. The third factor derived from the Job Problem instrument did not show a satisfactory level of reliability. Therefore, this factor did not appear in Table 14, and was dropped from the variable set for further analyses.

In Table 14, reliability estimates for newcomer's scales range from .67 to .93. There seems to exist no systematic difference among estimates derived from the six different monitoring points. All scales showed satisfactory levels of reliability coefficient at each time period. Especially, scales for Vertical Exchange, Job Need, and Role Disillusionment yielded consistently high internal consistency across all time periods. Table 15 displays that the scale reliability computed for supervisor's reports also reached a satisfactory consistency level across all the time periods. Especially, the Job Performance scale constructed by aggregating nine job behavior items displayed consistently high reliability. In Table 15, estimates range from .71 to .94, but for all scales, estimates derived from the fourth wave (W4) showed the highest level of reliability.

Tables 16 and 17 demonstrate another attempt to check reliability. Each table displays test-retest reliability calculated for newcomer's and supervisor's scales separately. In Table 16, test-retest correlation coefficients for newcomer's reports range from .24 to .83 with a median of .61. All coefficients are significant at the .05 level, indicating that the environment for career progress as perceived by the newcomer tends to remain relatively stable over the first three years in the DEPART organization. Especially, Table 16 indicates that career environment is perceived as highly stable between the two successive monitoring points (between W2 and W3; W3 and W4; and so on). But, as time passes, wave by wave (between W2, and W3, W4, W5 −; between W3, and W4, W5 −; and so on), the stability becomes eroded gradually. This erosion may be attributable to actual changes occurring in the environment over time rather than to instability of the scale itself, because Tables 14 and 15 show high internal consistency at all time periods. A typical change in environment is a disruption of vertical dyad linkage. Between Waves 6 and 7, more than half of our sample newcomers had supervisors different from those for the preceding periods, due to the extensive personnel mobility occurring in the organization. As shown in Table 16, this environmental change caused: (1) relatively low test-retest stability between W6 and W7, compared to the one between the other two successive periods, and (2) rather sharp drops in stablity between W7 and

Table 16

Test-Retest Reliability of the Factor Scale
Computed for Newcomer's Reports (N = 80)

Factor Scale	W2 with					W3 with				W4 with			W5 with		W6 with
	W3	W4	W5	W6	W7	W4	W5	W6	W7	W5	W6	W7	W6	W7	W7
Vertical Exchange	70	49	53	51	37	65	61	60	42	71	66	48	80	47	45
Job Problem: Frequency															
Dyadic Problems	53	34	46	48	24	57	67	56	38	62	53	36	64	29	46
Climate Problems	66	53	61	61	34	49	62	62	49	83	62	46	69	48	60
Job Problem: Severity															
Dyadic Problems	53	41	41	49	30	68	63	62	58	66	62	55	64	51	58
Climate Problems	70	53	57	63	48	66	61	59	59	75	68	66	77	63	64
Job Need: Receiving															
Leadership Support	80	65	60	61	54	73	73	65	66	78	73	69	75	71	73
Job Enrichment	55	43	34	39	41	59	50	46	43	73	66	44	70	47	44
Job Need: Preferred															
Leadership Support	52	48	46	45	40	64	68	61	47	67	66	46	73	57	60
Job Enrichment	33	30	35	37	40	42	59	46	46	52	55	41	64	54	57
Role Disillusionment															
Role Content	66	48	38	31	41	55	53	48	52	67	57	60	71	60	60
Profitability	79	63	61	57	57	64	60	56	60	65	49	65	74	61	62
Organizational Commitment															
Value of the Org.	78	57	61	59	42	72	70	70	54	82	78	74	83	60	60
Risk of Committing	78	60	57	62	52	71	67	68	56	72	64	70	76	55	62

Correlation Coefficient

Figures denote Pearson correlation coefficients with decimal points omitted.

Table 17

Test-Retest Reliability of the Factor Scale
Computed for Supervisors' Reports (N = 80)

Factor Scale	Correlation Coefficient														
	W2 with					W3 with				W4 with			W5 with		W6 with
	W3	W4	W5	W6	W7	W4	W5	W6	W7	W5	W6	W7	W6	W7	W7
Vertical Exchange	68	54	30	23	33	44	29	23	13	52	47	29	69	32	21
Job Need: Providing															
Leadership Support	64	53	32	34	27	52	38	38	20	56	48	28	61	33	25
Job Enrichment	69	39	36	30	23	49	40	22	22	56	48	33	53	39	31
Job Need: Preferred															
Leadership Support	65	41	21	21	32	57	35	32	44	55	52	42	65	44	52
Job Enrichment	65	47	44	22	35	38	32	15	23	59	31	25	65	46	40
Job Performance	70	32	22	15	31	59	37	34	41	56	64	55	69	44	46

Figures denote Pearson correlation coefficients with decimal points omitted.

all other monitoring periods. This second point is particularly true for the Vertical Exchange and Dyadic Problems scales: i.e., for Vertical Exchange, correlations between W7/W2, W3, W4, and W5 (.37, .42, .48, and .47 respectively) showed a considerable deterioration compared to those between W/6W2, W3, W4, and W5 (.51, .60, .66, and .80 respectively).

Table 17 displays test-retest reliability for supervisors' reports. It tells basically the same story as was found in the newcomer's reports. However, in general, test-retest stability of supervisors' reports tends to be lower compared to the ones for the newcomers. In Table 17, correlation coefficients range from .13 to .70 with a median correlation of .39. The cause of this relatively lower stability for supervisors' reports is again attributable to changes of the supervisor over time. For example, all supervisors responding at the W2 point to their newcomers were no longer in charge of the same newcomers at the W7 point. This indicates that as far as supervisors' reports are concerned, the "internal" continuity of the reports must be lost whenever the focal person changes his supervisor between any two points for the monitoring intervention. As stated earlier, more than half of the supervisors' reports lost this continuity between Wave 6 and Wave 7. Table 17 tells us that stability of supervisor's reports during that period suffered greatly due to the disruption of vertical dyad linkages. The impact of this supervisory change was most severe for the Vertical Exchange and Job Need Providing scales. However, despite a rather consistent loss of the internal continuity in supervisors' reports over time, Job Performance, and Job Need Preferred scales produced high, stable test-retest correlations, especially on and after the W3 period. The existence of this observed stability suggests that the supervisors' reports, regardless of changes in reporters, are picking up some "external" continuity involved in the subordinate's behaviors on his career role over time.

In sum, factor-analytically derived scales constructed for our analysis have shown satisfactory internal consistency across all time periods for monitoring. However, test-retest reliability of these composite scales showed considerable "shrinkage" over time, probably because of various changes which occurred both to the newcomer himself and to the environment for career development. This relative instability of responses across time periods may not be detrimental to our analysis. Rather, it implies dynamic processes of managerial progress during early stages of business careers, which will be subject to further exploration.

The design of statistical analysis for our study required the testing of three hypotheses stated in Chapter V regarding their strength and systematic capability in predicting various outcomes from the process of managerial career progress. For this purpose, predictors relevant to the testing of each hypothesis were constructed as a first step. Then, using each predictor as an independent variable, a series of one-way, repeated-measure ANOVA and correlation analyses were performed with a set of outcomes as the dependent variables.

II. Test of the Role Making Hypothesis

The role making hypothesis was tested using a Vertical Exchange (VE) scale reported by the focal newcomer during his first-year experience in the DEPART organization. The first-year VE score was constructed by computing an average of the second wave (monitored in November, 1972) and the third wave (monitored in March, 1973) VE scores. The second and the third wave monitorings corresponded to the middle and the last terms respectively within the first-year business calendar for the newcomer. The first wave data collected in June, 1972, two months after the start of recruits' career, were not included in the analysis, because of the experimental nature of the first wave study.

Using this first-year composite scale, subjects were divided into the following Three VE groups: High (n=28), Mid (n=29), and Low (n=23). Then, a repeated-measure analysis of variance was attempted with this VE category-measure as an independent variable and all outcome variables derived from the first years, fourth, fifth, sixth, and seventh monitoring as dependent variables. For this particular ANOVA design, the VE and Time factors were considered as fixed treatments, while the subject was regarded as a random factor to be crossed with the above Time factors. The ANOVA analysis required the nonadditive design (Winer, 1971), because it was expected that the nature of this phenomenon would produce interesting interaction effects (convergence and divergence) between predictors and the passages of time. Figure 6 displays stability of the three VE groups identified in the first year over the rest of the research periods. The ANOVA results suggest that the three VE groups identified in the first year remained as significantly different groups (p < .001) over the three-year research period. Figure 6 illustrates that those newcomers who reported a high level of vertical exchange with their supervisors in the first year tend to retain their high position almost unchanged over time. On the other hand, those who reported low and intermediate levels of exchange in the first year showed rather steady gains in vertical exchange over time, thus making the time effect on vertical exchange highly significant (p < .001). Moreover, a converging trend among three groups (especially between the Low and Mid VE groups) over the five time periods produced a significant

Figure 6

Stability of First Year Vertical Exchange over Time

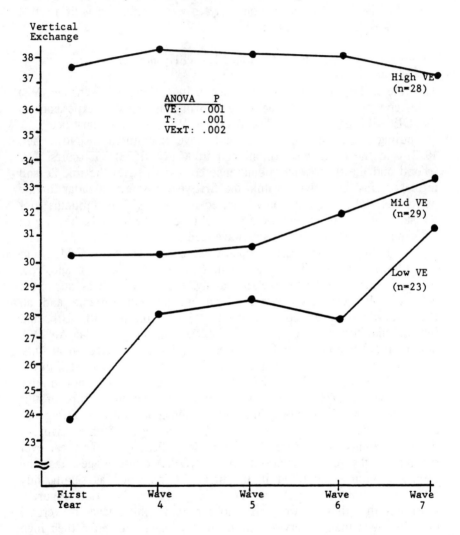

interaction effect (p < .002). In sum, Figure 6 indicates that the High VE group has been consistently different from the Mid and Low VE groups at all time periods. However the difference between the Mid and Low group tends to be less distinctive after the first year period. The significant interaction effect may indicate a bias or regression toward a mean. This problem will be discussed in the summary section.

1. Outcomes of Vertical Exchange

Table 18 shows a summary of a repeated-measure analysis of variance performed for a set of exchange outcomes. Except for the Job Problem Severity scales, the first-year vertical exchange had a strong, consistent effect upon the levels of exchange outcomes. That is, mean values shown in Table 18 indicate that the higher the first-year VE the higher the level of newcomers' receiving leadership support and job enrichment opportunities. Supervisor's reports endorsed this finding: they reported that those newcomers who experienced a high level of vertical exchange in the first year have been provided on the average with a high level of leadership support and with opportunities for job enrichment throughout the research period, compared to those who experienced the low or intermediate level of vertical exchange at the start of their career. In addition, supervisor's reports on vertical exchange indicated that newcomers' vertical exchange illustrated in Figure 6 can also receive an endorsement from the opposite party to the exchange. Furthermore, Table 18 tells us that the higher the first-year vertical exchange: (1) the less frequently the newcomer experiences dyadic problems, and (2) the more similar the response pattern becomes between the newcomer and his supervisor.

Figure 7 displays a pattern of mean changes over time for Dyadic Problems based on the three VE groups. The figure indicates that those who had Low vertical exchange during the first year tend to experience more problems with their supervisors throughout the remaining periods, compared to the High or Mid vertical exchange colleagues. Although three groups showed a converging trend by the end of the third year, this trend did not produce an effect strong enough to make interaction between VE and Time significant (p < .090). On the other hand, severity of problems felt by the newcomer did not show any significant difference among the three VE groups. This fact may imply the existence of communality of severe problems inherent in the newcomer's position. The severity of these problems may not be overcome even by the help of supervisors; the best thing supervisors could do is to reduce the frequency in occurrence of such problems.

Figure 8 illustrates mean differences for Leadership Support re-

Table 18

Effect of First Year Vertical Exchange (VE) Upon Exchange Outcomes over Time (T) (N=80)

| Variable | Mean for the VE Group | | | Probability | | |
	High (n=28)	Mid (n=29)	Low (n=23)	VE	Time	VExT
Newcomer's Report						
Job Need: Receiving						
Leadership Support	22.5	1.4	14.7	.001	.001	.023
Job Enrichment	25.4	20.6	18.0	.001	.001	.090
Job Problem: Frequency						
Dyadic Problems	28.9	31.4	34.4	.001	.148	.090
Climate Problems	18.8	20.0	20.8	.110	.001	.907
Job Problem: Severity						
Dyadic Problems	33.0	34.1	36.5	.093	.001	.189
Climate Problems	17.9	20.0	20.3	.214	.001	.109
Supervisor's Report						
Job Need: Providing						
Leadership Support	24.4	24.2	22.1	.001	.001	.648
Job Enrichment	28.2	26.8	25.8	.002	.002	.245
Vertical Exchange	40.3	39.7	37.8	.003	.001	.089
Agreement Measure						
Profile Similarity	38.0	44.2	49.2	.001	.001	.031

Figure 7

Frequency of Experiencing Job Problems Based on
the Vertical Exchange (VE) Group over Time (T)

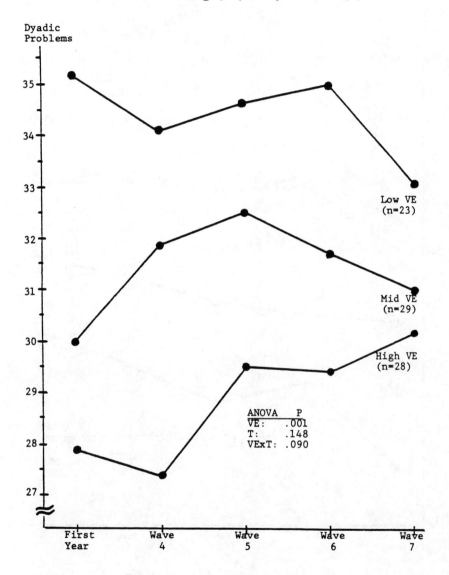

Figure 8

Leadership Support Reported by the Supervisor and His Subordinate Based on the Vertical Exchange Groups

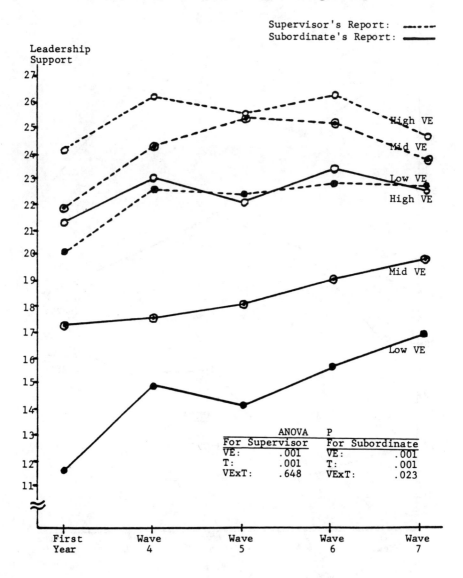

ported by the focal newcomer and his supervisor. In Figure 8, the pattern of mean differences indicates that the higher the first-year vertical exchange, the more leadership support the newcomer receives for the subsequent period of career development. The supervisor's report also endorses this pattern. However, Figure 8 indicates some problems concerning the "response sets." (1) Generally, supervisor's reports on his support behavior tend to be more lenient (an overall average for the supervisor's reports is 24.0), compared to those of newcomers (an overall average is 1.7). This indicates a "leniency tendency" involved in the supervisor's report, or a "stringency tendency" involved in the newcomer's report. (2) Supervisors' reports tend to be distributed more closely around the mean at each time period, while those of newcomers show more dispersion. For example, newcomers' reports at the seventh wave monitoring were found to be distributed with variance of 26.2, while those of supervisors had a variance of 16.3 at the same time period. As shown in Figure 8, the relatively small variance involved in supervisors' reports at all time periods may indicate another response bias called a "central tendency."

For our study, however, what is important is a *pattern* of responses between the supervisor and his subordinate. In other words, as long as this pattern is consistent, response biases as discussed above will not cause serious problems for our study.

Figure 9 illustrates mean profile-similarity scores for three vertical exchange groups over time. The "profile similarity" measure (Graen and Schiemann, 1977) was constructed by summing the absolute distance between supervisor's and newcomer's ratings (D) on 46 items, i.e., 34 Job Need (Receiving and Preferred) items and 12 Vertical Exchange items. Thus, the profile scores computed this way indicated that the greater the (D) score, the more dissimilar the response profile between the supervisor and his subordinate becomes. Figure 9 displays that for all VE groups, large leader-member disagreement which existed at the start of career development became narrowed very rapidly by the end of the third year ($p < .001$ for time effect). This is particularly true for the Low VE group. However, despite this converging trend that produced a significant intereaction effect ($p < .031$), the effect of the first-year vertical exchange remained valid ($p < .001$) throughout the research period.

In addition to the profile similarity scale, another form of agreement measure, a "pattern agreement" scale (Graen and Schiemann, 1977 and 1978) was also constructed based on a person-to-person, or a P-, correlation coefficient. However, this pattern measure that was reported to have a very strong relation with the vertical exchange in Graen and Schiemann's study (see Table 11) did not produce a sig-

Figure 9

Profile Similarity Based on the Vertical Exchange (VE) Group over Time (T)

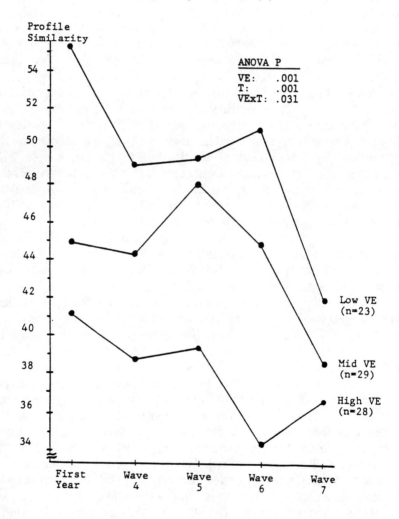

nificant result in our study. Yet, as shown in Table 19, the two agreement measures did show significant and meaningful relations in our study. That is, the smaller the (D) scores (i.e., the greater the profile similarity), the higher the pattern agreement between the leader and his subordinate.

Finally, it was found that vertical exchange achieved by the newcomer during his first year was also predictive of Job Challenge reported at the final research period after three years. Table 20 displays that the first-year vertical exchange has a strong, consistent effect upon the experience of job challenge three years later with respect to both increased centrality and task demand. Table 20 also displays that the supervisors' reports on the amount of their providing job-challenge episodes to their focal subordinate give endorsement to the newcomers' reports. Again, it is noted that the supervisors' reports involved response biases characterized by leniency and central tendencies.

2. Role Outcomes

Exactly the same analysis design as applied to exchange outcomes was repeated to test the effect of vertical exchange upon a set of role outcomes. Table 21 displays a summary of the ANOVA tests. Results shown in Table 21 indicate that the impact of first-year vertical exchange upon role outcomes is very strong and consistent during the three-year period of management progress within the DEPART organization. That is, those newcomers who received high vertical exchange during the first year in the organization, tend to show higher feelings of staying with the company (i.e., lower role disillusionment), higher organizational commitment, and lower levels of need deficiency over time, compared to those who experienced lower vertical exchange with their supervisors during the first year of their managerial career. Moreover, the supervisor's report indicated that the High VE group also shows high level of job performance and success potential over the three-year period, compared to the Mid and Low VE colleagues.

Figure 10 displays a pattern of mean differences for disillusionment with Role Content among three vertical exchange groups time. For this particular scale, low scores imply a tendency to feel like leaving the organization, i.e., high role disillusionment, while high scores imply the feeling of staying with the organization, i.e., low role disillusionment. Figure 10 indicates that those who experienced high vertical exchange in the starting year of their career, tend to show consistently lower level of disillusionment during the subsequent years, compared to those whose first-year experience produced only low or intermediate levels of vertical exchange with their supervisors. In Figure 10, the Low VE group,

Table 19

**Correlation Coefficient Between Profile Similarity (D)
and Pattern Agreement (P) Measures (N = 80)**

		Time Period		
FY	W4	W5	W6	W7
-.35	-.26	-.37	-.40	-.30

Note: P correlations were transformed into Z scores before calculation.

Table 20

**Effect of the First Year Vertical Exchange
Upon Job Challenge Reported at the
End of the Third Year**

| Variable | Mean for the VE Group | | | ANOVA P |
	High (n = 28)	Mid (n = 29)	Low (n = 23)	
Newcomer's Report				
Increased Centrality	26.5	19.5	18.0	.001
Task Demand	20.3	16.6	15.0	.002
Supervisor's Report				
Increased Centrality	27.9	26.4	23.4	.021
Task Demand	22.0	21.7	19.4	.040

Table 21

Effect of the First Year Vertical Exchange (VE)
Upon Role Outcomes over Time (T)
(N=80)

| Variable | Mean for the VE Group | | | Probability | | |
	High (n=28)	Mid (n=29)	Low (n=23)	VE	Time	VExT
Newcomer's Report						
Role Disillusionment						
Role Content	47.1	41.2	37.5	.001	.249	.063
Probability	31.3	30.3	28.9	.159	.19	.620
Organizational Commitment						
Value of Organization	44.8	41.8	38.6	.008	.682	.561
Risk of Commiting	16.4	14.6	14.6	.077	.085	.164
Need Deficiency						
Leadership Support	8.4	13.6	30.9	.001	.001	.019
Job Enrichment	2.7	5.4	13.9	.001	.276	.560
Supervisor's Report						
Job Performance	36.2	34.5	32.6	.003	.001	.089
Success Potential	11.5	11.2	10.6	.028	.228	.301

Figure 10

Role Disillusionment Based on the Vertical Exchange (VE) Group over Time (T)

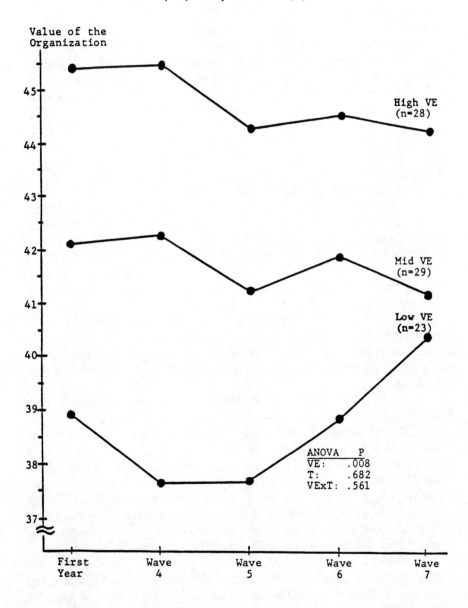

however, showed a steady step of recovery from disillusionment over time, thus making the combined effect between VE and Time almost significant ($p < .063$).

As shown in Figure 11, organizational commitment displayed basically the same trend as demonstrated by role disillusionment. In Figure 11, the "psychological value of the organization" has been felt to be consistently high by the High VE group, followed by the Mid, and Low VE groups. However, Figure 11 also indicates that by the end of the fifth wave of monitoring (the middle of the second year), all newcomers regardless of their vertical exchange positions, have experienced gradual decay in their felt values of the organization. This trend may indicate a process of adjustment by which the newcomer comes to accommodate his idealistic expectations with realities of the organization. After adjustment, the High and Mid groups maintained their positions, while the Low group showed a steady increase in commitment during the rest of the period until they almost reached the Mid group.

A need-deficiency scale (D^2) constructed as a measure of deficiency needs, or job satisfaction, produced a result consistent with the previous discussions. As shown in Figure 12, those who experienced low vertical exchange in the first-year have reported a high level of need deficiency during the subsequent years for career development, compared to those who experienced higher levels of vertical exchange. This is particularly true for the periods after Wave 5, during which the High and Mid VE groups have tended to convergence. Since speed in narrowing the need discrepancy has been much faster for the Low VE in comparison to the other two groups, the VE-by-Time interaction showed a significant result ($p < .019$). Again, this pattern may indicate a trend of regression toward the mean.

In addition to the Need Deficiency score, our research employed a single-item overall satisfaction scale to check the relationship between the two different satisfaction scales. An analysis variance test for this overall satisfaction scale produced basically the same result as we have seen for the need-discrepancy analysis. That is, the High VE group displayed the highest level of overall satisfaction followed by the Mid and Low VE groups (3.11, 2.27, and 1.96 for each VE group respectively; $p < .001$). Furthermore, converging mean satisfaction among three VE groups over time produced a significant interaction effect ($p < .010$), although the time effect remained at a marginally significant level ($p < .062$).

Table 22 displays the relationship between two satisfacton scales more clearly. In Table 22, correlation coefficients between D^2 scores and overall satisfaction produced a result supporting the hypothesized relationship between the two scales: the greater the D^2 score, the lower

Figure 11

Organizational Commitment Based on the
Vertical Exchange (VE) Group over Time (T)

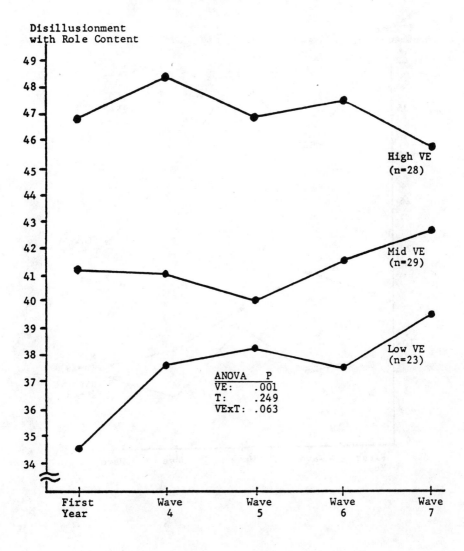

Figure 12

Need Deficiency (D^2) with Leadership Support
Based on Vertical Exchange (VE) Groups

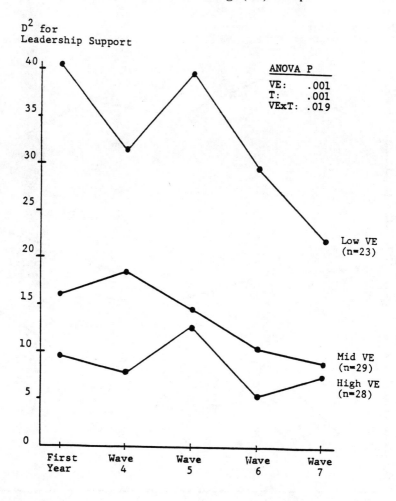

satisfaction becomes, and vice versa. Table 22 also indicates that overall satisfaction tends to have a stronger relationship with need fulfillment for the Leadership Support than for the Job Enrichment dimension.

Figure 13 displays mean performance ratings by the supervisor over time based on the three vertical exchange groups. The pattern of group differences shows a result quite consistent with previous discussions. That is, in Figure 13, those newcomers who could attain high exchange relations with their supervisors during the first-year period achieved higher job performance throughout all time periods, compared to those who could attain only an intermediate or low level vertical exchange during their critical first-year period. Supervisor's ratings on Success Potential also followed the same patterns as shown in Figure 13.

In Figure 13, performance ratings showed a slight decline for the High and Mid VE groups and a sharp drop for the Low VE group during the period between Wave 6 and Wave 7. Moreover, performance ratings for the Wave 7 produced the greatest variance in all time periods: i.e., variances involved in performance ratings for the First Year, Wave 4, Wave 5, Wave 6, and Wave 7 periods were found to be 21.2, 29.2, 25.0, 24.0, and 32.5 respectively. To explain this variation in performance ratings it will be assumed that the VE factor interacts with other factors during the period between the Wave 6 and W7 thus causing greater differentiation in performance ratings for that period. In the chapters that follow, the impact of individual potentials and the supervisor changes occurring between Wave 6 and W7 will be examined as possible interactive factors that may cause a decline and greater variation in peformance ratings at Wave 7.

Correlation coefficients computed between vertical exchange and job performance produced a result that supports the findings of the ANOVA test. Table 23 displays that the first-year vertical exchange has a consistent, positive correlation with job performance, both concurrently and over time. However, the magnitude of correlation seems to be greater for vertical exchange based on Waves 4 and 5 than that on the First Year. Table 23 indicates that vertical exchange consistently predicts job performance more strongly than job peformance predicts vertical exchange. Within the lower triangular matrix, only one correlation based on Wave 4 job performance reached a significant level in predicting vertical exchange at subsequent periods. On the other hand, within the upper triangular matrix, vertical exchange showed predictive validity of job performance across all time periods, regardless of the time period in which predictions were based. The above findings may suggest that the causal direction flows from vertical exchange to job performance, rather than the other way around. The more detailed causal analysis will be

Figure 13

Job Performance Based on the
Vertical Exchange (VE) Groups over Time (T)

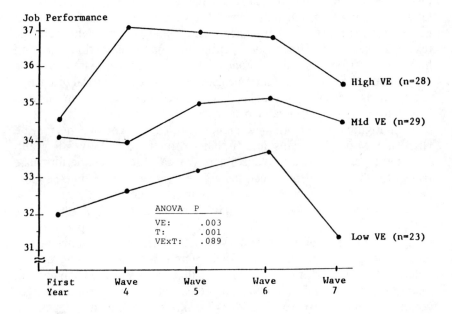

Table 22

Correlation Coefficient Between the Need Deficiency Scale and Overall Satisfaction at Five Different Time Periods (N = 80)

| D^2 Scale | Time Period | | | | |
	FY	W4	W5	W6	W7
Leadership Support	−.52	−.51	−.41	−.51	−.25
Job Enrichment	−.42	−.37	−.34	−.40	−.22

Note: For correlation coefficients with .22 or higher, $p < .05$; .28 or higher, $p < .01$.

Table 23

Correlation Coefficients Between Vertical Exchange and Job Performance Reported at Five Monitoring Periods (N = 80)

| Vertical Exchange | Job Performance | | | | |
	FY	W4	W5	W6	W7
First Year	.17	.25*	.21	.14	.27*
Wave 4	.11	.38**	.33*	.32	.36**
Wave 5	.05	.28**	.38**	.26*	.32**
Wave 6	.05	.20	.20	.16	.34**
Wave 7	.08	.21	.13	.16	.31**

The upper triangle displays predictive correlations based on vertical exchange, while the lower triangle displays predictive correlations based on job performance. The diagonal indicates correlation coefficients on a concurrent basis.

*$p < .05$
**$p < .01$

attempted in Chapter VIII using path analysis and dynamic correlation methods.

3. Career Outcomes

A set of career outcome measures based on company records were subject to the correlation analysis with the first-year vertical exchange. As discussed earlier, the company's performance appraisals corresponding to our fourth, fifth, sixth, and seventh Wave studies were available for this purpose. Based on this information, the relationships between company's appraisals ("internal" ratings) and job performance ("external" ratings) administered in our questionnaire were examined. Table 24 shows a correlation matrix for internal-external ratings.

In Table 24, performance ratings by our questionnaire tend to show greater stability than company appraisals. All test-retest correlations for our job performance scale (an upper triangular matrix) reached a significant level (except the one between W6 and W2), with a median correlation of .44. On the other hand, company's performance appraisals (a lower triangular matrix) produced significant correlations only between the two successive points; beyond the immediate successive points, all correlations became nonsignificant. A median correlation within the lower triangle was found to be somewhere between .11 and .24. Nonetheless, the internal-external ratings matched with the timings of monitoring produced all significant intercorrelations (a diagonal matrix). Moreover, agreement between the two ratings tends to become stronger as a function of time. In general, Table 24 indicates that; (1) both questionnaire ratings and company's appraisals picked up common variance associated with the newcomer's behavior on the job, but the overlapping area is far smaller than that left unexplained by each method; (2) as far as stability is concerned, performance ratings based on our questionnaire seem to be more reliable than company appraisals.

As discussed previously, company appraisals were transformed into a single *Performance Index* for the analyses of career outcomes. The second measure of career outcome, the *Potential Index*, was developed using information derived from company's reappraisal of newcomer's potential conducted at the end of the third year. As discussed in the instrument section, company's reappraisal involved evaluation of newcomer's potential after three years with respect to technical skill, administrative skill, interpersonal skill, energy, and intelligence, based on ratings by six to seven role-set members. These role-set raters consisted of superiors, peers, personnel staff members, and the focal newcomer himself. Since the five evaluative dimensions listed above have shown high intercorrelations, they were transformed into a composite scale for

Table 24

Internal and External Validity
of Performance Ratings (N=80)

Company's Appraisal		I W2 (11/72)	II W3 (3/73)	III W4 (7/73)	IV W5 (11/73)	V W6 (3/74)	VI W7 (2/75)
			Performance Ratings by Questionnaire				
I	n.a.	—	70	.32	.22	.15	.31
II	(9/72–3/73)	—	x	.59	.37	.34	.41
III	(4/73–8/73)	—	x	.21	.56	.64	.55
IV	(9/73–3/74)	—	x	.51	.35	.69	.44
V	(4/74–8/74)	—	x	.16	.24	.35	.46
VI	(9/74–3/75)	—	x	-.04	.11	.62	.38

^{x}Company appraisals at this time period showed no variance.

$^-$No company appraisals were made.

For rs to be significant at p < .05, r≥.22: at p < .01, r≥.28.

The lower triangle indicates test-retest reliability of company appraisals, while the upper trangle indicates that of the performance ratings based on our questionnaire.

The diagonal shows correlation between company appraisals and questionnaire ratings matched with the timing of monitoring waves.

each rater. Then, for our analysis, a single Potential Index was constructed by computing an average score across all raters.

Table 25 displays interrater agreement among key role-set members. Unlike the ordinary interrater agreement, the "multiple-rater" method used for the DEPART company's reassessment program involved a different team of raters for a different newcomer, with each rater representing a different position (as a supervisor, peer, staff, etc.) for evaluating. Correlation coefficients displayed in Table 25 indicate that agreement is very low among raters representing the three key evaluative positions, i.e., the focal newcomer himself, the supervisors, and a personnel staff member. This implies that raters tend to see many different aspects of a newcomer's potential, or that there is little common data upon which each rater is to rely for evaluation. Anyhow, Table 25 indicates that the Potential Index used for our study as a criterion of career outcome reflects the supervisor's evaluation most strongly, followed by the personnel staff members.

In addition to the two indices discussed above, the amount of *Bonus* each newcomer earned at the end period of research, and the *Right Type* scale rated by the supervisor at the seventh wave questionnaire survey were also employed as the third and fourth criteria of career outcomes. Table 26 displays an attempt to validate the final set of career outcomes based on Job Performance and Success Potential scales used for our questionnaire research. In Table 26 all career outcomes show stable, significant correlations with job performances and success potential, indicating that the career outcomes assessed at the end of the third year of newcomer's career do have a close relation with his past job performance monitored by our questionnaire at five different points in time. In other words, Table 26 indicates that the internal ratings based on our questionnaire predicted career outcomes after three years in a very consistent manner. In Table 26, correlations based on Wave 7 ratings implied "concurrent" prediction, thus the ratings showed the strongest correlations with all career outcomes, compared to the other "predictive" correlations, especially those for the first year.

Finally, an attempt was made to predict a set of career outcomes by computing correlation coefficients between each of the outcomes and the first year vertical exchange. Table 27 displays this result, together with predictive correlations based on vertical exchange at fourth, fifth, sixth, and seventh waves. Predictive correlations shown in Table 27 indicate that the First Year vertical exchange did predict newcomer's Potential and Right Type ratings assessed at the end of the third year. However, it failed to predict Performance Index and the level of Bonus after three years. Table 27 also indicates that instead of the First Year, both the

Table 25

Agreement on Newcomer's Potential Reassessed Among Raters Representing Three Different Evaluative Positions (N = 80)

		Rater's Position		
		I	II	III
I	Newcomer Himself	–	.13	.16
II	Supervisor	.13	–	.07
III	Personnel Office	.16	.07	–
IV	Potential Index	.05	.66*	.35

Figures denote Pearson correlation coefficients.
*p < .01

Table 26

Validity of Career Outcome Measures Based on Job Performance Scale at Five Monitoring Periods (N=80)

Job Performance Scale		Performance Index	Potential Index	Bonus	Right Type
First Year	I	.42	.38	.45	.33
	II	.41	.31	.40	.33
Wave 4	I	.46	.49	.52	.36
	II	.41	.39	.44	.33
Wave 5	I	.4	.43	.42	.33
	II	.41	.36	.32	.21
Wave 6	I	.51	.52	.49	.31
	II	.39	.42	.42	.25
Wave 7	I	.47	.65	.54	.76*
	II	.48	.60	.56	.72

For each wave, I and II indicate Job Performance and Success Potential scales respectively.

For correlation coefficients with .22 over, $p < .05$; with .28 or over, $p < .01$.

*These two correlations are based upon ratings by the same supervisor at the seventh wave research.

Table 27

**Predicting Career Outcomes, Job Performance and Success Potential
Assessed at the End of the Third Year Based on Vertical Exchange
Reported by the Newcomer at Five Different Points in Time (N = 80)**

Vertical Exchange	Perform-ance Index	Career Outcome Potential Index	Bonus	Right Type	Wave 7 Rating Job Per-formance	Success Potential
First Year	.13	.22:	.11	.28**	.27*	.25
Wave 4	.24*	.39**	.34**	.34**	.36**	.35**
Wave 5	.28**	.37**	.25*	.25*	.32**	.24*
Wave 6	.17	.25*	.19	.29**	.34**	.28**
Wave 7	.08	.0**	.16	.31**	.31**	.19

*p < .05
**p < .01

Waves 4 and 5 vertical exchanges did a better job in predicting all the career outcomes examined here. This finding coincides with the results shown in Table 23 in which the vertical exchanges based on Waves 4 and 5, rather than the First Year, predicted job peformance in the most significant manner.

In addition to career outcomes, Table 27 also displays correlation coefficients between vertical exchange and two ratings (Job Performance and Success Potential) derived from the final wave of our questionnaire research. These two ratings may be interpreted as career outcomes within our questionnaire method. As expected, "within-method" predictions produced consistently higher correlations, compared to those derived from "across-method" predictions.

In sum, the First Year vertical exchange predicted two career-outcome criteria out of four. That is, those who experienced high vertical exchange with the supervisor during their first year, were rated after three years: (1) as having higher potential, and (2) as being more a right-type person to progress in the DEPART organization. Although correlations with Performance Index and Bonus did not reach a significant level, the direction of impact of the First Year vertical exchange upon these outcomes was found in order. This result, together with the findings discussed earlier, suggests that for the newcomer, the quality of early-stage experience with his supervisor has a very important implication for his career success in later stages. As shown in Table 26, career outcomes may be predicted by early stage job performance and success potential ratings. But, the fact that vertical exchange can predict both job performance and career outcomes constitutes a more important contribution to the research and practice in the area of managerial career progress.

III. Test of the Disillusionment Hypothesis

The disillusionment hypothesis was examined based on the first factor (disillusionment with role content) of the Role Disillusionment (RD) measure reported by the newcomers during their first-year experience in the organization. The first-year RD scale was constructed by computing an average of the second and third wave reports on role-content disillusionment. Using the first-year RD score, subjects were divided into the follown three groups: High ($n=24$), Mid ($n=30$), and Low ($n=26$) RD groups. Then, taking this trichotomized RD measure as an independent variable, a repeated-measure ANOVA was performed to examine the RD group effect upon the outcome measures derived from our longitudinal investigation. The ANOVA for this test was based on the same design as used for the VE study.

Figure 14 illustrates stability of RD groups classified in the first year over the rest of the research periods. As discussed earlier, the scoring method for this particular scale was devised in such a manner that the higher the RD score, the lower the level of disillusionment, and vice versa. Figure 14 shows that three RD groups identified at the starting year of a newcomer's career, remained as significantly different groups (p < .001) over three years. Although the High disillusionment group members have shown steady recovery from their first-year disillusionment over time, they still remained as the most disillusioned group by the end of the third year. This indicates that if a group of newcomers were unfortunate enough to have an anemic role content that makes them "feel like quitting the company" in the first year, then they have to live with that disenchanted feeling at least during the first three years in their organizational career. In Figure 14, all groups showed a tendency of regressing toward an overall mean, thus making the RD-by-Time interaction significant (p < .003).

1. Exchange Outcomes

Table 28 displays a summary of a repeated-measure ANOVA based on the RD groups of the first year with vertical exchange and exchange outcomes as dependent variables. Table 28 indicates that those who had severe role disillusionment in the first year tended to show lower vertical exchange with their supervisor, lower leadership support and job enrichment, and higher frequency of experiencing dyadic problems in comparison to those who were relatively free from such disillusionment in their first year. However, supervisor's reports do not necessarily endorse what newcomers are reporting. That is, the supervisor's report displayed in Table 28 indicates that all newcomers have basically the same vertical exchange relations with their supervisors, and that they are provided with equal opportunity for job enrichment, despite the newcomer's report to the contrary. Only leadership support provided by the supervisor showed a barely significant (p < .045) group difference.

Figure 15 illustrates mean differences of vertical exchange reported by the newcomer over time based on the RD groups. The figures indicate a pattern of mean differences consistent with the hypothesis: the higher the role disillusionment, the lower the vertical exchange, and vice versa. Mean differences for leadership support and job enrichment displayed a pattern quite similar to the one illustrated in Figure 15, except that the convergency evolved in the Leadership Support scale between the Low and other RD groups produced a significant interaction effect (p < .029; see Figure 16). The Dyadic Problem scale also showed

Figure 14

Stability of First Year Role Disillusionment (RD) over Time (T)

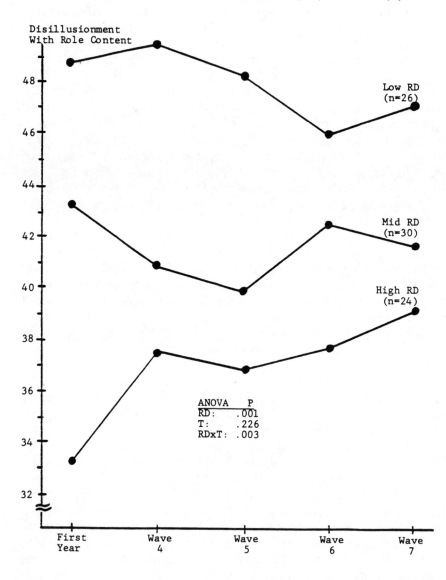

Table 28

Vertical Exchange and Exchange Outcomes Based on the First Year Role Disillusionment (RD) and Time (T) Factors (N=80)

| Variable | Mean for the RD Group | | | Probability | | |
	High (n=24)	Mid (n=30)	Low (n=26)	RD	T	RDxT
Newcomer's Report						
Vertical Exchange	28.2	32.8	36.2	.001	.001	.068
Job Need: Receiving						
Leadership Support	14.6	18.8	22.5	.001	.001	.029
Job Enrichment	18.2	21.7	24.5	.001	.001	.247
Job Problem: Frequency						
Dyadic Problem	34.0	31.6	28.7	.001	.149	.103
Climate Problem	20.0	20.0	18.8	.174	.001	.599
Job Problem: Severity						
Dyadic Problem	37.8	33.3	34.3	.311	.001	.527
Climate Problem	19.5	18.4	19.7	.602	.001	.157
Supervisor's Report						
Vertical Exchange	38.8	3.4	40.0	.354	.001	.371
Job Need: Providing						
Leadership Support	23.0	23.9	25.0	.045	.001	.972
Job Enrichment	26.6	26.7	27.6	.336	.003	.683
Agreement Measure						
Profile Similarity	49.9	43.1	37.1	.001	.001	.043

Figure 15

Vertical Exchange Reported by the Focal Based on Role Disillusionment (RD) over Time (T)

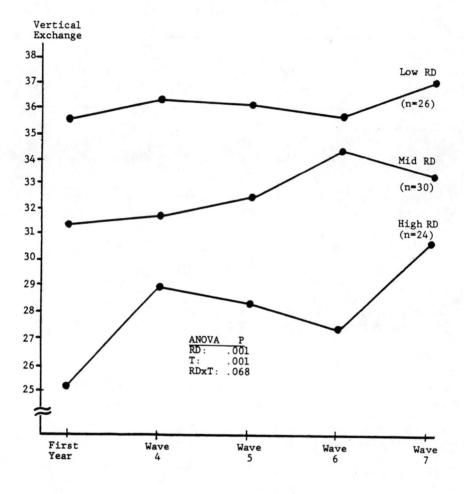

Figure 16

Leadership Support Reported by Newcomer
Based on Role Disillusionment (RD) over Time (T)

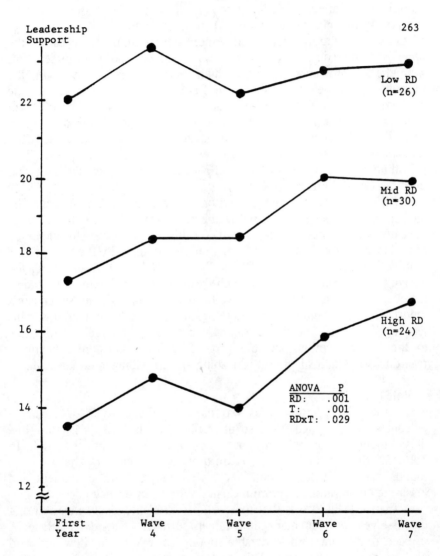

a consistent pattern where the higher the disillusionment, the higher the frequency of experiencing dyadic problems.

On the contrary, supervisor's reports suggest that a newcomer's feeling of disenchantment does not affect his treatment of the newcomer subordinate. For example, Figure 17 illustrates that after Wave 5 supervisors did not differentiate RD groups in their vertical exchange relations with the newcomer. In other words, from the eyes of the supervisor, newcomer's feeling of disillusionment did not hinder his willingness from engaging in a high vertical relationship with the subordinate. However, as shown in Figure 15, from the eyes of the newcomer, the quality of vertical exchange looks quite different depending upon whether he was "turned off" or "turned on" by the first year role experience. This inconsistency also holds true for the supervisor's report on job enrichment. The amount of supervisors providing leadership support showed a difference between the Low and the other two RD groups (p < .045).

Mismatch between the supervisor and his subordinate can also be seen in Job Challenge measured at the final wave of research. Table 29 indicates that a newcomer's report on his experience with increased centrality and task demand failed to gain endorsement by the supervisor's reports. Nonetheless, in Table 28 the Profile Similarity measure displayed a significant group difference with respect to the degree of leader-member agreement. However, as we have found already, the supervisor's report tends to be nondiscrminatory against disillusionment groups. This fact suggests that the difference in agreement may be largely attributable to the "misperception" on the part of highly disillusioned members regarding what their supervisors are doing and are willing to do for them.

2. Role Outcomes

The same ANOVA design as was used for the analysis of exchange outcomes was applied to test the effect of the first-year role dis-illusionment upon a set of role outcomes. Table 30 displays the result. In Table 30, the newcomer's reports are quite consistent with what we have found in the previous section: the higher the role disillusionment, the lower the organizational commitment and the greater the need deficiency.

Figure 18 illustrates that those who were highly disillusioned during the first year of their managerial career, suffered tremendous deficiency of need fulfillment with leadership support relative to the Low and Mid disillusionment colleagues. This finding is consistent with what other authors have found about the mechanism of disillusionment, i.e., the greater the discrepancy between what the newcomer expected to receive

Figure 17

Vertical Exchange Reported by the Supervisor Based on
the Role Disillusionment (RD) Groups over Time (T)

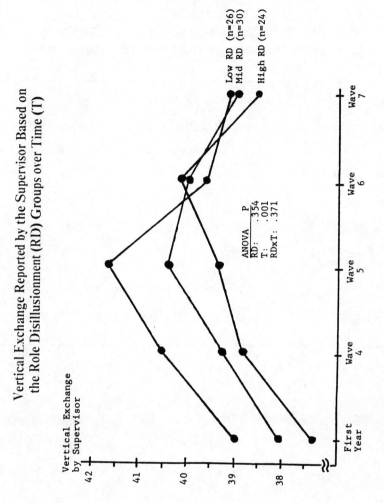

Table 29

**Job Challenge Reported at the End of the Third Year
Based on the First Year Role Disillusionment Group (N=80)**

| Variable | Mean for the RD Group | | | ANOVA P |
	High (n=24)	Mid (n=30)	Low (n=26)	
Newcomer's Report				
Increased Centrality	17.3	2.5	26.7	.001
Task Demand	14.3	17.0	20.8	.001
Supervisor's Report				
Increased Centrality	23.0	27.3	26.7	.085
Task Demand	20.0	21.9	21.3	.167

Table 30

Role Outcomes Based on the First Year Role Disillusionment (RD) and Time (T) Factors
(N = 80)

| Variable | Mean for the RD Group | | | | Probability | |
	High (n = 24)	Mid (n = 30)	Low (n = 26)	RD	T	RDxT
Newcomer's Report						
Organizational Commitment						
Value of Organization	37.4	41.6	46.5	.001	.675	.165
Risk of Commiting	14.4	14.9	16.4	.088	.091	.602
Need Deficiency						
Leadership Support	27.5	14.2	9.7	.001	.001	.002
Job Enrichment	12.4	5.6	3.2	.001	.268	.150
Supervisor's Report						
Job Performance	34.3	39.4	40.0	.030	.001	.371
Success Potential	11.2	10.8	11.5	.116	.223	.131

Figure 18

**Need Deficiency (D^2) with Leadership Support Based on
the First Year Role Disillusionment (RD) and Time (T)**

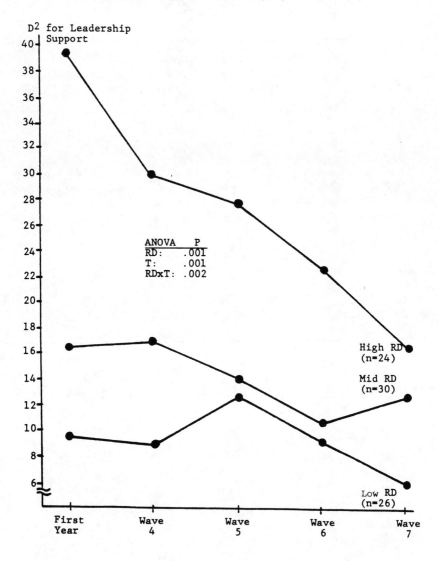

and what he actually did receive, the higher the disillusionment (Dunnette, 1973; Graen, 1776; Schein, 1964). However, as Figure 18 illustrates, among our sample newcomers, the severe need discrepancy in the first year became narrowed very rapidly over time, rather than widened, and lead to a turn-over in the end. This fact may suggest uniqueness of the Japanese organizational system for human resource development and utilization. The mean D^2 values for the Job Enrichment dimension indicated basically the same story as was told about the Leadership Support dimension in Figure 18. Moreover, it was found that mean differences for organizational commitment is also consistent with the preceding discussions. That is, those who experienced low role disillusionment in the first year have reported consistently high psychological value attached to their company, compared to those who experienced relatively high disillusionment at the start of their career.

Figure 19 illustrates mean performance ratings for three RD groups over time. In Figure 19, those newcomers who were the least disillusioned in their first-year experience showed a great progress in performance ratings by the beginning of the second year (Wave 4), and stayed as high performers throughout the rest of the research periods. The consistently high job performance achieved by the Low RD group seems to be the major source of variance that made the RD effect upon job performance significant ($p < .030$), because Figure 19 indicates that in the eyes of the supervisor, those newcomers who were most disillusioned do not necessarily seem to be the lowest performers. Rather, they were rated by the supervisor as having achieved a steady improvement in peformance beyond the level of Mid group members up to the Wave 6 point, except for the fact that at Wave 7, their performance level suddenly dropped to the lowest among RD groups. On the other hand, as far as the supervisor's ratings are concerned, the Mid RD group have been rather consistent bottom-level performers throughout the three-year research period.

Steady increase in performance ratings for the High disillusionment group up until Wave 6, can be interpreted as a part of the "catch up" process shown by this group's members. For example, in Figure 18, the High disillusionment group displayed a great reduction in need deficiency, while those in other groups remained basically unchanged in their need fulfillment during the three years. Moreover, as Figures 14, 15, and 16 illustrated, the High RD group have shown, respectively, a steady recovery from the first-year disillusionment, an increasing level of vertical exchange with the supervisor, and greater amounts of leadership support received from the supervisor, along with the progression of time for career development. However, the reason for the sudden decline in per-

Figure 19

Job Performance Based on
the Role Disillusionment (RD) Groups over Time (T)

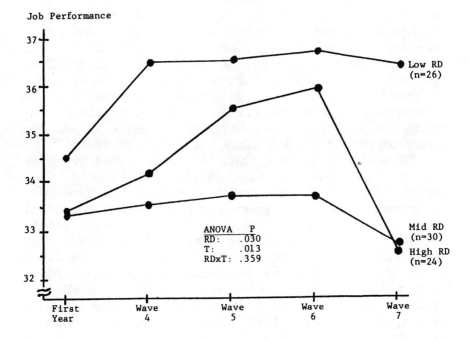

formance which occurred among the High RD group members between W6 and W7 is not known at this stage of analysis, and will be subject to further exploration.

Table 31 displays predictive correlations between role disillusionment and job performance. The first row of figures in the Table indicates that as long as the correlational analysis is concerned, there are no significant predictive relations between the first-year disillusionment and job performance during the subsequent periods. However, as we have seen in Figure 19, the ANOVA produced a significant result. This may suggest a contradiction between the two findings. But, both results are consistent: it is evident that the lack of meaningful correlations between the two measures is attributable to High and Mid RD members who created, as shown in Figure 19, an inverse relationship between role disillusionment and job performance during the period between the First Year and Wave 7.

Table 31 indicates that role disillusionment on and after Wave 4 did predict job performance for the subsequent periods. This finding suggests that the quality of disillusionment must be different between the first year and the rest of the periods. It may be that the first-year role disillusionment is a reaction to what the newcomer wished to have before joining the company. Therefore, disillusionment can be mainly a function of "unrealistic" expectation maintained by the newcomer before employment. As discussed earlier, mismatch between newcomer's and supervisor's reports based on the first-year role disillusionment, may give supportive evidence to this interpretation. Conversely, disillusionment on and after the second year may reflect the "reality" of actually anemic role-content that made some of the newcomers feel like quitting the company. Disillusionment at this stage also made it difficult for them to achieve high performance. The steady catch-up process shown by the High role disillusionment group suggests that they started to face the reality after the first-year experience.

3. Career Outcomes

Table 32 displays correlation coefficients between career outcomes (including W7 ratings) and role disillusionment monitored at five different time periods. As might be expected from the previous results shown in Table 31, the first-year role disillusionment predicted none of the career outcomes examined. On the contrary, role disillusionment after the First Year, especially at Wave 4 and Wave 5, tends to show rather consistent predictive correlations with career outcomes and Wave 7 ratings. This finding again gives support to the possible qualitative difference in the disillusionment phenomena between the first year, and

Table 31

Correlation Coefficients Between Role
Disillusionment and Job Performance
Reported at Five Different Points in Time
(N = 80)

Role Disillusionment[a]	Job Performance				
	FY	W4	W5	W6	W7
First Year	.17	.08	.08	-.03	.13
Wave 4	.07	.30**	.26*	.30**	.30**
Wave 5	.02	.26*	.36**	.27*	.33*
Wave 6	.12	.21	.21	.15	.27*
Wave 7	.10	.20	.09	.14	.35**

[a]Scaling of Role Disillusionment is made such that the larger the score, the lower the level of disillusionment.

The upper triangle displays predictive correlations based on role disillusionment, while the lower triangle displays predictive correlations based on job performance. The diagonal indicates correlation coefficients on a concurrent basis.

*p < .05
**p < .01

Table 32

Predicting Career Outcomes, Job Performance, and Success Potential Assessed at the End of the Third Year Based on Role Disillusionment Reported by the Newcomer at Five Different Points in Time (N = 80)

Role Dis-illusionment[a]	Perform-ance Index	Career Outcome			Right Type	Wave 7 Rating	
		Potential Index	Bonus			Job Per-formance	Success Potential
First Year	.03	.15	.03		.19	.13	.10
Wave 4	.24*	.41**	.27*		.33**	.30**	.27*
Wave 5	.25*	.38**	.14		.24*	.33**	.23*
Wave 6	.20	.31**	.28**		.22*	.27*	.23*
Wave 7	.06	.35**	.19		.22*	.35**	.25*

[a]Scaling for Role Disillusionment is made such that the greater the RD score, the lower the level of disillusionment.

*p < .05.
**p < .01.

the second and third years, as we discussed earlier. Among the outcome measures examined, the Potential Index derived from the reassessment at the end of the third year seems to be predicted best by the disillusionment scale based on each time period, except for the First Year.

In summary, the first-year role disillusionment failed to predict job performance and career outcomes for later stages of development within the DEPART organization. This may indicate that the newcomer's reaction to the environment of his career development during the first year tends to be illusory, or is primarily based on his unrealistic expectations rather than on reality testing. However, since the beginning of the second year, it started to reflect the quality of his role content and feedback on his role performance. Thus, disillusionment became real, producing significant predictive correlations between RD scale, and job performance and career outcomes thereafter.

IV. Test of the Assessment Center Hypothesis

For the purpose of testing the assessment center hypothesis, test scores derived from company's assessment of newcomers' potential conducted at the point of recruitment, were aggregated into a composite Assessment Scale (AS). The following four test scores were employed to construct the composite AS scale: (1) Intelligence scores derived from the Incomplete Sentences Blank, and scores from (2) an essay test, (3) an English test, and (4) an Interview. These four sets of scores were standardized with a mean 50 and a standard deviation of 20, then a AS score was computed by summing them and dividing the aggregate by four for each newcomer.

Table 33 displays intercorrelations among test scores and an AS composite. Table 33 indicates that the AS scale can be a fair representation of all other tests. Among various test results, the Interview showed the strongest intercorrelations among tests. Moreover, it produced the highest correlation with the AS Composite ($r = .81$). The result seems to be reasonable in view of the nature of the interview that the DEPART organization attempted. As discussed in Chapter V, a team of five company executives interviewed each applicant to make a final selection decision. For this purpose, they reviewed test scores and biographical data for each interviewee. Therefore, ratings derived from the interview session already denoted executives' judgment on overall potential of the newcomer. This is why the Interview came to show strong correlations not only with the other test scores, but also with our AS composite.

Table 33

**Intercorrelations Among Test Methods
and the AS Composite (N = 80)**

Test	Intelligence	Essay	English	Interview
Intelligence	–	.35	.17	.29
Essay	.35	–	.38	.48
English	.17	.38	–	.59
Interview	.29	.48	.59	–
AS Composite	.56	.77	.74	.81

For correlation coefficients with .22 higher, p < .05; with .28 or higher, p < .01.

1. ANOVA Results

Based on the composite assessment scale, a series of repeated-measure of ANOVA tests was performed to examine the effect of newcomers' potential assessed at the start of their organizational careers upon sets of outcomes derived from subsequent phases of their managerial career. Using the AS composite scores, subjects were divided into the following three groups: High (n = 27), Mid (n = 29), and Low (n = 24) potential groups. Then, repeated-measure ANOVA tests were attempted with this trichotomized AS scale as an independent variable, with outcome scales measured at five different monitoring points as dependent variables for the analysis.

Before presenting results of the analysis, a note on the method of classifying potential groups used for our study may be necessary. For the typical predictive study based on the assessment center model, assessees are usually rated and classified into two or three groups based on judgment by assessment staff members as to the degree of their potential to achieve a particular criterion outcome selected for prediction. Thus, predictive validity for this approach denoted the accuracy of staff judgment both in interpreting given assessment data and in making a "clinical" decision as to whether a particular newcomer has potential to attain a given outcome criterion. On the other hand, in our study the categorical judgment on potential for formulating a predictive decision is based on the "statistical" method, i.e., the mechanical grouping based on the standardized potential scores. In addition, usage of selection data as a basis of prediction may create a problem of range restriction in both predictor and criterion distribution. Whenever this problem occurs, prediction is expected to be negatively biased. This problem will be discussed in the summary section of this chapter.

ANOVA test results based on the above method classification produced no significant group effect as far as the newcomer's report is concerned. All newcomers, regardless of differences in their judged potentials, reported basically equal levels of job need received, job problems, job challenge, vertical exchange, organizational commitment, role disillusionment, and need deficiency. Moreover, the time effect did not make any significant change, as it interacted with the AS factor. On the contrary, the assessment factor displayed a very interesting effect upon supervisor's reports. Table 34 shows this result.

In Table 34, supervisors report that those newcomers who were judged to have High potential have been enjoying on average the higher level of vertical exchange with them during the first three years in the organization, compared to those who were judged to have Mid or Low potentials. Also, supervisors report that they have provided more oppor-

Table 34

**Supervisor's Report Based on Potential Groups
Identified by Selection Tests Upon Recruitment
(N = 80)**

Variable	Mean for the VE Group			AS	Probability Time	ASxT
	High (n = 27)	Mid (n = 29)	Low (n = 24)			
Job Need: Providing						
Leadership Support	24.7	23.7	23.5	.259	.001	.336
Job Enrichment	27.9	26.6	26.0	.062	.003	.936
Vertical Exchange	40.6	38.9	38.6	.012	.001	.082
Job Performance	35.4	35.0	33.1	.082	.012	.034
Success Potential	11.4	11.2	10.8	.174	.218	.042

tunities for job enrichment to the High potential subordinates than to the Mid and Low potential groups, although their reports failed to produce a significant group effect (p < .062). In addition, significant interaction effects observed for job performance and success potential in Table 34 suggest that differentiation among AS groups in terms of performance ratings by the supervisor might have taken place as a function of time.

Figure 20 illustrates mean vertical exchange scores reported by the supervisor over time based on three AS groups. In Figure 20, the High potential group showed also high level of vertical exchange reported by the supervisor except Wave 7, while the other groups remained basically the same. The sharp decline in vertical exchange reported by the High supervisor during Wave 6 and Wave 7 has partly to do with the disruption of vertical dyad linkages, which occurred in large scale during that period due to the extensive internal moblity of personnel. Anyhow, Figure 20 indicates that the subordinate potential, as the supervisor perceives it on the job, can be one of the factors to which the supervisor may attribute his vertical exchange activities with the subordinate. However, as discussed earlier, differential vertical exchange treatments reported by supervisors based on potentials seem to be too subtle to be noticed by their subordinates as such.

Figure 21 indicates that the differentiation in job performance might have taken place as early as the start of the newcomer's organizational career between the Low and the other two potential groups. By the end of the third year, the above process has broken into further ramifications quite consistent with potential ratings made at the start of the newcomer's career. Between Wave 6 and Wave 7, the Low group articulated as a result of precipitation in their job performance. This is more or less true even for the Mid group, while only the High potential group showed improvement in performance ratings during that period. Figure 22 illustrates mean success potentials rated by supervisors for each AS group over time by confirming the above story with a clearer picture. In Figure 22, relative positions among the three potential groups have shown stability, but with little differentiation until Wave 6: however, this process culminated in a "fan-shaped" differentiation at the end of the third year.

Table 35 also displays that the strength of association between selection tests and performance ratings is a function of time: Intelligence, Essay, and Interview came to show significant correlations with super-visors' ratings on job performance and success potential at Wave 7. Our composite AS scale, composed of standardized scores for Intelligence, Essay, English and Interview, also showed significant correlations at Wave 7. In addition, the AS composite produced significant predictive

Figure 20

**Vertical Exchange Reported by the Supervisor
Based on the Assessment Group (AS) over Time (T)**

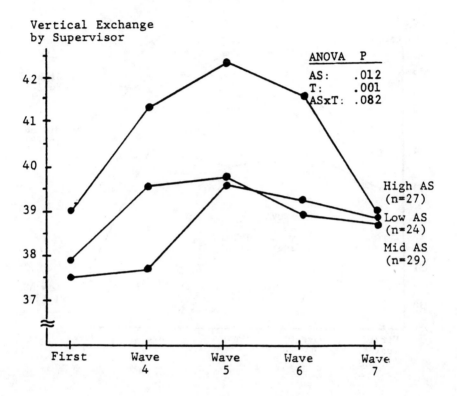

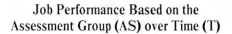

Figure 21

Job Performance Based on the
Assessment Group (AS) over Time (T)

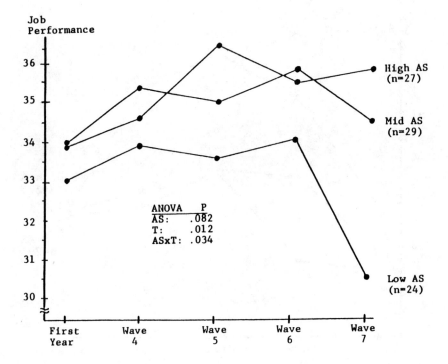

Figure 22

Success Potential Based on the
Assessment Group (AS) over Time (T)

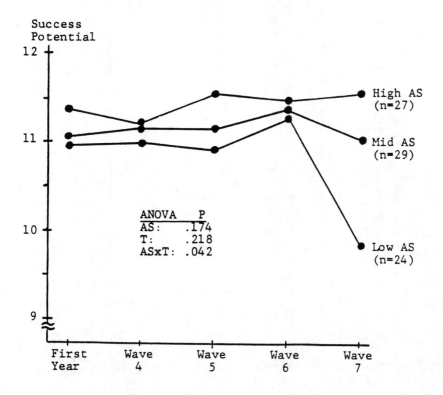

Table 35

Correlation Coefficients Between Selection Tests at the Point
of Recruitment and Job Performance and Success Potential Rated
by the Supervisor over Time Based on the Questionnaire (N=80)

| Test | Job Performance (I) and Success Potential (II) | | | | | | | | | |
| | First Year | | Wave 4 | | Wave 5 | | Wave 6 | | Wave 7 | |
	I	II	I	II	I	II	I	II	I	II
Intelligence	.11	.18	.17	.20	.25*	.16	.14	.17	.30**	.32**
Essay	.17	.16	.05	.02	.09	.05	.00	-.02	.25*	.29**
English	.14	.18	-.06	-.02	.17	.15	.04	.08	.12	.14
Interview	.07	.11	.05	-.01	.25*	.18	.14	.03	.41**	.37**
Personality Type[a]	.02	.09	.18	.23*	.07	.18	.05	.19	.09	.14
Conne	-.03	.01	.01	.08	.04	.03	-.11	.00	-.12	-.13
AS Composite	.18	.22*	.09	.07	.28**	.21	.13	.11	.38**	.39**

[a] A point biserial correlation coefficient.

* $p < .05$.

** $p < .01$.

correlations at First Year as well as at Wave 5, while the rest of the scales failed to show such consistency in predicting performance ratings over time. Interviews followed by the AS composite produced the two highest predictive correlation coefficients (.41 and .38 for job performance, and .37 and .39 for success potential, respectively) among all predictive correlations this study produced.

As discussed in the instrument section of Chapter V, the company's selection data provided the other two predictors, Personality Type and *Conne.* These variables were not utilized to construct an AS composite scale because of their unknown effects upon criterion outcomes. Table 35 displays the revealed effects of these variables upon job performance and success potential.

As discussed earlier, identification of a personality type was based on the clinical judgment of the newcomer's personality projected on the Incomplete Sentences Blank (Sano, 1969). Psychologists and personnel staff performed the task for our study. Information on a personality type originally displayed classification of newcomers into three modal personality types derived from the clinical theory of human personality: i.e., Epileptic, Schizophrenic, and Manic-depressive types (Sano, 1970 and 1975). For our study, however, only an Epileptic type was identified against others, because this particular personality is believed to be a "right type" for the DEPART organization and their business on the ground that this type of person tends to represent modesty, perseverance, predictability, social norms, and the like. In fact, about 81 percent of sample newcomers recruited by the DEPART were judged to belong to this personality type. However, as Table 35 displays, point biserial correlations computed between this personality type in contrast to others and performance ratings indicated only a weak relationship between the two.

A scale for *Conne,* or connection literary, implied the amount of outside intervention that an applicant might have had on his behalf to influence the hiring decisions of the DEPART company. In Table 35, this particular variable showed either negative or basically zero correlations with performance ratings over time, indicating that those who needed *Conne* to impact upon the company's hiring decision tended to be less effective performers after employment. This finding suggests that the DEPART company did employ less potent applicants who would not be hired without such *Conne* influence. As shown in Table 36, the impact of *Conne* upon the company's hiring decisions tell this fact more clearly: i.e., the less potential an applicant is judged to have, the more outside influence he needs to be exercised on his behalf in order to be hired.

Table 36

Relationship Between *Conne* Influence and
Assessment Tests for the Hiring Decision

Intelligence	Essay	English	Interview	AS Composite
−.14	−.35**	−.29**	−.33**	−.37**

*p < .05.
**p < .01.

2. Career Outcomes

Correlation coefficients calculated between a set of selection tests at the point of recruitment and career outcomes assessed in the end of the third year produced similar results as we discussed in the previous section. Table 37 displays that ratings for Intelligence and Interview, and our AS composite scale predicted all four career outcomes at a significant level. In Table 37, the highest predictive correlation appeared between Interview and Right Type ratings. This finding suggests that the executives' ratings at the interview for the final selection decisions were endorsed by the immediate supervisor's evaluation after three years regarding the extent to which each newcomer seems to be the right-type person to progress in the DEPART organization. Conversely, the Potential Index based on the company's reassessment of newcomer's potential conducted at the end of the third year, could only gain significant, but relatively low, endorsement from the test information. The AS composite that was found to be the best scale for predicting job performance in the previous section, could show only .26 correlation with the Potential Index. This relatively low correlation between the two potential scales may be attributable to the difference in methods between the two potential ratings (i.e., "multiple-test" method versus "multiple-rater" method). But the results also suggest that the potential identified at the start of the newcomer's career does not necessarily predict accurately the increasing value of personal resources of the newcomer during the subsequent periods for career development.

In Table 37, the negative effect of hiring *Conne* persons is evidently displayed. Although correlation coefficients did not reach a significant level, the *Conne* scale showed a consistent negative effect upon all career outcomes.

In sum, the composite potential scale based on the selection test

Table 37

Correlation Coefficients Between Selection Tests at the Point of Recruitment and Career Outcomes Assessed after Three Years (N = 80)

| Test | | Career Outcome | | |
	Perform-ance Index	Potential Index	Bonus	Right Type
Intelligence	.23*	.22*	.34**	.31**
Essay	.19	.20	.12	.22*
English	.05	.04	.15	.05
Interview	.21	.21	.25*	.42**
Personality Type[a]	.11	.17	.21	.05
Conne	−.13	−.09	−.16	−.16
AS Composite	.24*	.26*	.30**	.34**

[a] A point biserial correlation coefficient
*p < .05.
**p < .01.

information could predict all career outcomes assessed after three years in the newcomer's organizational career. Given the fact that performance ratings monitored by our questionnaire also showed higher correlations at the end of the third year, it is expected that the first stage of career differentiation might have happened among our sample newcomers at the end of their three-year experience in the DEPART organization. As discussed in Chapter V, the end of the third year incidentally denoted the time when newcomers are promoted to the Grade 3 level and assume the responsibility of section leaders. In fact, the follow-up study revealed that they were all promoted to that position after three years automatically. However, results of our study told an inside story about what actually happened to the newcomer by the end of the third year. In other words, the first promotion which occurred to newcomers on an across-the-board basis was accompanied by the undercurrent of differentiation in actual progress within the organization.

V. Summary of Results

Table 38 indicates that among the three hypotheses examined, the role making hypothesis represented by the first-year vertical exchange scale, VE(FY), produced the strongest and most consistent results in explaining the outcomes of career development. Out of the 23 variables tested, the VE(FY) measure demonstrated a *significant and hypothesized effect* upon the 18 variables. In addition, every factor derived from each instrument employed in our study was found to have a meaningful relationship with vertical exchange, except Job Problem Severity factors. Especially, the first-year vertical exchange was found predictive of all outcome variables reported by the supervisor throughout the research period.

On the other hand, the AS factor representing the assessment center hypothesis did not produce any significant effect as far as the newcomers' reports were concerned. However, this factor did show an interesting impact upon job perfomance and success potential of the newcomers as rated by the supervisor. That is, the AS factor predicted very clearly the differentiation among newcomers that occurred at the end period of the third year with respect to job performance and success potential (see Figures 21 and 22). No other predictors could detect the outcroppings of this differentiation process which could have been reasonably expected to happen at some point during the period of establishment within the organization. Unfortunately, however, due to the inability of the AS factor in explaining the newcomers' reports, we still have not answered "how" this process came into being. This question will be answered in the next chapter by examining the combined effect between the VE (FY) and AS factors upon the outcomes of development.

Table 38 displays that the RD(FY) factor that represents the disillusionment hypothesis produced exactly the same pattern of effects as that of the VE(FY) factor, as far as the newcomers reports are concerned. The similarity of results was found attributable to the high intercorrelation between the two factors ($r = .73$). However, Table 38 indicates that the RD(FY) factor does not have as consistent an influence upon the supervisor responses (see Figures 17 and 19) as did the VE(FY) factor, despite the high intercorrelation between the two. Moreover, the correlation analysis shown in Table 31 indicated that the RD(FY) has no predictive power for job performance. This finding may imply that although about 50 percent of the variance overlaps between the VE(FY) and RD(FY) factors, the remaining 50 percent of the variance for each factor tells quite a different story about supervisors' reports. In other words, variance for the VE(FY) explains both the newcomers' and supervisors' reports, while variance for RD(FY) explains only the newcomers' report. Furthermore, this finding suggests that the quality of the first-year vertical exchange might have been the cause of both role disillusionment (among many other newcomers' reports) and job performance (among other supervisors' reports), rather than the first-year role disillusionment being the cause of job performance and vertical exchanges.

Table 38 suggests that the time factor might have produced considerable impact upon the process of career development. To identify the pattern of time effect, trend mean changes over the five monitoring periods were examined for variables that registered a significant time effect. Table 39 displays the result. In Table 39, leadership support, job enrichment, and vertical exchange reported by the newcomer showed a monotonically increasing mean trend over time. On the other hand, need deficiency and profile similarity scales displayed a monotonically decreasing trend, indicating that the need deficiency and profile "dis-similarity" steadily decreased as a function of time.

The above findings suggest that all newcomers as a group have seen that their role positions become more and more "resourceful" (leadership support, job enrichment, and vertical exchange) as a function of time. In addition, the above process was accompanied by the gradual adjustment of discrepancy between what they wanted and what they actually received. As a result of this adjustment and actual improvement of their resource conditions, the way (or "profile") newcomers perceived their role situation, became closer and closer to the one the supervisors perceived. Interestingly, job problems experienced and felt by newcomers

Table 38

The ANOVA Test Results for the Role Making,
Disillusionment and Assessment Center Hypotheses (N = 80)

Dependent Variable	Factor Corresponding to Each Hypothesis			
	VE (FY)	RD (FY)	AS	Time
Newcomer's Report				
Job Need: Receiving				
Leadership Support	**	**	x	**
Job Enrichment	**	**	x	**
Job Problem: Frequency				
Dydadic Problem	**	**	x	x
Climate Problem	x	x	x	**
Job Problem: Severity				
Dyadic Problem	x	x	x	**
Climate Problem	x	x	x	**
Vertical Exchange	**	**	x	**
Job Challenge				
Increased Centrality	**	**	x	-
Task Demand	**	**	x	-
Organizational Commitment				
Value of Organization	**	**	x	x
Risk of Committing	x	x	x	x
Role Disillusionment	**	**	x	x
Role Content	**	**	x	x
Probability	x	**	x	x

Table 38 (continued)

The ANOVA Test Results for the Role Making, Disillusionment and Assessment Center Hypotheses (N = 80)

Dependent Variable	Factor Corresponding to Each Hypothesis			
	VE (FY)	RD (FY)	AS	Time
Need Deficiency				
Leadership Support	**	*	x	**
Job Enrichment	**	**	x	x
Supervisor's Report				
Job Need: Providing	**	*	x	**
Leadership Support	**	*	x	**
Job Enrichment	**	x	x	**
Vertical Exchange	*	x	x	—
Job Challenge				
Increased Centrality	*	x	x	—
Task Demand	*	x	x	—
Job Performance	**	x	***	**
Success Potential	*	x	***	x
Profile Similarity	**	**	x	**

$*$ $p < .05$;
$**$ $p < .01$;
$***$ Significant interaction at $p < .05$.
 x Nonsignificant;
 — Not applicable.

Table 39

Trend Means over Time for the Variables that Registered a Significant Time Effect (N=80)

| Variable | Mean for the Time Period | | | | | ANOVA P |
	FY	W4	W5	W6	W7	
Newcomer's Report						
Job Need: Receiving						
Leadership Support	17.1	18.7	18.3	19.7	22.8	.001
Job Enrichment	20.3	21.3	21.0	22.3	22.8	.001
Job Problem: Frequency						
Climate Problem	17.9	20.4	20.4	21.3	19.2	.001
Job Problem: Severity						
Dyadic Problem	33.8	34.1	35.5	35.5	33.0	.001
Climate Problem	17.9	18.6	19.4	20.3	19.8	.001
Need Deficiency						
Leadership Support	21.1	18.3	18.3	14.1	12.0	.001
Supervisor's Report						
Job Need: Providing						
Leadership Support	22.2	24.5	24.6	249	23.8	.001
Job Enrichment	26.5	27.2	27.5	27.5	26.2	.003
Vertical Exchange	38.1	40.0	40.5	40.0	38.9	.001
Job Performance	33.7	34.7	35.2	35.3	33.9	.012
Profile Similarity	46.5	43.7	45.7	42.9	38.8	.001

tended to increase in intensity as the process of career development evolved. This finding suggests that tasks assigned to the newcomers became more and more important and complex, thus causing more problems for them.

The pattern of time effect reported by the supervisor by the time of W6 tends to endorse the newcomer's perception on the effects of time. But, all supervisors' reports shown in Table 39 registered a decline during the period between W6 and W7. This decline was found attributable to the extensive disruption of old leader-member relations, and the start of new ones, which took place during the period.

Table 40 displays a summary of correlation studies performed to examine predictive validity of our three predictors. As we have seen already, career outcomes and supervisors' ratings at the final period of research were best predicted by the AS composite scale representing the assessment center model: (1) it showed significant correlations with all outcome variables examined, and (2) with each of the outcome variables, the AS scale produced stronger correlations than the other two predictors. The first-year vertical exchange showed the second best position in its consistency of predicting career outcomes, while the RD(FY) scale produced no significant predictive correlation at all.

However, considering all results shown in Tables 38 and 39 together, it will be concluded that the role making hypothesis represented by the VE(FY) scale emerges as the strongest hypothesis when explaining the process of managerial progress of newcomers during their first three years in the organization. It predicted exchange outcomes and role outcomes during the first three years, as well as career outcomes at the end of the third year. Conversely, the other two hypotheses could explain only a part of the entire sequence of outcomes derived from the process of managerial career development.

Two methodological biases which might have been involved in the present analysis need to be discussed. One of the biases is the tendency of regression toward the mean. As discussed earlier, some of the newcomers' reports that registered significant interaction effects between the predictor and time factors seem to have been affected by this bias. When a bias of regression toward the mean occurs, predictive validity of the VE(FY) scale summarized in Table 38 was checked against this bias with respect to the outcome measures reported by the newcomer. The testing procedure required the following three steps: (1) Newcomers' reports for the First Year were subject to the one-way ANOVA tests based on the trichotomized VE(FY) scale. Whenever this analysis produced a significant result, then (2) newcomers' Wave 7 reports were examined using the same ANOVA design to check if the first-year

Table 40

Summary of Predictive Correlation Coefficients for
Career Outcomes and Wave 7 Ratings Based on the
VE (FY), RD (FY), and AS Scales (N = 80)

| Predictor | | Career Outcome | | | Rating at Wave 7 | |
	Perform-ance Index	Potential Index	Bonus	Right Type	Job Per-formance	Success Potential
VE (FY)	.13	.22*	.11	.28**	.27*	.25*
RD (FY)	.03	.15	.03	.19	.13	.10
AS	.24*	.26*	.30**	.34**	.38	.39**

*p < .05.
**p < .01.

difference based on the VE(FY) factor was maintained in the end of the final wave of our research; (3) at the same time, variability of criterion distribution was compared between the First year and Wave 7 based on the coefficient of variation ($V = S/X$). A rule of thumb to judge the bias of regression toward the mean was established in such a manner that the bias is involved: when the group difference at the First Year based on the VE(FY) scale disappears at Wave 7, while variance in criterion measures at Wave 7 either increases or remains at the same level, compared to that observed at the First Year.

Table 41 displays the result of analysis. According to the above criteria, a tendency of regression toward the mean occurred for the Value of the Organization and Frequency of Dyadic Problems. For these variables, significant group differences existing at the First Year were washed away by Wave 7, while variations remained basically at the same level between the two time periods. This result indicates that predictive validity of the VE(FY) scale for these two outcome variables must be discounted by the bias of regression toward the mean. Table 41 suggests that for other variables, the VE(FY) are free from the regression bias, including those variables that registered significant VE-by-Time interaction effects.

The second methodological problem for the present analysis is that a negative bias might have been involved in the predictive validity of the AS composite scale, due to the possible range restriction in the predictor as well as the criterion distributions. This problem is attributable to the fact that the data used for creating the AS composite scale were derived from the company's selection tests, and thus the AS predictor tends to have very high intercorrelations with the selection batteries (see Table 33). If the bias of range restriction occurs, predictive validity of the AS scale will be an underestimate of population correlation coefficients. For the present study, predictive validity of the AS scale ranged form .24 to .34 in terms of correlation coefficients (see Table 37). This range seems lower than that reported by the past assessment center studies summarized in Table 6. Range restriction in a "technical" sense may be one of the possible reasons for the relatively low predictive validity of our AS scale. Although, recruiting *Conne* people helped stretch the range toward the lower end in both predictor and criterion distributions (see Tables 36 and 37 for negative correlations between *Conne* and AS and career outcome scales). The second reason may be attributable to the "built-in" restriction in criterion distribution, due to the company's policy of slow promotions. For the present study, this restriction implies that three years may be too short in the DEPART organization to see the full

Table 41

Examination of the Trend of Regression Toward a Mean
Using Three VE (FY) Groups Based on the Comparison
of ANOVA Results Between the First Year and Wave 7

Newcomer's Report		Mean for the VE(FY) Group				ANOVA P	$\underline{V}$
		Low (n=23)	Mid (n=29)	High (n=28)	Overall (N=80)		
Org. Commitment:							
Value of Org.	FY	38.8	42.1	45.4	42.3	.011	.19
	W7	40.4	41.1	44.3	42.1	.150	.18
Disillusionment:							
Role Content	FY	34.6	41.1	46.9	41.3	.001	.17
	W7	39.5	42.6	45.9	42.9	.004	.16
Job Need:							
*Leadership Support	FY	11.6	17.3	21.3	17.1	.001	.33
	W7	16.9	19.8	22.5	19.9	.001	.26
Job Enrichment	FY	15.5	20.1	24.4	20.3	.001	.24
	W7	20.7	22.3	25.2	22.8	.007	.23
Need Deficiency:							
*Leadership Support	FY	41.4	16.5	9.2	21.1	.001	.94
	W7	21.9	8.7	7.1	11.9	.001	1.27
Job Enrichment	FY	16.0	5.9	2.2	7.5	.001	1.41
	W7	10.7	3.7	3.6	5.7	.008	1.63
Frequency of:							
Climate Problems	FY	35.2	30.0	27.8	30.7	.001	.19
	W7	33.1	31.0	30.2	31.3	.183	.18
*Vertical Exchange	FY	23.8	30.3	37.6	31.0	.001	.20
	W7	31.2	33.1	37.2	34.0	.005	.20

*Results of repeated ANOVA tests produced the significant VExT interaction effects.

V   Coefficient of variation $(V=S/\overline{X})$.

differentiation among newcomers in terms of hard criteria of career progress.

Considering the possible built-in bias, an attempt was made to create more variance in criterion distribution. For this purpose, four career outcome measures displayed in Table 37 were standardized and aggregated into a single career outcome index. Then, a correlation coefficient between this index and the AS potential scale was computed. The result yielded a .54 correlation between the predictor and the criterion index, indicating that the relatively low predictive validity of the AS potential scale displayed in Table 37 can partly be attributable to the built-in restriction of criterion distribution in the DEPART organization.

Finally, it must be noted that a very low turnover rate among our sample of newcomers enabled us to maintain possible full-range criterion variance "after" employment. On the other hand in the AT&T study, for example, investigators lost 104 recruits (38%) by the end of the research period. Moreover, the 52 recruits (20%) were forced to leave because of their low performance, perhaps making criterion distribution positively skewed.

Chapter VII

Interaction Between Factors of Progress

This chapter will examine the causal relationships among the factors of career progress. As summarized in Table 38, the results reported in Chapter VI suggested that vertical exchange explains the various outcomes derived from the process of career progress in a very consistent manner. On the other hand, role disillusionment failed to explain performance ratings and other outcomes reported by the supervisor, as well as career outcomes measured at the end of the third year. Conversely, the AS potential scale predicted performance ratings and career outcomes consistently, but it failed completely to explain the outcomes reported by the newcomer. The discussion presented in Chapter IV was based on the assumption that the three factors of career progress examined in our study were casually independent of each other. Now, however, it becomes necessary to determine causal relationships among the VE(FY), RD(FY), and AS factors. To answer this question, independence of causal impact was examined for each factor by holding the effect of the remaining two factors constant (Blalock, 1964).

I. Partial Predictive Validity
Figure 23 illustrates hypothetical relationships among three factors. The first possible causal linkage derived from Figure 23 suggests that the potential factor assessed upon employment is the ultimate cause of whatever happens after employment. If this is true: (1) the potential factor will have significant correlations with the first-year vertical exchange and disillusionment, as well as with outcomes for the subsequent time periods, and (2) it will still predict outcomes after the effects of the first-year vertical exchange and role disillusionment are partialed out. The findings reported in Chapter VI suggest that the first condition partially holds true for the AS potential factor. Thus, the focus of analysis is directed toward examining the partial correlations between the AS factor and the outcome variables, holding the effect of other factors constant. The next causation states that the first-year vertical exchange determines outcomes of career development for the later time periods, as well as role disillusionment for the first year. The direction of influence shown by arrows A and B in Figure 23 corresponds to this

Figure 23

Causal Relationships Among Factors of Career Progress

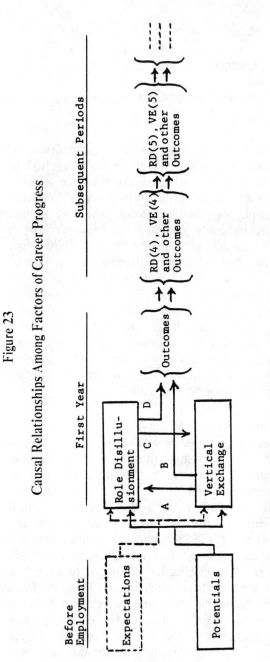

Figure 23. Causal Relationships Among Factors of
Career Progress

hypothesis. If this causal linkage holds true, we will expect that the first year vertical exchange remains predictive of outcome variables after the effects of potential and disillusionment factors are controlled. The third alternative causation states that the first-year role disillusionment determines both the first-year vertical exchange and outcomes for the subsequent time periods (see C and D arrows in Figure 23). Again, for this hypothesis to be true, the first-year disillusionment must remain predictive of outcome measures after the potential and the first-year vertical exchange are controlled.

For the present analysis, the three hypotheses stated above will be tested by computing partial correlation coefficients between one of the VE(FY), RD(FY) and AS factors, and outcome variables for the subsequent time periods, holding the remaining two factors constant. An examination of intercorrelations among the above three factors at a zero-order level indicated that the AS potential factor correlates with the VE(FY) and RD(FY) factors by .18 and .10 respectively, while the VE(FY) correlates with the RD(FY) factor by .73. In Figure 23 the AS factor is regarded as exogenous to the process of career development. Moreover, zero-order correlations and the results reported in Chapter VI suggest that the AS potential factor may be causally independent of the remaining two factors. Thus, the main focus for the present analysis is in determining the causal direction between the VE(FY) and RD(FY) factors. Figure 23 displays another exogenous factor, *career expectations* maintained by the newcomer before employment, as a source of causal effect upon RD(FY) and VE(FY) factors. Unfortunately, however, data corresponding to this factor are not available in our study. Therefore, partial correlations obtained for the present analysis need to be inter-preted by considering the possible impact of this fourth factor.

To prove that the VE(FY) factor *alone* is the cause of the outcomes for the subsequent time periods, the following two conditions must be met: (1) the VE(FY) factor must remain predictive of outcome levels after the effect of both RD(FY) and AS factors are partialed out, and (2) the RD(FY) factor should lose predictive validity of outcomes after the effects of the VE(FY) and AS factors are removed. When the first condition is true, while the second one is false, it can be judged that each factor has *independent* predictive validity. On the other hand, when the first condition is false, while the second one is true, the two factors are regarded as *interdependent*. In this case, causal influence must follow the two-way path.

Table 42 displays partial correlation coefficients computed between the VE(FY) factor and a selected set of outcome variables reported by the newcomer for the subsequent periods of career progress, with the

Table 42

Correlation Coefficients Between the VE(FY) Scale and a Set of Variables
Reported by the Newcomer at Five Different Time Periods, Controlling the
RD (FY) and AS Potential Factors (N=80)

Newcomer's Report	FY	W4	W5	W6	W7
			Time Period		
Value of Organization	-.35 (-.27)	-.02 (.35)	-.06 (.30)	-.09 (.23)	-.03 (.25)
Role Disillusionment	x (.73)	.20 (.52)	.16 (.46)	.33 (.52)	.06 (.41)
Leadership Support	.33 (.70)	.32 (.53)	.39 (.59)	.40 (.59)	.28 (.52)
Need Deficiency with Leadership Support	-.30 (-.62)	-.33 (-.45)	-.20 (-.35)	-.37 (-.50)	-.20 (-.37)
Vertical Exchange	1.00 (1.00)	.51 (.62)	.44 (.61)	.47 (.60)	.23 (.43)

Figures in parentheses denote zero-order correlation coefficients.

For partial correlations with $r \geq .23$ and $r \geq .28$, $p < .05$ and $p < .01$, respectively.

For zero-order correlations with $r \geq .22$ and $r \geq .28$, $p < .05$ and $p < .01$, respectively.

x Control variable

effect of the RD(FY) and AS potential factors upon outcomes held constant. Table 42 also includes the zero-order correlation coefficients between the VE(FY) and outcome measures. As far as the zero-order correlations are concerned, the VE(FY) factor can predict the newcomer's reports at five different time periods in a very consistent manner; all zero-order correlations were found significant at the .05 level, and 21 coefficients out of the 24 examined, reached the .01 level of significance.

The partial correlation coefficients shown in Table 42 indicate that the VE(FY) factor remains predictive of vertical exchange for the subsequent time periods, even after the effects of RD(FY) and AS factors are partialed out. This finding suggests that the levels of vertical exchange for Wave 4, Wave 5, and so on, are caused mainly by the VE(FY), the first-year vertical exchange. Likewise, the VE(FY) factor showed significant partial predictive validity for both leadership support and need deficiency. On the other hand, the VE(FY) lost its predictive power over organizational commitment (the "psychological value of the organization") after the effects of RD(FY) and AS factors were removed. Partial correlations between the VE(FY) and disillusionment for the later time periods reduced its magnitude relative to the zero-order corrrelations, but the influence of the VE(FY) remained significant even after the effect of role disillusionment itself was removed together with the effect of the AS potential factor. In sum, the results shown in Table 42 indicate that the first condition necessary to identify the independent effect of the VE(FY) factor was met for leadership support, need deficiency and vertical exchange itself. This condition seems to hold more or less true for role disillusionment, while for organizational commitment this condition did no prevail.

To examine the second condition discussed earlier, partial correlation coefficients between the RD(FY) factor and the outcomes for the subsequent time periods were computed while holding the effects of VE(FY) and AS factor constant. Table 43 displays the results. In Table 43, the RD(FY) factor failed to show any significant relation to leadership support, need deficiency, and vertical exchange after the effect of VE(FY) as AS factors were partialed out. But, for the psychological value of the organization and role disillusionment scales, the RD(FY) factor still remained predictive after the other factors were controlled. The above results combined with those shown in Table 42 may point to the following conclusions.

(1) *Single Independent Causation.* Within the system of three factors of career progress, the first-year vertical exchange was found to have a single independent causal effect upon leadership support, need deficiency, and the vertical exchange which developed after the first year.

Table 43

Correlation Coefficients Between the RD (FY) Scale and a Set of Variables
Reported by the Newcomer at Five Different Time Periods, Controlling the
VE(FY) and AS Potential Factors (N=80)

Newcomer's Report	Time Period				
	FY	W4	W5	W6	W7
Value of Organization	.68 (.64)	.39 (.50)	.38 (.46)	.34 (.40)	.27 (.36)
Role Disillusionment	1.00 (1.00)	.32 (.56)	.27 (.50)	.09 (.43)	.34 (.51)
Leadership Support	.50 (.75)	.13 (.47)	.11 (.49)	.10 (.49)	.18 (.49)
Need Deficiency with Leadership Support	-.38 (-.66)	-.02 (-.35)	-.08 (-.31)	-.00 (-.37)	-.10 (-.34)
Vertical Exchange	x (.73)	-.08 (.41)	.03 (.46)	-.05 (.41)	.12 (.39)

Figures in parentheses denote zero-order correlation coefficients.

For partial correlations with $r \geq .23$ and $r \geq .28$, $p < .05$ and $p < .01$, respectively.

For zero-order correlations with $r \geq .22$ and $r \geq .28$, $p < .05$ and $p < .01$, respectively.

x   Control variable

For those variables, both conditions (1) and (2) discussed earlier were satisfied. First, the VE(FY) showed significant predictive correlations after the effects of the RD(FY) and AS factors were partialed out, and second, the RD(FY) failed to remain predictive after the VE(FY) and AS factors were controlled. On the other hand, the RD(FY) was found to have a single causal effect upon the psychological value of the organization reported by the newcomer for Wave 4, 5, and so on. By the same token, the RD(FY) factor remained predictive of value of the organization after the VE(FY) and AS factors were controlled, while the VE(FY) failed to show predictive validity after the effects of RD(FY) and AS were partialed out.

(2) *Multiple Independent Causation.* It may be safe to say that role disillusionment on and after Wave 4 was caused independently both by the VE(FY) and RD(FY) factors, because each factor remained predictive of role disillusionment for the subsequent time periods after the remaining factor was controlled together with the AS potential factor. In other words, the first condition was true, but the second one was false, both for the VE(FY) and RD(FY) factors. Under these circumstances, role disillusionment after the first year can be best described by a "linear combination" of VE(FY) and RD(FY) factors.

The results displayed in Tables 42 and 43 also suggest that both the VE(FY) and RD(FY) factors have independent effects upon leadership support, need deficiency, and psychological value of the organization as reported by the newcomer during the first year period. An interesting question to be asked is why did the independent effect of the RD(FY), which appeared on leadership support and need deficiency during the first year suddenly wash away for the subsequent time periods, while on organizational commitment the effect was maintained over time. Likewise, why is it that the VE(FY) lost partial predictive validity for organizational commitment, while its effect remained significant for leadership support and need deficiency over time?

In Chapter VI, we hinted that the first-year disillusionment might have been caused by an emotional reaction of the newcomer faced with the reality of his career role that confronted his idealistic expectation maintained prior to employment. If this is the case, expectation may be another independent source of variance for role disillisionment, and probably for organizational commitment. On the other hand, the results shown in Table 43 indicate that expectation and subsequent disillusionment did not affect reality. That is, the effect of role disillusionment upon leadership support and need deficiency disappeared after the vertical exchange variable that represents one of the most important conditions on the real job was controlled. Conversely, the results displayed in Table 42 indicate that the resource conditions for career progress, vertical exchange and leadership support, are predictable by the VE(FY) factor independent of the newcomer's disillusionment with his first-year career role. This finding suggests that the first-year disillusionment seems to have remained as a feeling of resentment or as a minor trauma experience within the mind of each individual resulting in a significant influence upon organizational commitment, but not necessarily affecting the reality conditions after the first year.

In sum, the partial correlation analyses produced the necessary evidence to evaluate the hypothetical causal influence illustrated in Figure 23. (1) The first-year vertical exchange (arrow B) was found to be a single, independent cause of leadership support, need deficiency with leadership support, and vertical exchange itself for the subsequent time periods, while (2) the first-year role disillusionment (arrow D) was found solely responsible for organizational commitment. (3) On the other hand, for role disillusionment, the results of the analysis suggest that one of the causal influences may flow from A to D, with expectations being the other possible source of variance for the disillusionment phenomenon. (4) None of the variables examined produced results that indicate a C-to-B causal linkage. As shown in Table 43, the RD(FY) factor cannot be a cause of vertical exchange, while the reverse seems to be more likely. (5) As might be expected from the results shown in Table 38, the AS potential factor produced no significant results upon newcomer's reports in terms of either zero-order correlation or partial correlation coefficients.

The same design of partial correlation analysis as applied to the newcomer's reports was performed for job performance rated by the supervisor at five different points in time. Table 44 displays the results of this analysis. In Table 44 the partial correlations between each factor and job performance produced basically the same results as those derived from the zero-order correlation analysis. This indicates that both VE(FY) and AS factors have a causal effect upon job performance independent of each other and of the RD(FY) factor. Conversely, none of the correlations reached a significant level between RD(FY) and job performance. Table 44 also displays partial and zero-order correlation coefficients between each factor and selected career outcomes.

Again, the AS potential factor predicted the career outcomes most consistently after the effects of VE(FY) and RD(FY) factors were partialed out. On the other hand, the effect of VE(FY) upon the Potential Index was washed away after the remaining factors were controlled.

To examine whether the VE(FY) factor remains predictive of job

Table 44

Partial Correlation Coefficients Between Each of the Three Predictors, and
Job Performance and Career Outcomes, Holding Other Predictors Constant
(N=80)

Inde- pendent Variable	Control Variable	Job Performance					Career Outcome		
		FY	W4	W5	W6	W7	Pot. Index	Bonus	Per. Index
VE(FY)	AS	.02	.28*	.17	.23*	.21	.12	.09	.13
	RD(FY)	(.17)	(.25*)	(.21)	(.14)	(.27*)	(.22*)	(.11)	(.13)
AS	VE(FY)	.16	.08	.28*	.14	.38**	.27*	.31**	.24*
	RD(FY)	(.18)	(.09)	(.28**)	(.13)	(.38**)	(.26*)	(.30**)	(.24*)
RD(FY)	VE(FY)	.09	-.16	-.09	-.19	-.09	.00	-.07	-.09
	AS	(.17)	(.08)	(.08)	(-.03)	(.13)	(.15)	(.03)	(.03)

Figures in parentheses show zero-order correlation coefficients.

   * p<.05 .
  ** p<.01 .

performance over time, after the effects of the other two factors were removed, a repeated-measure ANOVA was performed with the trichotimized VE(FY) scale as an independent variable, and the residual gain performance scores for each time period as a dependent variable in the analysis. Residual gain scores (Y-Y) were computed as discrepancy scores between the raw performance ratings (Y) and their least-square estimates (Y) based on the RD(FY) and AS factors. The design of ANOVA tests for this study was the same as the one used in Chapter VI, except that the residual gain performance scores were subject to analysis instead of uncorrected performance ratings. Table 45 displays the result of the ANOVA, together with results of the similar analyses using the RD(FY) and AS factors for ANOVA tests.

The residual performance scores corresponding to each factor of the ANOVA were distributed with a mean zero within each time period. Thus, in Table 45 the time effect upon performance was removed although the interaction effect between time and each factor remained valid as a standardized form. Results shown in Table 45 indicate that the VE(FY) factor remained predictive of job performance *over time* even after the effects of the RD(FY) and AS factors were partialed out (p < .006). A pattern of mean differences among three VE groups seems to be basically the same as the one based on the unadjusted performance ratings (see Figure 13). The High VE group members remained as the highest performers followed by the Mid and Low VE colleagues. However at Wave 7 the difference between the High and Mid groups disappeared after the effects of RD(FY) and AS factors were removed, while the difference between the Low and the other two groups became more conspicuous.

In Table 45, holding the other factors constant, the AS potential factor also produced a significant effect upon job performance by interacting with the time factor. This result again is consistent with what we found based on the raw performance scores (see Figure 21). That is, a divergence between Low AS and the other two groups over time yielded a significant AS-by-Time interaction affect upon the residual performance scores (p < .044). Conversely, in Table 45 the RD(FY) factor lost its predictive validity when the effects of VE(FY) and the AS factor were held constant. It must be noted that as shown in Figure 19, this factor produced a significant result for the uncorrected performance ratings. This finding suggests that the effect of the first-year role disillusionment upon job performance over time is basically random, once the VE(FY) and AS factors were controlled. The fact that the RD(FY) also failed to explain leadership support, need deficiency and the vertical exchange reported by the newcomer may point, together with the above evidence,

Table 45

ANOVA Results for Residual Job Performance Scores Computed by
Controlling VE(FY), AS, and RD (FY) Variables Taken Pair-Wise (N =80)

Control Variable	Factor for ANOVA		Mean Residual Score for Job Performance						ANOVA P	
			FY	W4	W5	W6	W7	Average		
AS and RD(FY)	VE(FY)	L(n=23)	-1.58	-2.27	-1.84	-1.69	-2.16	-1.90	VE:	.006
		M(n=29)	.63	-.67	.11	-.02	.92	.19	Time:	1.000
		H(n=28)	.64	2.56	1.40	1.40	.83	1.37	VExT:	.345
VE(FY) and RD(FY)	AS	L(n=24)	-.39	-.13	-1.13	-.74	-2.77	-1.03	AS:	.268
		M(n=29)	.30	.65	-.13	.58	.80	.44	Time:	1.000
		H(n=27)	.02	-.59	1.14	.04	1.60	.44	ASxT:	.044
VE(FY) and AS	RD(FY)	L(n=27)	-.28	.69	.10	.45	1.24	.44	RD:	.554
		M(n=29)	.92	.46	.48	.06	-.89	.21	Time:	1.000
		H(n=29)	-.51	-1.03	-.49	-.47	-.42	-.58	RDxT:	.557

The L, M, and H denote the Low, Mid, and High groups respectively.

to the conclusion that the independent effect of the first-year disillusionment upon the process of career development may be very limited, despite the arguments to the contrary (Dunnette, et al., 1973; Graen, 1976; Porter, et al., 1975; Schein, 1964).

In sum, the results of the partial correlation analyses suggest that the three predictors explored in our study determine the three different aspects associated with the entire process of career progress within the organization: vertical exchange is mainly responsible for resource acquisition (leadership support, job enrichment, job challenge, etc.) and job performance, while the AS potential is more predictive of job performance and complex, career outcomes. Conversely, the first-year role disillusionment was found causally related only to organizational commitment, implying that disillusionment with one's career role during the first year may affect his attitude to the organization for the subsequent time periods. These findings may point to the notion that most outcomes of career progress can be better explained by "combining" the two most influential factors (i.e., VE(FY) and AS potential factors) of career progress. A scenario regarding how our sample newcomers behaved under this combined effect may look like the following. First, the experience of high vertical exchange relations with the supervisor during the first year provided the newcomer with extra resources to perform a better job and to develop his career role position. Second, high performance enabled the newcomer to acquire more resources for role activities for the next phase of development. In this way, an upward spiral of role development was triggered by high vertical exchange during the first year. The above two processes could be accelerated, if the newcomer were equipped with high potential together with high vertical exchange relation. Third, it is expected that the first-year experience enabled the high exchange newcomers to learn the basic skills and knowledge necessary to develop their own role: i.e., setting a high performance standard, negotiating for resources, hard work and contribution, and expanding personal influence with their supervisors and colleagues. Once these critical tools for promoting one's role position can be learned by experience, they would be applicable to new assignments with different supervisors. Fourth, the critical first-year experience of the leader-member relationship might have enabled successful newcomers to experience "psychological success" (Hall, 1968) which plugged in these people toward a path of self-propelled higher-order need fulfillment. Especially, this might have been the case for those newcomers who could have high vertical exchange relations with their supervisors combined with high potentials for growth during the first-year. Accordingly, this success experience might have reinforced the "self-esteem" (Korman,

1967) of the high potential newcomers. In the next section, this scenario will be tested by examining the combined effect between the VE(FY) and the AS potential factors upon the outcome of career progress.

II. Interaction Between the First-Year Vertical Exchange and the Potential Factors

Examination of the combined effect between the VE(FY) and the AS factors requires an assumption on the "pattern of the combined effect upon outcome variables." An *additive* model (Winer, 1971) assumes that the AS potential factor has an equal magnitude of effect upon the dependent variables at each level of the VE(FY) factor. In other words, this model assumes that the effect of potential is the same (i.e., adds an equal effect) to both high and low vertical exchange members in predicting outcome variables. The effect of potentials interpreted this way may be called a *general adequacy hypothesis* on individual potentials. This is the hypothesis advanced by Korman to explain how the assessment center method works. He stated that assessment ratings may be predicting "the general level of adequacy with which the person will be able to function in a complex environment and the extent to which he will be able to handle the various stresses" (Korman, 1968, 316–317). However, evidence raised in our study suggests that the general adequacy hypothesis has little explanatory power. As summarized in Table 38, the results of our analysis produced no significant AS potential effect upon newcomer's reports, indicating that potential cannot make any significant difference in the newcomer's coping behavior with the environmental pressures and stresses.

An alternative, *nonadditive* model (Winer, 1971) assumes that the effect of the AS potential factor upon the outcome variables is a function of the level of leader-member relations. This model suggests that the potential factor emits different effects upon the outcome variables depending upon the level of vertical exchange between the leader and his member. An interpretation of an individual's potential based on this model may be called a *partial adequacy hypothesis*. Our alternative hypothesis simply states that potential is just "potential"; it needs additional conditions for its realization. For the present study, vertical exchange will be considered as one of the conditions necessary to augment the partialness of an individual's potential. Under this hypothesis, it is assumed that those newcomers with High potentials accompanied by High vertical exchange relations with their supervisors (the High-High group) will be in the most favorable position to make progress within the organization. On the other hand, those newcomers who were judged to have High potentials, but were denied its realization by Low vertical relations (the High-Low group) will be precipitated into the worst situation for career development. Because, under this situation, the higher-order needs (needs for self-esteem, autonomy, self-actualization, etc.) that the High potential individuals would seek to fulfill are prone to frustration more easily. Thus, those with High potential, but with Low vertical exchange, will come to experience the most severe disillusionment, need deficiency, and decay in organizational commitment. Probably, under those circumstances, job performance will also suffer.

The remaining groups, the Low potential with High vertical exchange (the Low-High group) and the Low potential with Low vertical exchange (the Low-Low group), will be expected to find their position between the two extreme groups discussed above. More precisely, the Low-High group may take a superior position over the Low-Low group, because of the complementary effect of high vertical exchange that the Low-High group can enjoy. In summary, our partial adequacy hypothesis based on the interaction between potential and vertical exchange factors predicts that those newcomers with High potential accompanied by High vertical exchange will be in the best position for the managerial progress, followed by, in order, the Low-High, Low-Low, and High-Low groups.

The above prediction is based upon the consideration of the impact of leader-member relations upon potential. In terms of factor analysis, vertical exchange denoted two dimensions of a leader-member relation characterized as *dyadic contingency* and *job latitude*. The first factor denoted supervisor's recognition of the newcomer's potential, his understanding of the newcomer's expectations and problems, and his willingness to help the subordinate, while the second factor denoted the newcomer's latitude, autonomy, and influence on the job. Therefore, if the high potential newcomers could enjoy the high vertical exchange in terms of the above two dimensions, they would be most likely to achieve the highest level of career progress within the organization. Conversely, if High potential newcomers were placed in a constrained vertical relation, they would feel that their potential was denied, and be discouraged more severely than the low potential newcomers under similar conditions. This *discouragement effect* for the high potential newcomers may be attributable to the negative reaction derived from the unfulfilled potential or self-esteem. In Chapter VI, it was found that High potential newcomers as a group show no significant differences from low potential newcomers in their reports. This result was produced probably because in the previous analyses we could not consider the above discouragement effect occurring to a part of the High potential newcomers. Thus, the positive AS effect reported by the High vertical exchange group might have been offset by the negative one experienced by the low vertical exchange group.

The partial adequacy hypothesis, as specified above, was tested using a two-way, repeated-measure ANOVA design based on the AS and VE(FY) factors. For the purpose of testing, sample newcomers were first divided into two groups based on the AS scale. Then, they were cross-tabulated into four groups using the second VE(FY) scale, so that the classification could produce subgroups relevant to the examination of our hypothesis. Subgroup entries based on the above cross-tabulation produced a little unbalanced distribution due to a slight intercorrelation between the two classification scales $(r = .18)$. Therefore, random sampling was performed in order to balance the subgroup entries. This procedure reduced our sample size from 80 to 61, with the following distribution for each subgroup: The High AS and High VE(FY) group, i.e., the High-High group $(n = 15)$, likewise the High-Low group $(n = 16)$, the Low-High group $(n = 14)$, and the Low-Low group $(n = 16)$.

Based on the above classification, a repeated-measure ANOVA was performed with the dichotomized AS and VE(FY) scales as independent variables, with all outcome variables measured at five different points in time as dependent variables. As far as the main effects (effects of AS, VE(FY), and Time factors) are concerned, the results should appear basically the same as those observed in Chapter VI, although reduction in sample size due to random sampling for the present analysis may cause changes between the two analyses. The purpose of the analysis for this study, however, was not to examine the main effects but to test the interaction effects between the AS and VE(FY) factors, or among the AS, VE(FY), and Time factors, upon outcomes to see the "partial" impact of the potential factor. The AS, VE(FY), and Time factors were fixed, with the subject being random and crossed with Time for the ANOVA design.

1. Partial Adequacy: Newcomer's Reports

Figure 24 displays stability of the vertical exchange scale over five different points in time based on the four subgroups of newcomers derived from the classification method discussed earlier. Figure 24 clearly illustrates that the four subgroups of newcomers identified at the starting year of their careers were found to have maintained their positions over time in accordance with the prediction based on the partial adequacy hypothesis. That is, in Figure 24, those newcomers who were judged to have High potential and in addition were provided with High vertical exchange during the first-year period (the H-H group), achieved

Figure 24

Stability of Vertical Exchange Reported by
the Newcomer Based on the First-Year Vertical Exchange (VE)
and Assessment (AS) Groups over Time (T)

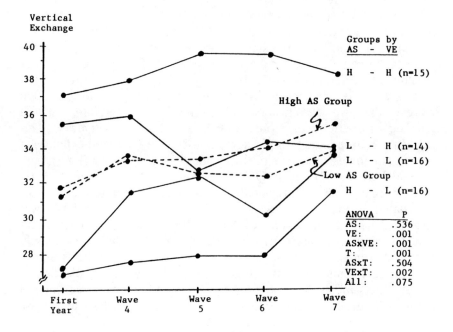

the highest, and even an increasing level of vertical exchange with their supervisors over the subsequent periods for career development. On the other hand, those who were judged to have High potential but experienced a constraint during the first year in realizing their potential due to Low vertical exchange relations with their supervisors (the H-L group), were precipitated into the lowest level of vertical relations for the remaining research periods. As predicted, the other two groups, the Low potential and High vertical exchange (the L-H group), found their respective positions between the two extreme groups. Moreover, even between the L-H and L-L groups, the effect of the first-year VE was in order, although it seems to be less conspicuous during and after Wave 4.

The mean vertical exchange reported by each of the group members over time produced a pattern of differences predicted by our hypothesis, i.e., among the four groups, the H-H group members achieved the highest level of vertical exchange across all time periods, followed in order by the L-H, the L-L, and the H-L groups. This pattern of group differences produced a highly significant interaction effect between the AS and VE(FY) factors (see the ANOVA results reported in Figure 24), indicating that the effect of the first-year vertical exchange is completely different depending upon the newcomer's position on the AS potential scale. In addition, a trend of divergence between the H-H and the other three groups over time made the interaction among all factors (AS×VE×T) approach a significant level (p < .075). As we have found in Chapter VI: (1) the main AS effect (see dotted trend lines for the High and Low AS groups in Figure 24) produced no significant effect, and (2) the VE(FY) and Time factors, including the interaction between the two, yielded highly significant effects upon vertical exchange for the subsequent time periods reported by the newcomer.

The stability test displayed in Figure 24 indicates that the potential factor alone would not aid the newcomer in achieving a high level of vertical exchange during the early stages of career development. Figure 24 clearly suggests that in addition to high potential, the newcomer also needs a high quality of leader-member relations during his first year in the organization in order to put himself on the highest position of vertical exchange for the remaining periods of career progress. More than that: when the High potential newcomer is unfortunately forced to have Low vertical exchange with his supervisor during the first year, the despondency caused by this conflicting dyadic experience turns him into the most constrained subordinate during his early years in the organization. However, for the Low potential newcomers, whether or not they had high vertical exchange during the first year does not seem to produce as dramatic an effect as that which occurred to the High potential colleagues.

Table 46 displays a summary of ANOVA results for outcome variables reported by the newcomer. In Table 46, the straight AS effect does not show any significant impact upon newcomer's reports, indicating that the "general adequacy" hypothesis regarding the function of newcomer's potential is untenable from the eyes of the newcomer. The other main factors, VE(FY) and Time, displayed exactly the same pattern of effect as we have seen already in Chapter VI. On the other hand, the interaction between the AS and VE(FY) factors produced significant effects for the Job Need, Job Problem, and Role Disillusionment scales. This finding suggests that our alternative, "partial adequacy" hypothesis may better explain the effect of individual potentials upon the process of career development as seen by the newcomer.

Figure 25 illustrates how the partialness of the AS potential factor affects the leadership support reported by the newcomer. The pattern of group differences shown in Figure 25 indicates very clearly that those newcomers who were judged to have high potentials and could enjoy high vertical exchange relations during the first year (the H-H group) received the highest level of leadership support throughout the three-year period for their career development. Conversely, those who were rated to have high potentials but were deprived of the high quality leader-member relations at the start of their career (the H-L group), have remained as the bottom group consistently with respect to the amount of leadership support received from their supervisors. Although the situation for this group's members seems to have improved since Wave 5, the end of the second year, they were still left with the lowest level of leadership support at the end of the third year. For the low potential newcomers, the lack of good vertical relations with their supervisors seems to be less detrimental than for the High potential colleagues. In Figure 25, the L-L group showed a consistently higher position than the H-L group, followed by the L-H newcomers who were judged to have low potentials but could augment their role positions with the help of the vertical exchange with the supervisors. The combined effect between the AS and VE(FY) factors ($p < .001$) described above, produced a pattern of group differences that suggests all four groups may be significantly different, with the H-H being the highest followed by the L-H, the L-L, and the H-L groups. Moreover, the convergence between the L-H and H-L groups over time made the overall interaction effect approach a significant level ($p < .057$). Figure 26 displays the pattern of interaction discussed above more clearly. The figure indicates that the direction of the effect of a potential factor may reverse depending upon the new-

Table 46

Summary of ANOVA Results for Newcomer's Reports over Time (T) Based on the Classification by AS and VE(FY) Scales (N = 61)

Variable	AS	VE	T	ASxVE	ASxT	VExT	All
				Probability			
Job Need: Receiving							
Leadership Support	–	**	**	**	–	–	–
Job Enrichment	–	**	**	**	–	–	–
Job Problem: Frequency							
Dyadic Problem	–	**	–	*	–	–	–
Climate Problem	–	–	**	–	–	–	–
Job Problem: Severity							
Dyadic Problem	–	–	**	–	–	–	–
Climate Problem	–	–	**	–	–	–	–
Role Disillusionment							
Role Content	–	**	–	**	–	–	–
Profitability	–	–	–	–	–	–	–
Organizational Commitment							
Value of Organization	–	**	–	–	–	–	–
Risk of Commiting	–	–	–	–	–	–	–
Need Deficiency							
Leadership Support	–	**	**	–	–	**	–
Job Enrichment	–	**	–	–	–	–	–

– Nonsignificant
*$p < .05$.
**$p < .01$.

Figure 25

Leadership Support over Time (T)
Based on the AS and VE(FY) Groups

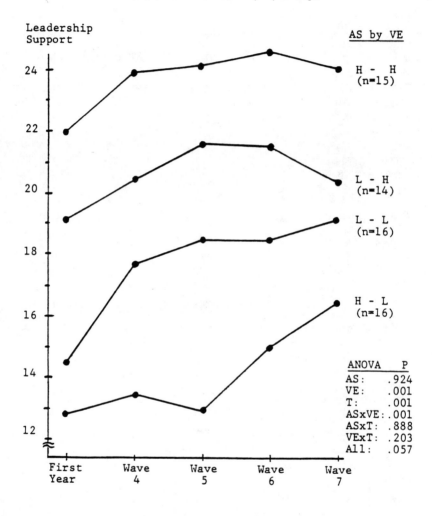

Figure 26

**Combined Effect Between the AS and VE(FY) Factors
Upon Leadership Support Reported by the Newcomer**

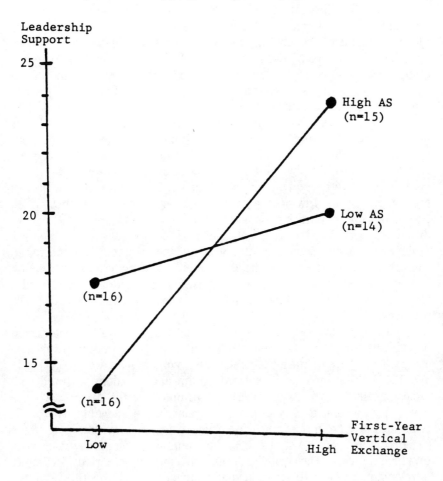

comer's position on the vertical exchange. If the VE(FY) is Low, the higher the potential, the lower the leadership support received by the newcomer. But, if the VE(FY) is High, the higher the potential, the greater the leadership support.

Figure 27 illustrates the mean job enrichment scores among the four groups over time. In Figure 27, the H-H and the H-L groups remained in their respective positions predicted by our partial adequacy hypothesis. Conversely, during and after Wave 4, the two Low potential groups became less distinctive, and tended to differ not so much from each other as from the H-H and H-L groups. This pattern of interaction was found significant at the $p < .001$ level.

Figure 28 displays the frequency of experiencing dyadic problems between the newcomer and his supervisor as reported by the four comparison groups. In Figure 28, the high potential newcomers, combined with the high first-year vertical exchange, reported on the average the lowest frequency in experiencing dyadic problems, while the high-potential and low-exchange newcomers reported the highest level. Again, the low potential newcomers as a single group appeared to have differences vis-à-vis the H-L and the H-H groups, although all group differences which existed at the start of the process have narrowed considerably by the end of the third year. The pattern of interaction between the AS and VE(FY) factors illustrated in Figure 29, produced a significant effect ($p < .021$) upon the frequency of experiencing dyadic problems.

Partialness on the effect of a potential factor was also documented very clearly in terms of role disillusionment. Figure 30 displays a comparison of trend means for four subgroups. In Figure 30, the H-H and the H-L groups again showed contrasting positions as predicted, indicating that high potential can contribute greatly to enhancing a newcomer's feeling to stay with the company, when and only when, it is reinforced by the high vertical exchange experience at the start of the career. Otherwise, the strong feeling of quitting the company dominates the high potential newcomers throughout the early periods of career development. The two low potential groups (the L-H and the L-L) that maintained a middle position between the above extreme groups showed a convergence during and after Wave 5. The pattern of group differences discussed above produced a highly significant interaction effect between the AS and VE(FY) factors upon disillusionment with role content ($p < .001$). The interaction pattern was found to be basically the same as the one we saw in Figure 26. Furthermore, the convergence between the L-H and the L-L groups (incidentally, they diverged from the H-H and the H-L groups respectively) made the interaction effect

Figure 27

Job Enrichment over Time (T) Based on the AS and VE(FY) Groups

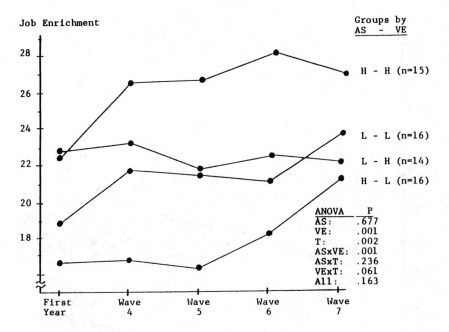

Job Enrichment

Groups by
AS - VE

H - H (n=15)

L - L (n=16)

L - H (n=14)

H - L (n=16)

ANOVA	P
AS:	.677
VE:	.001
T:	.002
ASxVE:	.001
ASxT:	.236
VExT:	.061
All:	.163

First Year Wave 4 Wave 5 Wave 6 Wave 7

Figure 28

Frequency of Experiencing Dyadic Problems over Time (T)
Based on the AS and VE(FY) Groups

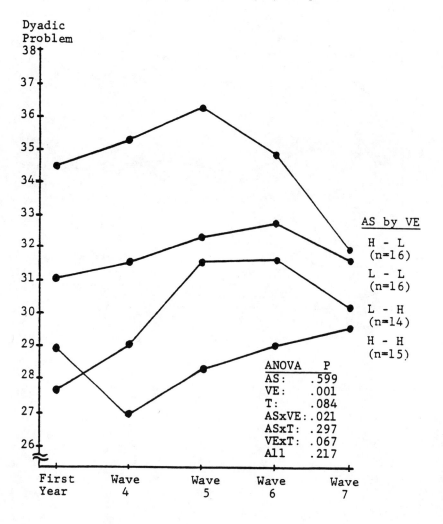

Figure 29

**Combined Effect Between the AS and VE(FY) Factors Upon
Dyadic Problems Experienced by the Newcomer over Time (T)**

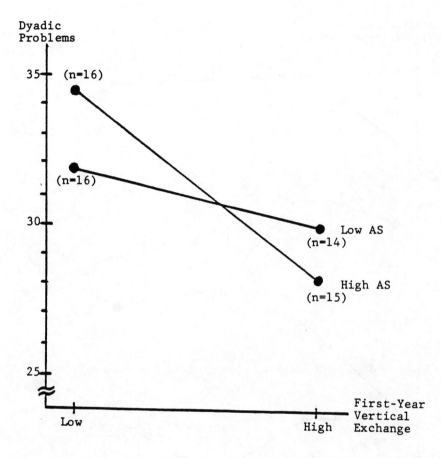

Figure 30

Disillusionment with Role Content Over Time (T)
Based on the AS and VE(FY) Groups

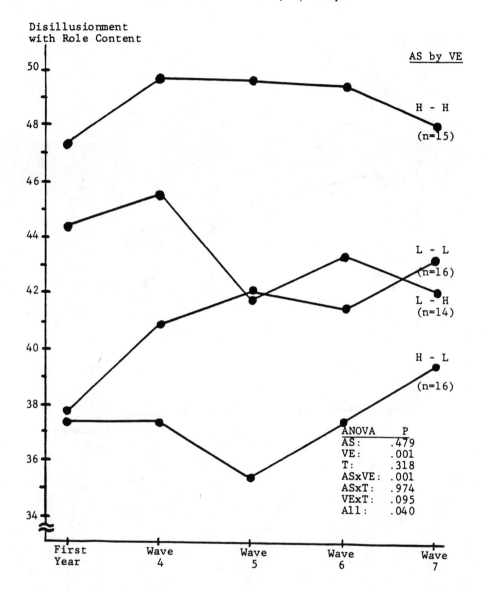

among all (AS×VE(FY)×Time) factors significant for the newcomer's feeling of disillusionment.

The analysis on need deficiency also produced a result supporting our partial adequacy hypothesis. For example, the mean need deficiency scores (D^2) of leadership support for the H-H, the L-H, the L-L, and the H-L groups were 6.7, 10.7, 22.1, and 29.9 respectively. The pattern of mean D^2 differences displayed in Figure 31 is quite consistent with what our hypothesis predicts, but the statistical result for the interaction between the AS and VE(FY) factor did not reach a significant level (p. < 082). The analysis for organizational commitment (the psychological value of the organization) also produced a pattern consistent with our partial adequacy hypothesis, with means of 46.5, 44.3, and 39.4 for the H-H, the L-H, the L-L, and H-L groups respectively. However, the F-test for the interaction effect did not reach a significant level. Finally, none of the Job Problem Severity scales produced significant interaction effects, although the H-L group members tended to report slightly higher levels of severity relative to the other three group members.

In sum, the "partial adequacy" hypothesis advanced for the present study gained support from the newcomer's report on leadership support, job enrichment, dyadic problems experienced, and role disillusionment. The pattern of group differences for need deficiency was also found to be consistent with what our hypothesis predicted, but the statistical analysis did not reach a significant level. Conversely, the "general adequacy" hypothesis maintained by the conventional assessment center approach completely failed to predict newcomer's responses during the period of career development. The ANOVA results discussed in this section suggest that the partialness of the potential factor may produce at least the following three distinctive subgroups when it interacted with the vertical exchange during the first year: i.e., (1) the High potential-High exchange group (the H-H group), (2) the L-H and the L-L (probably as a single group), and (3) the H-L group. For our study, these three groups taken in order denote the level of effectiveness with which each group member will function in a complex environment for career progress, as long as the newcomer's reports are concerned. Next, the supervisors' reports will be examined regarding how superiors deal with the combined effect between the newcomers' potential and vertical exchange.

2. Partial Adequacy: Supervisor's Reports
Table 47 displays a summary of the ANOVA results for the supervisor's reports based on the same design of analysis as was applied to the newcomers' reports. In Table 47, the main factors produced the same pattern of effects for supervisors' reports as was seen already in Table 38,

Figure 31

Need Deficiency with Leadership Support over Time (T)
Based on the AS and VE(FY) Groups

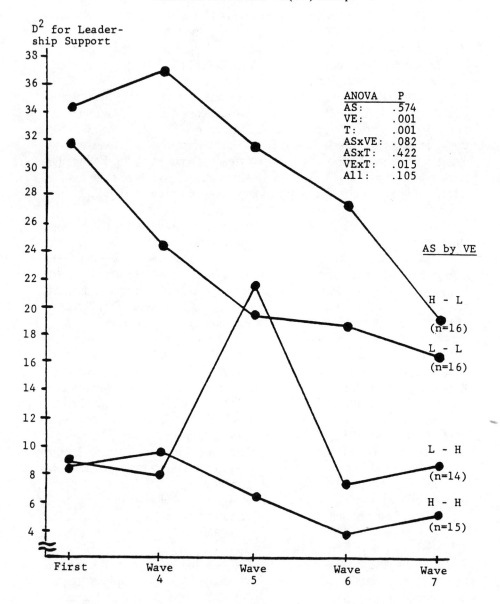

D^2 for Leadership Support

ANOVA   P
AS: .574
VE: .001
T: .001
ASxVE: .082
ASxT: .422
VExT: .015
All: .105

AS by VE

H - L
(n=16)

L - L
(n=16)

L - H
(n=14)

H - H
(n=15)

Table 47

Summary of ANOVA Results for Supervisor's Reports over Time (T) Based on the Classification by AS and VE(FY) Scales (N = 61)

Variable	AS	VE	T	Probability ASxVE	ASxT	VExT	All
Job Need: Providing							
Leadership Support	–	**	**	–	–	–	–
Job Enrichment	–	**	*	–	–	–	–
Vertical Exchange	**	**	**	–	*	–	–
Job Performance	–	**	*	–	*	–	*
Success Potential	–	*	–	–	–	–	–

– Nonsignificant
* p < .05.
** p < .01.

except that the interaction effect between the AS and Time factors (AS×T) upon success potential did not reach a significant level (p<.093). The interaction effect among all (AS×VE×T) factors upon job performance produced a significant result, suggesting that the differentiation among four subgroups may develop over time. For the other supervisors' reports, the interaction between the AS and VE(FY) factors or among all factors, did not show significant effects. However, these findings do not necessarily imply that the "partial adequacy" hypothesis does not work for supervisors' reports. A closer look at the pattern of group mean differences revealed that the partial effect of a potential factor produced a significant difference between the H-H and the other three groups for supervisors' reports in a very consistent manner.

Figure 32 illustrates one such result. In Figure 32, the supervisors reported that those newcomers who were judged to have a high potential and at the same time had a high vertical exchange with their supervisors during the first year (the H-H group), were provided with constantly higher levels of leadership support over the three years, compared to the other group members. From the eyes of the supervisor, the newcomer's potential can function only when it is reinforced by high vertical exchange. Otherwise, potential has no significant effect, i.e., the H-L, the L-H, and the L-L groups are seen as basically homogeneous, forming a distinctive group in contrast to the H-H group. Although this pattern of interaction between the AS and VE(FY) factors did not reach a significant level (p < .137), the mean differences among the four subgroups as shown below suggested that the partial adequacy hypothesis may work in its weaker form for the supervisors' reports: 26.3, 23.3, 23.9, and 23.0 for the H-H, the H-L, the L-H, and the L-L groups respectively.

The supervisor's report for job enrichment followed exactly the same pattern as the one for leadership support. The supervisor reported that only the H-H group is different in the amount of job enrichment provided among all the newcomer groups. Figure 33 illustrates the group means for job enrichment reported by the supervisor, based on the AS and VE(FY) factors. Although the combined effect between the two factors shown in Figure 33 produced an interaction pattern supporting our hypothesis, the statistical result again did not reach a significant level (p < .092). The vertical exchange reported by the supervisor showed a result similar to the one discussed in Figure 32. Figure 34, illustrating the mean vertical exchange scores for four subgroups reported by the supervisor, indicates that only the H-H group members have achieved distinctly high exchange relations with their leaders over time. In addition, for the rest of the group members the supervisor recognizes no differential dyadic relations.

Figure 32

Leadership Support Provided by the Supervisor over Time (T) Based on the AS and VE(FY) Groups

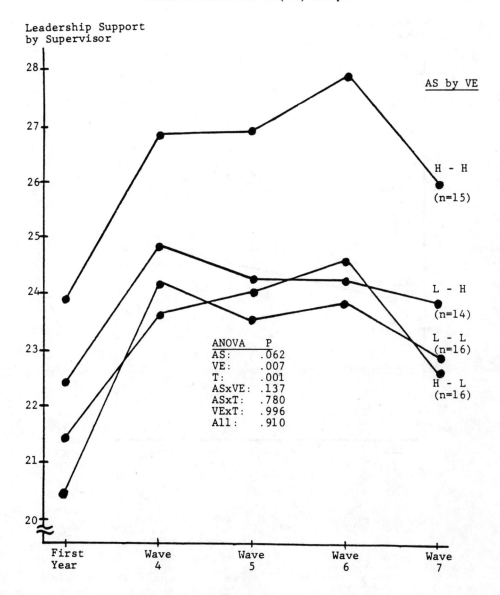

Figure 33

Combined Effect Between the AS and VE(FY) Factors
Upon Job Enrichment Reported by the Supervisor

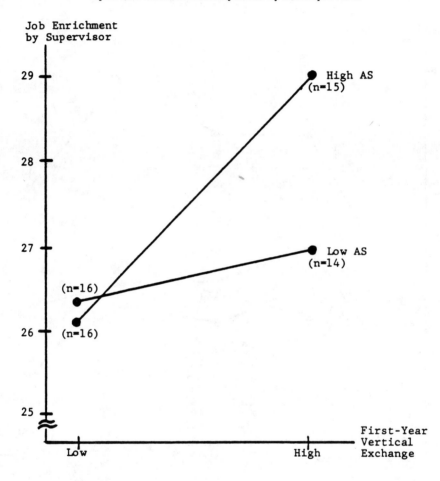

Figure 34

Vertical Exchange Reported by the Supervisor Based on the AS and VE(FY) Groups over Time (T)

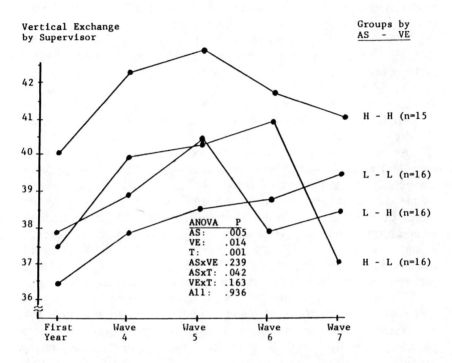

Figure 35 illustrates the mean performance ratings provided by the supervisor over time for the four comparison groups. As pointed out earlier, performance differentiation between the H-H and the other three groups over time, especially between the H-H and the L-H groups, produced the significant interaction effect among all factors (p < .052). In Figure 35, the process of ramification which occurred after Wave 4 led the H-H group to the increasing level of performance over time, while the other three groups either decreased or remained stationary in their performance level relative to the H-H group.

In Chapter VI, we raised the questions: (1) why did job performance drop between Wave 6 and Wave 7, even among newcomers with High vertical exchange with their supervisors (see Figure 13), and (2) why did variation in job performance show the highest level at Wave 7? As an answer to the above questions, it was assumed that the individual potential might have interacted with vertical exchange during the period between Wave 6 and Wave 7. Figure 35 displays that interaction did occur between the AS and VE(FY) factors. It became salient during and after Wave 5, separating the H-H group from the other group members. As a result, (1) job performance showed the greatest variation at the end of the research period, and (2) the exacerbation of job performance for the L-H group produced a declining performance trend for the High vertical exchange group as a whole.

Finally, success potential showed a result consistent with the other supervisors' reports discussed above. The H-H group members have been rated by their supervisors as having the highest levels of success potential, compared to the rest of the group members. The average potential ratings were found to be 11.7, 11.0, 10.7, and 10.7 for the H-H, L-H, L-L, and H-L groups respectively, but this group difference was too subtle to make the AS-by-VE(FY) interaction effect significant.

3. Job Challenge and Career Outcomes

A two-way ANOVA with the 2-by-2 factorial design based on the AS and VE(FY) factors was performed for the analysis of job challenge and career outcomes measured at the end of the third year. Subgroup entries were exactly the same as those for the preceding analyses, except that they were not repeated over time. The hypothesis to be tested is also the same: if the potential factor is to have only a partial effect, those newcomers who have potentials and high vertical relations with their supervisors simultaneously at the start of their careers, would report (a) the highest level of job challenge associated with their career roles, and (b) the highest career outcomes by the end of the third year. On the other hand, those with high potentials but with low vertical exchange

Figure 35

Job Performance Based on the AS and
VE(FY) Groups over Time (T)

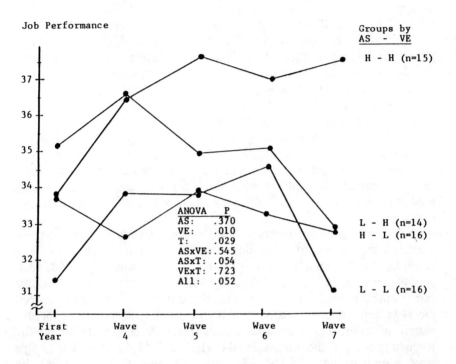

Job Performance

Groups by
AS - VE

H - H (n=15)

L - H (n=14)
H - L (n=16)

L - L (n=16)

ANOVA   P
AS: .370
VE: .010
T: .029
ASxVE: .545
ASxT: .054
VExT: .723
All: .052

First   Wave   Wave   Wave   Wave
Year   4   5   6   7

during the first year, would report the lowest level in job challenge and career outcomes.

Table 48 displays the result of the ANOVA tests conducted for job challenge reported by the newcomer and his supervisor at Wave 7. The pattern of effect for main factors seems basically the same as the one reported in Table 38, except that the amount of newcomer's task demand as reported by his supervisor failed to reach a significant level. The interaction between the AS and VE(FY) factors did not show a significant effect for all variables tested. However, examination of mean values among the four subgroups suggested that the pattern of group differences is very consistent with what our partial adequacy hypothesis predicted: the H-H is the highest followed by the L-H, the L-L, and the H-L groups. Since job challenge for the H-L group was scored so low the overall mean for the High AS group (the H-L and H-H groups combined) turned out to be lower than that for the Low AS group. This result apparently contradicts what the "general adequacy" hypothesis predicts, but is in order from the point of view of the "partial adequacy" hypothesis.

Analysis on career outcomes produced similar results, but for these outcomes the pattern of group differences was found less clear-cut. For example, the Potential Index produced a set of means, 53.5, 49.4, 48.8, and 49.3 for the H-H, L-H, L-L, and H-L groups respectively. For this career outcome measure, it seems that the difference exists only between the H-H and the rest of groups, although the interaction effect for this pattern of differences did not reach a significant level ($p < .184$). For the Right Type scale, the means for the H-H, L-H, L-L, and H-L groups were found to be 10.5, 9.9, 8.3, and 9.5 respectively. Again, the difference seems to exist between the H-H and other groups, but the interaction effect was found far from the significant level ($p < .609$), compared to the main effects based on the VE(FY) ($p < .029$) and AS ($p < .095$) factors. For the other career outcome measures, the Performance Index and Bonus, partial effects of the potential factor were less conspicuous. Rather, the effect of the main factors seemed predominant, although none of the effects reached a significant level for the nonadditive ANOVA design.

III. Patterns of Interaction

The preceding discussion suggests that the process and outcomes of career progress can be better predicted by considering the combined effect among what are believed to be the determinants of progress. This finding suggests that career development within the organization may

Table 48

Job Challenge Reported for the Wave 7 Monitoring
Based on the AS and VE(FY) Groups

Variable	Group Mean								Probability		
	AS		VE(FY)		ASxVE				AS	VE(FY)	ASxVE
	Low	High	Low	High	HH	LH	LL	HL			
Newcomer's Report											
Job Challenge											
Increased Centrality	22.9	20.9	18.1	25.7	25.9	25.4	20.3	15.9	.230	.001	.133
Task Demand	18.0	17.4	15.7	19.6	20.5	18.8	17.2	14.3	.661	.008	.110
Supervisor's Report											
Job Challenge											
Increased Centrality	26.0	26.2	24.5	27.6	29.0	26.3	25.6	23.4	.878	.041	.104
Task Demand	21.5	21.4	20.7	22.2	22.5	21.9	21.1	20.4	.969	.157	.522

Sample size: HH (High AS - High VE) = 15, LH=14, LL=16, and HL=16.

involve a lot of conditionality. Therefore, theoretical statements for predicting managerial progress need to be made in such a way that progress (or the loss of it) may occur among a group of individuals characterized by the factor A, *if* conditions X, Y, . . . are present (or are not present). As we found in the preceding discussion, the partial adequacy hypothesis tested for our study suggests that a high level of career progress occurs among high potential newcomers if they can achieve high vertical exchange relations with their supervisors during their first year in the organization. Furthermore, our hypothesis suggests that the lack of high vertical relations will have a more severe impact upon the high potential newcomers than upon the low potential colleagues, because the sense of frustration caused by the constrained relations becomes much greater among the former group members. Thus, according to our hypothesis, when working in its strongest form, the High-potential and High exchange newcomers are expected to show the highest position, probably followed in order by the L-H, the L-L, and the H-L groups, with respect to the level of outcomes from the process of career progress. The preceding analysis also identified two other patterns of interaction between the AS and VE(FY) factors in addition to the above. All of these patterns can be classified into the following three categories. (1) Only the high potential newcomers supported by the high vertical exchange (the H-H group) show a high level of progress. The rest of the newcomers are basically the same and distinctive only from the H-H group. (2) The H-H group will show the highest level and the H-L group will become the lowest group, with the two low potential groups (the L-H and L-L groups) being placed between the highest and the lowest as a homogeneous group. (3) All four groups can be significantly different in accordance with the following order in relation to their level of career progress: the H-H, the L-H, the L-L, and the H-L groups.

1. Characterizing a Pattern of Group Differences.

To identify what pattern of interaction was actually created by the nonadditive effect of the AS potential factor, a series of t-tests were performed for characterizing a predominant pattern of differences among the four subgroups. Table 49 displays a summary of these statistical analyses. The table consists of results derived from the four different statistical analyses. The first column displays results of a one-way ANOVA designed to test whether or not four subgroups have a difference among themselves, when they are considered as independent groups for career progress. The remaining six columns show results of t-tests for the examination of a pattern of group differences. A set results

Table 49

One-Way ANOVA Based on the Four Comparison Groups
Followed by t-Test for the Pair-wise Comparison (N=80)

| | | t-Test | | | | | |
| | | I | | | II | | III |
Variable	ANOVA	1/2	2/3	3/4	1/2+3	2+3/4	1+2+3/4
Newcomer's Report							
Job Need: Receiving							
Leadership Support	**	**	–	*	**	**	**
Job Enrichment	**	**	–	**	**	**	**
Job Problem: Frequency							
Dyadic Problem	**	–	–	–	**	*	**
Climate Problem	–	–	–	–	–	–	–
Job Problem: Severity							
Dyadic Problem	–	–	–	–	–	–	–
Climate Problem	–	–	–	–	–	–	–
Job Challenge							
Increased Centrality	**	*	*	–	**	–	**
Task Demand	*	–	–	–	**	–	*
Role Disillusionment							
Role Content	**	*	–	**	**	**	**
Profitability	–	–	–	–	–	–	–
Organizational Commitment							
Value of Organization	**	–	*	–	–	*	**
Risk of Committing	–	–	–	–	–	–	–

Table 49 (continued)

One-Way ANOVA Based on the Four Comparison Groups
Followed by t-Test for the Pair-wise Comparison (N = 80)

Variable	ANOVA	t-Test I 1/2	2/3	3/4	II 1/2+3	2+3/4	III 1+2+3/4
Need Deficiency							
Leadership Support	**	–	*	–	**	**	**
Job Enrichment	**	–	**	*	–	**	**
Vertical Exchange	**	*	**	**	**	**	**
Supervisor's Report							
Job Need: Providing							
Leadership Support	**	–	–	*	–	**	**
Job Enrichment	**	–	–	*	–	**	**
Job Challenge							
Increased Centrality	–	–	–	–	–	–	*
Task Demand	–	–	–	–	–	–	–
Vertical Exchange	**	–	–	**	–	**	**
Job Performance	*	–	–	–	–	–	**
Success Potential	–	–	–	–	–	–	*

For t-test, numbers 1, 2, 3, and 4 denote the H-L, L-L, L-H, and H-H groups, respectively.
– Nonsignificant
*p < .05.
**p < .01.

covered by t-test I denotes the significance level for the difference-of-means test between any two groups taken pair-wise among the four comparison groups: i.e., the H-L group (or group No. 1 in Table 49), the L-L group (No. 2), the L-H group (No. 3), and the H-H group (No. 4). The next two columns covered by t-test II display the results of pair-wise comparisons among the following three groups, the H-L, the L-L and L-H combined, and the H-H groups. Likewise, the last column displays the results of the difference-of-means test between the H-H and the rest of the groups combined into a single group.

In Table 49, group numbers were assigned in an ascending order according to the level of mean values expected for each group: that is the previous analyses revealed that in most cases, the H-H group (No. 4) yielded the highest mean values followed by the L-H (No. 3), the L-L (No. 2), and the H-L (No. 1). Therefore, suppose a difference-of means test between groups No. 1 and No. 2 (the 1/2 comparison for the t-test I) produced a significant result, then this fact further implies that the 1/3 and 1/4 comparisons would show much higher levels of significance. Or, suppose the 1/2 comparison fails to reach a significance level, it is very likely that the 1/3 and 1/4 comparisons would yield significant results. In Table 49, however, these peripheral results are not displayed. Instead, the table shows results covering the comparisons between the two immediate successive groups. A set of results under t-test II was derived in the same manner. For this series, three groups taken pair-wise were compared: the H-L, the L-H and L-L combined as a single group, and the H-H groups. Finally, t-test III compared the H-H group with the other three put together as a single group.

The one-way ANOVA and a series of t-tests were performed using factor scales aggregated over the research periods. An aggregated value was computed for each scale by summing scores at Waves 2, 3, 4, 5, 6, and 7, and dividing the aggregate by 6. For the job challenge scales that were administered only at Wave 7, the original scores were used for the analysis without any further modification.

The t-test I series is designed to tap the pattern of group differences as might be exemplified by the one illustrated in Figure 25: all four groups are significantly different from each other with the H-H group being the top, followed in order by the L-H, the L-L, and H-L groups. This is the strongest case in which the partial adequacy hypothesis might work. The t-test series II is designed to examine a pattern of group differences displayed by Figure 27 or Figure 30. For this case, the H-H and L-H groups may be distinctive vis-à-vis the two middle groups (the L-L and the L-H) that are assumed to be basically homogeneous. Lastly, t-test III is designed to depict a pattern illustrated by Figure 32: that is, the H-H group may be significantly different from the other three that are assumed to be a single homogeneous group. This pattern may correspond to a weaker expression of the partial adequacy hypothesis. The alternative pattern that may belong to this case is the one in which the L-L consititutes the bottom group vis-à-vis the other three groups. However, this pattern of group differences did not appear in our study.

Test results shown in Table 49 indicate that the strongest form of group differences did not appear on any of the outcome variables. A factor variable, vertical exchange reported by the newcomer, reached a significance level in all three comparisons, indicating that the four groups identified based on the AS and VE(FY) factors at the start of the career, remained as mutually different groups with respect to the vertical exchange for the subsequent periods. Leadership support reported by the newcomer followed basically the same pattern as the one for vertical exchange, except that the 2/3 comparison (the difference between the L-L and L-H groups) for this variable reached only a marginal level of significance (p < .068). This finding is very reasonable because leadership support should be the outcome most closely connected with the process of vertical exchange.

Results derived from t-test II suggest that for many of the newcomers' reports, significant group differences exist among the top H-H group, the middle L-L and L-H groups, and the bottom H-L group. Among the newcomers' reports that registered a significant group difference using an ANOVA test, more than half of them were found to have a pattern of group differences like those discussed above. Especially, the newcomers' reports on leadership support, job enrichment, role disillusionment, and need deficiency displayed a very clear differentiation among the three test groups. These results seem to be consistent with the pattern of mean differences illustrated in Figures 24, 25, 26, 27, and 30. However, none of the supervisors' reports endorsed this three-group differentiation as reported by the newcomer. In Table 43, the supervisors' reports suggested that the H-H group may be significantly different from all other groups, but the H-L group was regarded as homogeneous with the Low potential groups.

Finally, results of t-test III suggested that the significant group differences that the ANOVA test detected may be best summarized as the difference between the H-H group, and the other three groups taken together as a single unit. As shown typically in Figures 32 and 33, this pattern is one of the weaker expressions of our hypothesis. However, the result of t-test III is very consistent: both newcomers and their supervisors agreed that the H-H group members maintained the highest position vis-à-vis the other group members on the ladder for managerial progress during the three years with respect to almost all outcome areas examined in our study. Especially, the supervisors' reports consistently distinguished the H-H group from the others throughout all the series of t-tests. Moreover, in Table 43 the supervisors' reports on centrality and success potential reached a significant level for t-test III, while the ANOVA result denied the existence of overall group difference for both the centrality ($p < .076$) and the success potential ($p < .165$) scales.

The same sets of analyses were performed for career outcomes, with results that support the finding reported in Table 43. That is, the ANOVA test disclosed the existence of significant differences (at the .05 level) among four groups with respect to the Potential Index and Right Type scale. In addition, a series of t-test produced a pattern of group differences identical to the one displayed by the Job Performance scale in Table 49, except that the level of significance remained at the .05 level for both Potential Index and Right Type. This finding suggests that the H-H group members again achieved the higher level of career outcomes compared to the other three group members who were considered to be homogeneous and distinctive as a single group from the H-H. However, the other two career outcome scales, the Performance Index and Bonus, did not show a sign of significant differences for both the ANOVA and the t-tests.

2. A Comparative Perspective

Interaction between potential and vertical exchange factors examined based on newcomers in the DEPART organization, produced the following two results. The first one is represented by a strong combined effect between high potential and high vertical exchange upon career progress. This particular combination gave rise to the significantly high level of outcomes derived from the process of managerial progress, compared to the other possible combinations based on the above two factors. This pattern of group differentiation was endorsed by the supervisors' as well as the newcomers' reports very extensively. The second finding is featured by the *negative* effect of high potential upon progress which occurred under a condition of constrained leader-member relations. As Table 49 indicates (t-test II) this negative effect separated the H-L group not only from H-H, but also from the remaining two Low potential groups. However, this pattern of differentiation occurred only for the outcomes reported by the newcomer.

The findings in Table 49 point to a characterization of the system for managerial resource development operating in the DEPART organization. Figure 36 illustrates key characteristics for the DEPART system (Figure A), in comparsion to those for the alternative system (B) reported

Figure 36

Two Different Systems for Managerial Career Development:
Noncompensatory (A) and Compensatory (B) Systems

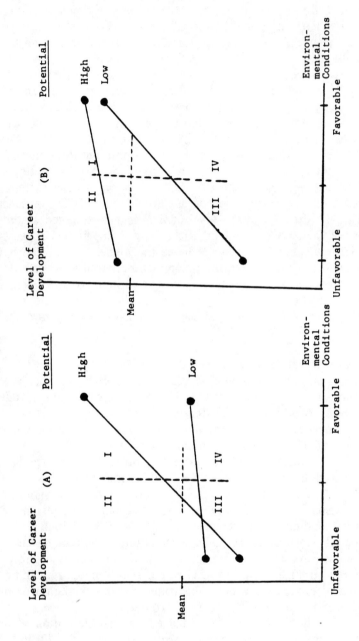

by Bray, et al., (1974) in their study at AT&T. Figure (B) was developed by roughly converting the AT&T report summarized for our study by Table 5 in Chapter II into a framework comparable to our results. As will be discussed later, these two studies may differ in detail, but they are basically similar in that the interaction effect between the newcomer's potential and environmental conditions upon the level of career progress was explored by using a method of longitudinal investigation.

System (B) will be best characterized as a *compensatory system* where the lack of potential in relative terms does not hamper the career progress if the environmental conditions are favorable enough to complement the loss of potential. Likewise, for this system if an individual has high potential, a relatively high level career progress can be maintained even under the unfavorable environmental conditions. Because, as Figure 36 displays, under this circumstance the strong potential effect comes to offset the environmental impact that may impede his progress. However, progress would be hard to come by when the newcomer who lacks potential is put under the environment with little stimulus for development. Conversely, the high potential combined with a high level stimulus condition constitutes the best position for career progress. Under the compensatory system, practices for human resources development are said to be directed toward supplying internally a large pool of managerial talent with homogeneous capability within a given period of time. In Figure (B), management attempts at achieving the above goal may require a strategy which minimizes the number of people who may end up in the III and IV quadrants, by manipulating the potential factor and environmental conditions.

On the other hand, the system shown in Figure (A) is characterized by the *noncompensatory* relation between factors. The high level of career progress occurs only for those who have favorable environmental conditions combined also with high potentials for development, otherwise development would be seriously constrained. Especially, in the worst situation (see Figures 26 and 33) potential may complement the environmental conditions in a "negative" manner: newcomers' reactions (role disillusionment, for example) faced with the unfavorable conditions for career progress become stronger among the high potential newcomers than among the low potential colleagues. The *noncompensatory system* is directed toward producing a relatively small group of high-flying managerial talent, by maximizing a yield at quadrant I. However, it is apparent that this system may involve greater manpower costs due to: (1) the underutilization of the high potential employees by limiting opportunities for development, and (2) the waste of managerial resources by not pushing those employees who may lack the potentials but were given favorable conditions for career development. These manpower costs are expected to become a grave concern for the DEPART organization that is utilizing the noncompensatory system under the principle of lifetime employment.

However, it must be noted that the above results may be attributable partly to the difference in the context of research involved between the present study and the management progress study at AT&T (Bray, et al., 1974). (1) Our study covered the first three years of newcomers' progress within the organization, while the AT&T study did the first eight years. It may be that the contrasting results shown in Figure 36 are partly attributable to differences in the time period covered by each study: that is, the DEPART newcomers may eventually show a pattern of differentiation characterized by Figure (B) in eight or more years. (2) During eight years, the 38 percent or 104 newcomers left the Bell Telephone companies either voluntarily or by forced terminations, while in the DEPART company, only one newcomer left the organization during the three-year research period (see Tables 2 and 12 for turnover figures in each study). Moreover, Bray and his associates (1974) reported that out of the 104 recruits who left the Bell System, 52 of them were forced to leave because of poor job performance, or because they were judged not to have potential for advancement. This indicates that about 20 percent (52 out of a total of 172) of the criterion distribution, corresponding to the lower-tail of total distribution was truncated due to the forced termination of less successful recruits (perhaps the remaining part of the distribution included only relatively successful recruits). This may be another reason why the final pattern of group differentiation in the AT&T study appeared to have the pattern as shown in Figure (B). In other words, if the DEPART organization tried to correct the outcome distribution by "cutting off" a part of its lower tail, then, the corrected distribution might look like Figure (B).

3. Need Strength and Career Progress

More discussion will be required to explain why in the DEPART organization those newcomers who were judged to have high potentials became affected so badly in later phases when they were exposed to the constrained leader-member relations during the first year of their careers. One of the explanations for the above phenomena is that the constrained interpersonal environment in the first year might have an adverse motivational effect upon the high potential newcomers, because they were deprived of opportunities to experience higher-order need fulfillment. This proposition will be examined using *need preference for job enrichment* reported by the newcomer as a measure for higher-order need strength in our study.

According to Alderfer's (1969 and 1972) theory on higher order need strength, the proposition stated above can be interpreted as a *frustration-regression* hypothesis. This hypothesis states that the higher-order need frustration leads to the arousal of lower-order needs, accompanied by withdrawal from the desire for higher-order need fulfillment. According to the theory, it is expected that the H-L group members may show the most regressed desire for the fulfillment of job enrichment need for the present study, because they are the most frustrated in many aspects of the career environment in the DEPART organization.

On the other hand, the H-H group members who are found to be the least frustrated, are expected to show the highest need strength for job enrichment because, according to Maslow (1954 and 1962), higher-order needs will never be satisfied: the more one gets, the more one wants. Based on the above theoretical considerations, a prediction was made regarding the strength of need for job enrichment in the following manner. (1) The H-L group members may show the lowest need level because they are the most frustrated and thus might have withdrawn from higher-order need fulfillment. On the other hand, (2) the H-H group members may show the highest need level, because they are most satisfied. (3) The L-H and the L-L group members whose need frustration is found to be at an intermediate level will follow their H-H colleagues.

Figure 37 illustrates the mean need strength for job enrichment reported by the four group members over time. Interestingly, the ANOVA result indicated that the main effects based on the AS and VE(FY) factors have no significant impact at all: regardless of the differences in potential and vertical exchange, all newcomers showed basically the same amount of need for job enrichment. However, the combined effect between the above two factors produced a highly significant result (p < .003). Figure 37 indicates that the frustration-regression hypothesis seems to be predictive of the mean job enrichment needs reported by the high potential groups over time. The H-L group members reported the lowest need level for job enrichment (except for Wave 7), while the H-H group members remained at a much higher level across all time periods. This finding may point us to the following explanation. Upon recruitment, the high potential newcomers as a single group may all have high expectations about their career role in the DEPART organization, because according to the *self-esteem theory* (Korman, 1967) if a person has a high level of potential, he will rate the

Figure 37

Strength of Need for Job Enrichment Reported by the Newcomer Based on the AS and VE(FY) Factors

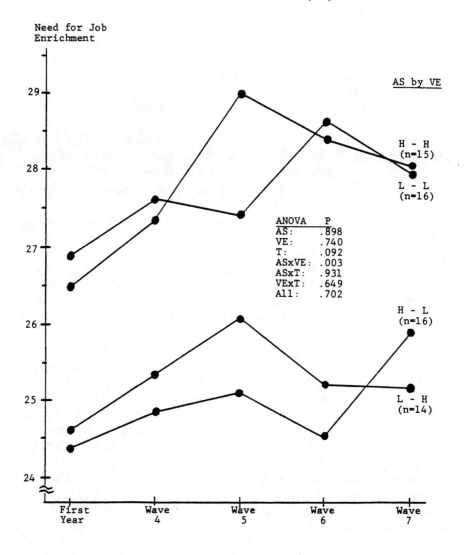

value of his potential (or self esteem) as high, and thus set the targets for performance and career-related activities much higher than otherwise would be the case. The career environment during the first year, however, would not allow all high potential newcomers to try out their potentials. Only those who could enjoy high vertical exchange relations with their supervisors had opportunities to do so. Remember that factor-analytically, high vertical exchange denoted clarity in *dyadic contingency* and *high job latitude* (see Chapter VI). The first factor was characterized by the supervisor's recognition of the newcomer's potential, his understanding of the newcomer's expectations and problems, and his willingness and discretion in helping the newcomer. Whereas, the second factor implied the newcomer's latitude given by the supervisor to get the job done, his contribution, influence, and autonomy on the job. Therefore, it is probable that the high potential newcomers who could achieve high vertical exchange with the supervisor during the first year had chances to reinforce their high expectations by one of the most important environmental conditions for role development.

As we have found already, this first-year incident predicted the outstanding position of the H-H group members with respect to almost all the important outcome measures evaluated during the subsequent period for career progress. Moreover, the present analysis disclosed that their need for job enrichment also stayed at a high level over time, suggesting that their satisfaction with the need for job enrichment has driven them to desire the same need more.

Conversely, for the remaining half of high potential newcomers who failed to achieve high vertical exchange relations with their supervisors (the H-L group), the story seems to be completely different. Those H-L newcomers could not get their supervisors to recognize their potentials, expectations, and problems, and thus their supervisors were not willing to exercise authority to help their subordinates. As a result, this group of newcomers saw their role positions as constrained and lacking autonomy, influence, and chances for contribution. It is expected that the failure in materializing high expectations might have plagued the H-L group newcomers into the most severe feeling of relative deprivation at the start of their career. Results shown in this study tell more about what happened to this group of newcomers. As we discussed already, throughout the research period they reported the lowest leadership support and opportunities for job enrichment. They were the most disillusioned. They experienced the highest levels of job problems, need deficiency, and lack of job challenge (see t-test II in Table 43).

All these findings suggest that the high level of frustration, which occurred to this group of newcomers forced them to withdraw from active participation in the process of their role development, despite their high potentials for doing so (or, because of this very reason). Withdrawal from higher-order needs may be inevitable for them, because the more they aspire under the constrained career environment, the more severely their self-esteem will be wounded by the reality of their situation. However, it must be noted that in spite of this drawback in their need level, the H-L group members still have suffered the highest level of deficiency with job enrichment between what they want and what they actually received.

The frustration and regression that occurred to the H-L group of newcomers, however, was not necessarily recognized by their supervisors. This insensitivity of the supervisors is partly attributable to the nature of the low vertical exchange that tends to create discrepancies in terms of feedback and expectation (Graen, 1976) and to communication gaps caused by various noises (Schiemann, 1977). However, the basic reason seems to be in the system of human resource development itself: as shown in Figure 36, the DEPART system had a tendency to pay attention (at least during the first three years) only to a small group of people who have potentials and who are fortunate enough to have favorable environmental conditions for career development.

In Figure 37, if the frustration-regression hypothesis is equally applicable to the low potential groups, the L-L members who are considered to be experiencing higher need frustration should report a more regressed need level, compared to their L-H group colleagues. However, what Figure 37 displays is in opposition to the above prediction. Moreover, the L-L group members report just as high need levels as those reported by the H-H group members. Why does the relationship between the frustration level and need strength come to show an opposite function between the high and low potential groups? In other words, why is it that the higher the frustration, the weaker the higher-order need for the high potential newcomers, while for their low potential colleagues, the higher the frustration, the stronger the higher-order need? Figure 38 (A) displays mean need strength for job enrichment reported by four groups' members. The figure illustrates clearly the pattern of interaction implied by the above question. Trend lines for the high and low potential groups cross each other at almost a right angle, producing a highly significant interaction ($p < .003$) upon the level of need strength.

To explain the above phenomenon, we need to consider the relationship between a person's capability to get the job done and his desire for higher-order need fulfillment. For some of our low potential newcomers working under the high vertical relations with their super-

Figure 38

Interaction Effect Between Potential and First-Year
Vertical Exchange Upon Strength of Need for Job Enrichment

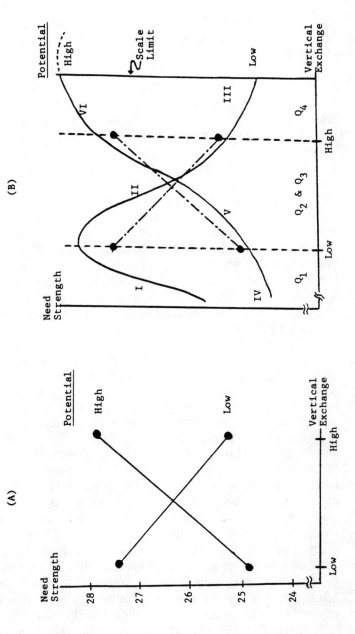

visors, demanding more job enrichment may only cause work overload, because their jobs could be already enriched as a result of high vertical exchange, just as much as, or more than, their present abilities and knowledge can handle. Under this work overload situation, high vertical exchange may only contribute to the oversaturation of job enrichment. On the other hand, when the vertical exchange relation is low enough to arouse need for more job enrichment among the low potential newcomers, then their need level will increase until it reaches the saturation point.

Figure 38 (B) illustrates a hypothetical need curve for low potential newcomers, in which the highest point for higher-order need appears at a relatively lower level on the vertical exchange scale. On the other hand, for the high potential newcomers, the saturation point for the job enrichment need is expected to appear on the very high level of vertical exchange. In Figure 38, (B), it is assumed that the peak point for the high potential newcomers may not be identified because of the scale limit imposed on our vertical exchange measure. Conversely, the intermediate and low levels of vertical exchange are assumed to produce frustration among high potential newcomers, thus eroding their desire for higher-order need fulfillment.

The hypothetical need curves shown in Figure 38 (B) were evaluated in the following manner. First, sample newcomers ($N = 80$) were divided into three groups such that the first (Q_1) and the fourth (Q_4) quartiles represent very low and very high vertical exchange relations respectively, while the second and third quartiles combined (Q_2 and Q_3) represent the intermediate level of vertical exchange. Then, the relationships between the first-year vertical exchange, and need for job enrichment (averaged over research periods) were examined for each of the three VE groups controlling the level of potential (high versus low) based on the AS scale. Therefore, as shown in Figure 38 (B), the above method of classification produces six groups for comparison: consisting of very low (I), intermediate (II), and very high (III) vertical exchange groups for the low potential newcomers, and likewise very low (IV), inermediate (V), and very high (VI) vertical exchange groups for the high potential newcomers. Finally, within each group a mean need score and a correlation coefficient between need and vertical exchange were computed in order to examine whether each group can represent a respective portion of need curves as Figure 38 (B) illustrates.

If our hypothesis on the saturation of higher-order needs is true, then: (1) correlations between vertical exchange and need strength will show positive coefficients for the I, IV, V, and VI groups, while for the II and III groups, the correlations should be negative. Moreover, (2) a pattern of mean differences should appear to be consistent with those illustrated by the dotted lines in Figure 38 (B). Table 50 displays results of an empirical examination conducted based on the first-year vertical exchange, and need for job enrichment averaged across six research periods during three years.

Table 50

Relationship Between the First-Year Vertical Exchange and Average Need Strength for Job Enrichment Based on the High and Low Potential Groups (N = 80)

	Low Potential Group			High Potential Group		
	I	II	III	IV	V	VI
	Low VE	Mid VE	High VE	Low VE	Mid VE	High VE
	(n = 12)	(n = 20)	(n = 7)	(n = 11)	(n = 17)	(n = 13)
Correlation[a]	.49*	−.01	−.37	.02	.30	.66*
Mean Need Strength	27.9	25.7	26.0	25.1	25.8	29.3

[a]Pearson correlation coefficients between need strength and first-year vertical exchange for each group.
*$p < .05$ (one-tailed test).

In Table 50, all correlation coefficients show signs consistent with our prediction. That is, for the I, IV, V, and VI groups, correlations between vertical exchange and need strength displayed a positive direction, suggesting that in the area covered by these groups, need strength tends to increase as the first-year vertical exchange increases. On the other hand, in the areas covered by the II and III groups, the direction is reversed. Need strength tends to decrease as the first-year vertical exchange increases. The above result combined with the pattern of mean differences among groups shown in Table 50 indicates that for low potential newcomers, the optimal level of vertical exchange leading to a peak desire for higher-order need satisfaction is located somewhere between Q_1 and Q_2, while for high potential newcomers the optimal exchange is at the Q_4 area.

In summary, the above discussion may point to the following conclusion. The interaction effect as shown in Figure 38 (A) occurred because vertical exchange beyond a certain level caused saturation in higher-order need and work overload for the low potential newcomers. On the other hand, for their high potential colleagues the same VE level still could cause frustration. Moreover, since the VE scale used for the present analysis is based on the first-year measure, the results imply predictive relationships: frustration or saturation caused by the first-year vertical exchange determines the average strength of the higher-order needs of the newcomer during the subsequent period for career development. During the first year, even the low potential newcomers might have felt strong frustration and regression in their higher-order needs when they were placed under the highly constrained leader-member relations. Their need strength started to increase as vertical exchange relations improved over time. On the other hand, those low potential newcomers who had higher vertical relations with their supervisors during the first-year assignments felt themselves "stretched" beyond what they thought was the optimum level of the workload. Therefore, they had no strong need to aspire to a more enriched job for the subsequent periods of role development. Conversely, high potential newcomers who also had high vertical relations during the first year kept wanting more job enrichment opportunities throughout the period for their role development, probably because they were in the forefront of career progress among their colleagues. They never felt themselves stretched enough on their career roles. The process of development for this group can best be described in terms of what Hall and Nougaim (1968) called the *success syndrome*. On the other hand, for the rest of the high potential newcomers, their experiences of a low vertical exchange during the first year had a strong *discouragement effect* upon them. This experience forced them to adjust their aspirations to a more regressed level than their initial expectations could hope for, for the subsequent phases of organizational career development.

Chapter VIII

Causal Examinations

I. The Impact of Structural Variables of the Organization and the Impact of Personal Background Variables Upon Leader-Member Exchange Processes

The preceding discussion suggests that vertical exchange represents one of the critical aspects of the developmental process and that it has a strong independent effect upon the outcomes of career development. However, the research diagram displayed in Figure 4 implies that the vertical exchange process may be influenced by the structural and personal background variables. It is the purpose of the present study to examine the extent to which the effect of the vertical exchange discovered in the previous chapters is independent of the structural aspects of the organization and of the personal background variables.

Figure 39 illustrates the hypothetical function of vertical exchange. If vertical exchange actually operates independently of structural and personal background variables, then (a) the supervisor's report on what he is doing vis-à-vis his subordinate with respect to vertical exchange activities, must be one of the major sources of variance in the newcomer's report on the same subject. This implies that in terms of a formula of regression analysis, the supervisor's report on vertical exchange can make a significant contribution to explaining the newcomer's report on vertical exchange (arrow A), after contributions of structural and personal background variables are controlled. By the same token, (b) the newcomer's report on his exchange activities can add a significant contribution to explain what the supervisor is doing on the same subject, after the effects of exogenous variables are held constant (arrow B). Next, if our hypothesis is true, (c) what the supervisor is doing on exchange activities must have a significant, additional contribution to make in explaining the newcomer's reports on outcomes (arrow C) after the contributions of the input variables are controlled. Likewise, (d) the supervisor's reports on outcomes must be explained in terms of the newcomer's exchange activities in the same manner (arrow D).

Before testing the above hypotheses, the nature of the impact

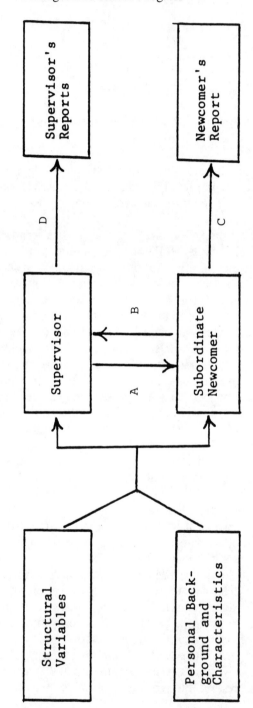

Figure 39

Flow Diagram on the Direction of Influence
Among Causal Variables

derived from the structural and personal background variables upon newcomers' and supervisors' report must first be examined. The regression analysis was used for this purpose. Structural variables for the analysis were measured during the period of Wave 4 research, while personal background variables were derived from the company's records on newcomers upon recruitment. Dependent variables for regression analyses consisted of newcomers' and supervisors' reports at the period of Wave 4. Dependent variables were classified into the following two groups with respect to their relationships with the vertical exchange scale. (I) Variables that have positive correlations with vertical exchange: Organizational Commitment (OC), Role Disillusionment (RD), Job Need (JN, Receiving and Preferred reported by the newcomer; Providing and Wanting reported by the supervisor), Job Performance, and Success Potential. (II) Variables that have negative correlations with vertical exchange: Need Deficiency (D^2), and Job Problem (JP, Frequency and Severity). Correlations computed between the vertical exchange reported by the newcomer and the dependent variables listed above, based on the Wave 4 data, support the present variable classification system. Below is a list of the independent variables which were entered into the regression. In the list, the hypothesized directions of the effect of each dependent variable upon the Group I and II dependent variables were specified.

Structural Variables of the Organization

(1) *Supervisor's Status.* Supervisor's status was measured by a six-point scale corresponding to formal positional status of the supervisor. Since it is expected that the higher the status, the greater will be the positional resources of the supervisor for distribution among his subordinates, *ceteris paribus* the status variable is expected to have a positive contribution to the group I dependent variables and a negative contribution to the group II dependent variables.

(2) *Supervisor's Age.* The older the supervisor, the greater may be the interpersonal distance or generation gap between him and his subordinates, thus producing a negative effect upon group I and positive effect upon group II variables.

(3) *Supervisor's Education.* A dummy variable was created with college or over equal to 1, and others zero. The college dummy may show positive and negative contributions to the group I and II variables respectively. In general, the college graduate supervisor may have stronger positive influence over his college graduate subordinate, because of the communality of the educational background, and the higher potential to develop in the organization.

(4) *Supervisor's Tenure.* *Ceteris paribus* higher tenure of the supervisor implies slower speed in his career development. Thus, the supervisor's tenure years will have negative and positive effects upon group I and II variables respectively.

(5) *Supervisor Change.* During the period between Wave 3 and Wave 4, about 40 percent of the newcomers changed the supervisors with whom they had vertical exchange. To evaluate the effect of this change, values of 1 and 0 were assigned to those newcomers whose dyadic relations remained the same and whose dyadic relations changed during that time period, respectively. Sine disruption in dyadic relations is assumed to have a negative effect upon the level of vertical exchange, it is expected that the supervisor change dummy will take on positive and negative signs for group I and II variables respectively.

(6) *Job Type.* Newcomers were distributed to a variety of jobs to start their career in the DEPART organization. Table 11 presented in Chapter V indicates that sales jobs based on the shop floor represent one of the largest categories (about 70 percent) of the newcomers' jobs. For the purpose of regression analysis, a dummy variable for the job type was created with assigning 1 to the sales jobs and zero to all others. The company's policy emphasized "serving" the customer and learning the company's "trade." Sales is regarded as a critical part of the activities for practicing this policy. Information obtained by interviews with newcomers and their supervisors seemed to endorse the above statement; most of them believed that DEPART men should have experience with one of the sales shops before they are promoted to a middle management level; some newcomers complained about doing supportive functions while their colleages were learning their trade. Based on the above consideration, it was hypothesized that the job type dummy may have a positive contribution to the group I variables and a negative contribution to the group II variables.

(7) *Unit Size.* Number of employees headed by the First level manager (see Figure 6 in Chapter V for the structure of a work unit) was defined as the size of a work unit. It was found that the work units to which the newcomers were assigned had 11 employees on the average. Based on the assumptions that unit size may have a positive correlation with the amount of resources (manpower, budget, responsibilities, etc.) available to each member within the unit, it was hypothesized that the size variable would make positive and negative contributions to group I and II variables respectively.

(8) *Percent Male.* Number of male employees relative to total number of employees in the unit was calculated as a second measure of unit size. Based on the same assumption as used for unit size, the

percentage of males was hypothesized to have a positive contribution to the group I dependent variables and a negative contribution to the group II variables.

(9) *Dummy Variables for Work Locations.* Work locations listed in Table 11 were assigned to a value of zero if they fell in the Tokyo area, and a value of 1 if in the Osaka, Kyoto, and Kobe areas. This recode procedure created three dummy variables corresponding to the last three work locations, with the first acting as a basis for contrast. However, no prediction was made regarding the hypothetical effect of work location dummies, because the variable itself is so complex that no concrete data were available to predict directions of a locational effect.

Personal Background Variables

(1) *Assessed Potentials.* The AS potential variable was introduced into the regression. Although previous results suggest that the effect of a potential factor depends on the level of vertical exchange, it was hypothesized that on the average the AS factor may make a positive contribution to the set of dependent variables grouped as I, and a negative contribution to the group II dependent variables.

(2) *Personality Type.* As discussed earlier, DEPART people had a belief that a person characterized by features of an Epileptic type of personality (modesty, perseverence, social norms, etc.) would have a tendency of fitting better into their organization and with the nature of their business. In fact, about 80 percent of our sample of newcomers were found to belong to this personality type. A dummy variable was created to account for the effect of this particular personality type. It was hypothesized that the personality dummy variable will have positive and negative effects for the group I and II variables respectively.

(3) *Conne.* The *Conne*, or connection literary, implied an outside pressure for employment exercised on behalf of some of the newcomers whose potentials generally fall below the acceptable level for recruitment. Thus, this variable displayed negative correlations with job performance and career outcomes (see Tables 35 and 37) rated after employment. Company records showed that out of the 85 newcomers recruited, 15 of them had *Conne* influence of varying degrees. For the present analysis, this variable was hypothesized to have negative and positive effect upon group I and II variables respectively.

(4) *Age.* Among newcomers, age was distributed within a limited range: about 80 percent of them were between 23 and 24, with a mean age of 23.6. The age difference did not indicate variation in prior work experiences, but it commonly denoted whether the newcomer had *rōnin* experience or not. This particular experience implied that if a person

failed to pass the entrance examination for college once, then he had to spend a year or two attending preparatory school until he finally succeeded in passing the entrance examination. A study conducted by Wakabayashi and his associates (1977) reported a negative effect of the *rōnin* experience upon the process of students' assimilation to college. Similar findings have been reported by many authors (Orihara, 1967; Sumiya, 1967; Vogel, 1963). Since the overwhelming majority graduated from college in four years, the age difference at the point of recruitment suggested that the higher the age, the longer were the years of the *rōnin* experience the newcomer might have. Although no direct evidence exists to suggest the persistence of the negative effect of *rōnin* beyond college life, it was hypothesized for the present study that such an effect may persist. Thus, the newcomer's age will contribute negatively to group I and positively to group II dependent variables.

(5) *Universities.* Information on universities from which new-comers graduated produced three dummy variables. (1) University, private ($=1$) versus public ($=0$). (2) Major, LAS ($=1$) versus engineering fields ($=0$). (3) University location, Osaka area ($=1$) versus others ($=0$). For these variables, no hypotheses were developed as to the direction of their effects upon the dependent variables, because it seemed too speculative to do so.

1. Structural Effect

Table 51 displays newcomers' reports regressed on the structural variables of the organization. The regression analysis for the present study had two purposes: one was to test how consistently each independent variable produced the hypothesized direction of effect, regardless of its size of contribution upon a set of dependent variables. The second was to evaluate how much of the variance in the dependent variables could be explained by a set of structural variables. To answer the first question, the probability that a regression coefficient for a given independent variable takes on the hypothesized signs was tested against a null hypothesis that states the probability of appearing positive (p) or negative (q) is random ($p = 1-q = .50$) upon each of the regression analyses. For example, in Table 51 our hypothesis states that the coefficients for "Sup Status" will show positive signs to newcomer's reports on VE, OC, RD, JN(R), and NJ(P) variables (group I variables are listed above the dotted line in Table 51), and negative signs to D^2, JP(F) and JP(S) variables (group II variables are listed below the dotted line). Whereas the null hypotheses states that within each group of variables the chances for those variables appearing to be positive or negative is random. This null hypothesis, then, will be rejected if the

Table 51

Newcomer's Reports Regressed on Structural Variables of the Organization Based on the Wave 4 Data (N=80)

Newcomer's Report		Sup Status	Sup Age	Sup Edu	Sup Ten	Sup Change	Job Type	Unit Size	% Male	Osaka	Kyoto	Kobe	R	F
VE	I	.10	.21	-.19	-.32	.14	-.12	-.03	.08	.08	-.16	.16	.45	1.54
OC	I	.04	-.23	.05	.11	.16	-.10	-.01	.08	-.24	-.09	.12	.33	.77
	II	.11	-.01	-.15	-.21	.07	.05	.08	.07	-.14	-.03	.26	.35	.86
RD	I	.26	-.13	-.01	-.07	.11	-.22	-.01	.13	-.19	-.15	.16	.46	1.67
	II	.36*	-.15	-.11	-.23	.19	.01	.01	.22	-.18	.15	.27*	.49*	1.96
JN(R)	I	.34*	-.14	.01	-.04	.04	-.39**	-.14	.04	.03	-.01	.07	.53*	2.47
	II	.16	.13	-.13	-.19	.04	-.10	.01	.20	.04	.03	.21	.36	.90
JN(P)	I	.15	-.01	-.05	.05	.21	-.14	-.19	.08	-.11	.17	.09	.40	1.21
	II	.13	.05	-.12	-.07	.04	-.21	-.15	-.10	.02	.09	.15	.33	.33
D²	I	-.21	.17	-.09	.08	.12	.17	.08	.01	-.10	.22	.12	.45	1.55
	II	-.08	-.20	.02	.18	-.07	-.21	-.16	-.42	-.06	-.01	-.06	.37	1.00
JP(F)	I	-.11	.02	.10	.05	-.08	.10	-.02	-.27	-.05	.01	-.10	.36	.90
	II	.04	-.24	.18	.23	-.14	-.15	.11	-.20	.25	.11	.18	.34	.91
JP(S)	I	.01	-.26	.26	.31	.07	.14	-.05	-.15	-.20	-.01	-.12	.42	1.34
	II	-.03	-.30	.38*	.55**	.03	-.14	-.11	-.33	.06	.13	-.12	.45	1.56
Sign Test		.004	.500	.996 (.018)	.004	.018	.941 (.151)	.696	.004					

Figures denote beta weights.

Figures in parentheses show probability for the alternative hypothesis.

- Nonapplicable.

*p<.05 .

**p<.01 .

probability of the hypothesis being false (or true for the alternative testing hypothesis) is less than .05 in terms of a binominal distribution. For the second question, multiple correlation coefficients (R) were tested using F statistics with 11 and 68 degrees of freedom for the numerator and the denominator respectively.

Results of the sign tests shown in Table 51 indicate that supervisor's status, his tenure years, supervisory change, and percentage of male employees in the unit, produced a significantly large number of positive signs as predicted by our hypothesis. For example, beta weights for Supervisor's Status all showed positive signs for the group I variables indicating that the higher the supervisor's status, the higher the vertical exchange, organizational commitment, feeling of staying and so on, reported by the newcomer. For group II variables, Supervisor's Status also showed consistent effects in that the higher the supervisor's status, the lower the need deficiency and job problems, although for two of the dependent variables, Supervisor's Status produced signs contrary to our hypothesis. However, the results of the sign test indicated this error (2 out of 15) is small enough to reject the null hypothesis at the $p < .05$ level.

On the other hand, supervisor's age, his educational background, job type and unit size failed to show hypothesized effects at a significant level. Moreover, Supervisor's Education and Job Type variables produced a pattern of effects indicating that an alternative hypothesis might be true. That is, contrary to our predictions, *ceteris paribus* college graduate supervisors and sales type jobs tend to have negative impacts upon newcomers' reports on vertical exchange and outcomes of career progress. Table 51 also indicates that newcomers working in the Kobe area are significantly different ($p < .004$) in contrast to their colleagues working in the Tokyo area. However, this observed locational effect is beyond the plausible explanation.

The results of F tests indicate that the organizational structure variables as a whole have made significant contributions to the newcomer's disillusionment with the profitability of the organization (RD-II), and leadership received (JN(R)-I). Structural factors explained 24 and 28 percent of variance in the above two dependent variables respectively. For the latter variable, results indicated that leadership support received by the newcomers will be the highest for those working under high status and young supervisors, for non-sales jobs, within a smaller work unit. For dependent variables other than the above two, the explanatory power of structural factors remained nonsignificant, with R^2s ranging from .11 to .21.

Table 52 displays results of the regression analyses and sign tests applied to the supervisors' reports. In Table 51, the sign tests for

Table 52

Supervisor's Reports Regressed on Structural Variables
of the Organization Based on the Wave 4 Data (N=80)

Supervisor's Report	Independent Variable												
	Sup Status	Sup Age	Sup Edu	Sup Ten	Sup Change	Job Type	Unit Size	% Male	Osaka	Kyoto	Kobe	R	F
VE	-.08	.01	.20	.05	-.04	-.13	.01	-.10	.06	-.13	.13	.32	.68
JN(P) I	.04	-.12	.19	.17	.09	-.21	.03	.07	-.07	.02	.02	.29	.58
JN(P) II	-.40*	.40	.10	-.14	.13	-.11	.06	.03	-.22	-.34*	-.02	.44	1.48
JN(W) I	-.11	.16	.08	-.14	.25	-.06	.10	.12	-.01	.06	.12	.37	1.01
JN(W) II	-.19	.29	.20	-.13	.24	-.12	.19	.04	-.24	-.29*	.03	.49*	2.00
Performance	-.22	.07	.09	.05	.11	-.07	.10	-.45	.09	.04	-.01	.31	.66
Success	-.22	.09	.01	-.05	-.01	-.28*	.10	-.20	.19	.06	-.01	.43	1.43
Sign Test	.992 (.062)	.992 (.062)	.008	.500	.227	(.008)	.008	.500	-	-	-		

Figures denote beta weights.

Figures in parentheses show probability for the alternate hypothesis.

- Nonapplicable.

* $p < .05$.

supervisors' education and unit size produced significant results consistent with our hypotheses.   This indicated that supervisors with college education who are in charge of large work units tend to give more vertical exchange, provide more opportunities for job needs, see their newcomers as wanting more opportunities for need satisfaction, and rate newcomers' performance and success potential higher.   However, the above reports are contradictory to what the newcomers reported in Table 52:   they say the opposite is true for supervisor's education, and what is important is the percentage of male employees in the work unit rather than the size of the unit itself.   For status, age, and tenure of the supervisor, the results are not only nonsignificant, but also contradict what the newcomers reported.

Supervisor's Change and Job Type are the only two variables that produced a similar pattern of effects between the newcomers' and supervisors' reports.   A dummy variable for supervisory change (coded change$=0$, nonchange$=1$) displayed a consistent positive effect upon leader-member units when dyadic relations remained unchanged between Waves 3 and 4, although the sign test for the supervisor's reports failed to reach a significant level ($p < .227$).   As to the effect of job type, our hypothesis was not endorsed by either the newcomer or his supervisor, but both parties agreed that the alternative hypothesis may be true: it is the non-sales jobs that have a positive contribution to the vertical exchange and outcomes for career progress.

The R^2s for supervisor's reports ranged from .08 to .24.   A regression for the supervisor's report on the job enrichment wanted by his newcomer ($R^2=.24$) reached a significance level, while all other reports failed to do so.   The location dummy for Kyoto picked up significant negative contributions to supervisors' reports on job enrichment, but again no plausible explanation is readily available for this observed phenomenon.

In sum, results displayed in Tables 51 and 52 suggest that: (1) structural variables of the work organization combined into a linear form of equation, explained maximally 28 and 24 percent of the variance for newcomers' and supervisors' reports respectively. (2) Supervisor's Change and Job Type produced consistent effects across reporters.   However, for Job Type an alternative to the hypothesized effect was found to be true. (3) The patterns of effects of structural variables are different depending upon the reporter's position.   (a) Supervisor's status and his educational level had an opposite effect between the supervisor and his subordinate. (b) Supervisor's tenure and percentage of male employees showed the hypothesized effects upon newcomers' reports, but no consistent effect upon supervisors' reports. (c) Conversely, unit size had an hypothesized effect upon supervisors' reports, but again no effect upon newcomers' reports.

2. Effect of Personal Background Variables

The same design of regression analysis as was applied to the structural variables was used to examine the effect of personal background variables upon newcomers' as well as supervisors' reports. Table 53 displays beta weights and multiple correlation coefficients derived from regressing the newcomer's reports on the background variables of the newcomer himself. The result of the sign tests shown on the last row in Table 53 indicates that the hypothesized effects of the personality type of the newcomer and his age tested against randomness of the effects, reached marginal level of significance. This result implies that the personality type preferred by the DEPART organization tends to have an hypothesized positive effect upon the outcomes reported by the newcomer. Also, the hypothesized effect of spending extra years to finish college was supported by a negative contribution that the age variable displayed, whereas the AS potential and *Conne* variables failed to produce a predicted pattern of effects. The R^2s computed for the newcomers' reports ranged from .04 to .15, however, none of them reached a significance level.

Table 54 displays the result of the regression analysis applied to the supervisors' reports. Sign test for AS potential and personality type variables reached a significance level indicating that potential and a personality type preferred by the DEPART organization had a consistent positive effect upon the outcomes reported by the supervisor. The university variable had a consistent negative contribution to the vertical exchange and outcomes reported by the supervisor. This finding implied that the private university graduates tend to have lower vertical exchange and job needs, and lower ratings with respect to job performance and success potential, compared to their colleagues who graduated from national or public universities.

In Table 54, a regression for vertical exchange reached a significance level ($R^2 = .19$), indicating that the supervisor's willingness to engage in a vertical relation with his subordinate is partly determined by the personal background of the newcomer. Especially if the newcomer is considered to have high potential (together with the public university background), his supervisor appears more willing to have a high level of vertical exchange with him, than would otherwise be the case. A significant contribution that the AS potential factor ($p < .01$) had upon the supervisors' vertical exchange for the present regression analysis gives support to the ANOVA result reported in Chapter VI with respect to the

Table 53

Newcomer's Reports at Wave 4 Regressed on Personal Background Variables of the Newcomer (N = 80)

Newcomer's Report		AS	Per Type	Conne	Age	Univ	Major	Univ Location	R	F
					Independent Variable					
VE		.16	.18	.07	-.14	-.21	-.04	-.12	.32	1.14
OC	I	-.03	-.08	.03	-.06	.02	.14	.04	.26	.72
	II	-.15	-.09	-.15	.12	.16	.14	.17	.28	.90
RD	I	.06	.09	-.01	-.14	.12	.10	-.04	.20	.42
	II	-.24	-.15	-.08	-.17	.01	.13	.14	.35	1.46
JN(R)	I	.07	.11	.09	-.15	-.28*	-.06	-.18	.34	1.33
	II	.08	.06	.11	-.16	-.20	.03	-.12	.28	.87
JN(P)	I	.18	.02	.18	.12	-.02	.07	.05	.25	.68
	II	.01	-.04	.12	.05	-.05	.13	.06	.20	.44
D^2	I	.08	-.19	.01	.22	.27*	.14	.24*	.39	1.84
	II	.05	-.05	-.07	.18	.18	.01	.23	.32	1.17
JP(F)	I	.06	-.09	.01	.17	.13	-.05	.17	.27	.80
	II	.33**	-.06	.15	-.01	.17	.04	-.20	.38	1.52
JP(S)	I	.15	-.09	.05	.12	.15	-.02	.16	.28	.85
	II	.15	-.17	.08	.01	.19	.11	-.07	.26	.73
Sign Test		.849	.059	.500	.059	–	–	–		

Figures denote beta weights
- Nonapplicable.
 * p < .05.
** p < .01.

Table 54

Supervisor's Reports at Wave 4 Regressed on Personal Background Variables of the Newcomer

Supervisor's Report		AS	Per Type	Conne	Age	Univ	Major	Univ Location	R	F
								Independent Variable		
VE		.35**	.12	.06	−.01	−.24*	−.10	−.12	.44*	2.42
JN(P)	I	.03	.05	−.13	.08	−.13	−.02	.01	.22	.51
	II	.21	.21	−.01	.07	−.16	−.13	−.01	.33	1.25
JN(W)	I	.17	.01	.04	.01	−.26	.15	−.07	.24	.64
	II	.22	.16	−.02	−.03	−.21	−.09	.05	.34	1.35
Performance		.12	.19	.05	−.14	−.04	.09	−.12	.29	.96
Success		.14	.25*	.12	−.04	−.11	.13	−.19	.38	1.71
Sign Test		.008	.008	.773	.500	−	−	−		

Figures denote beta weights.
− Nonapplicable
* $p < .05$.
** $p < .01$.

effect of AS potential upon supervisors' vertical exchange (see Figure 20 in Chapter VI). For the other dependent variables, the R^2s ranged from .05 to .15, but none of them reached a significance level.

In sum, the pattern of personal background effects again produced an inconsistency between the newcomer and his supervisor. The AS potential factor produced a hypothesized positive effect upon the newcomers' reports. In addition, the negative effect of age was endorsed by the newcomer, but the supervisors' reports indicated that the effect might be random. On the other hand, the personality type preferred by the DEPART company produced a consistent effect between the newcomers' and the supervisors' reports. One of the interesting findings is that supervisor's willingness to engage in a vertical relation with his subordinate was significantly influenced by his evaluation of "what kind of person his subordinate is." Especially, for the DEPART supervisors, newcomers' potentials and one of the educational background factors were found critical for this evaluation.

A question may be raised as to why some of the structural and background variables showed an opposite effect between the newcomers' and supervisors' reports. A problem of perception or attribution seems to be involved in this question. For example, supervisor's status, age, education, and tenure are considered as "given constraints" in the eyes of the newcomer. Thus, these characteristics of the supervisor become part of the structure of the work unit, and the newcomer may attribute whatever happens to one of these characteristics. On the other hand, from the eyes of the supervisor, these characteristics are partly a "personal background" of his own. Thus, they may directly constrain his behaviors and perceptions. The same problem may happen to the personal background variables of the newcomer. More research will be required to explore the process of perception, communication, and attribution under various constraints for career development.

3. Critical Contribution of Vertical Exchange

A flow diagram on directions of causal influence among the variables of career progress illustrated in Figure 39 may imply the following four propositions: (a) the supervisor's report on vertical exchange, VE(S) has a significant independent effect upon the vertical exchange of the focal newcomer, VE(F), (b) simultaneously, the VE(F) has a significant independent effect upon the VE(S), (c) the VE(S) also has an independent effect upon the outcomes reported by the focal newcomer, O(F), and conversely (d) the VE(F) has an independent effect upon the outcomes reported by the supervisor, O(S). In a functional form, the above propositions can be stated as follows:

$$\begin{array}{llllll}
VE(F) & = & f & (VE(S), & C_1, & \ell_1) & - & (a) \\
VE(S) & = & g & (VE(F), & C_2 & \ell_2) & - & (b) \\
O(F) & = & h & (VE(S), & C_3 & \ell_3) & - & (c) \\
O(S) & = & k & (VE(F), & C_4 & \ell_4) & - & (d)
\end{array}$$

For the above equations, C denotes control variable consisting of the structural and personal background variables discussed earlier, while ℓ implies disturbance factors specific to each equation. Functional relations between the VE and the dependent variables implied in the above equations were tested by evaluating the significance level of contribution that the VE variables add in terms of R^2 to each of the dependent variables. For this purpose, "net" contributions of VE(F) and VE(S) variables were examined after the effects of control variables were removed by using regression analysis. Table 55 displays a summary of results.

The first colum (R_1^2) in Table 55 displays the R^2s derived from regressing each of the dependent variables on the 11 structural variables as listed in Tables 51 and 52. The second column (R_2^2) also displays the R^2s for each dependent variable obtained by using the 18 control variables; the first 11 variables consisted of the structural variables, and the last 7 consisted of the personal background variables listed in Tables 53 and 54. The third and fourth columns indicate respectively an increment (R_d^2) in the coefficient of multiple determination between R_1^2 and R_2^2, and a significant level of R_d^2 tested using a F statistic. The last four columns present results corresponding to the testing of the four hypotheses stated above. The hypotheses testing was based on two sets of analyses. First, for testing the effect of the supervisors' vertical exchange upon the subordinates' responses [hypothesis (a) and (c)], the VE(S) variable was introduced into the regression equations for the newcomers' reports, followed by the 18 control variables. Then the R_3^2 was computed based on the total 19 independent variables. Next, the contribution of the VE(S) upon the newcomer's report was evaluated by computing the difference between R_2^2 and R_3^2. Finally, this increment (R_d^2) was subjected to the significance test using F statistic. For the second part of the analyses, the effect of the focal newcomer's vertical exchange [hypotheses (b) and (d)] was evaluated by introducing a VE(F) variable into the regression equations for the supervisor's reports. Procedures following after this step were exactly the same as those for the first part of the analyses.

In Table 55, the F tests for the contribution of personal background variables (see the third column) reached a significance level only for the VE(S), vertical exchange reported by the supervisor. For this dependent variable, personal background variables as a whole added 20 percent

Table 55

Contribution of Vertical Exchange to Newcomer's and Supervisor's Reports after Structural and Personal Background Variables are Controlled (N=80)

Subjects' Reports		Structural Variables R^2	Variable Set Structural plus Personal Background Variables			Structural plus Personal plus Vertical Exchange[a]			t^6
			R^2	R^2	F	R^2	R^2	F	
Newcomer's Report									
VE (F)		.20	.26	.06	.72	.31	.05**	4.39	*
OC	I	.11	.18	.07	.75	.24	.06**	4.82	*
	II	.12	.19	.07	.76	.26	.07**	5.72	*
RD	I	.21	.25	.04	.45	.31	.06**	5.30	*
	II	.24	.35	.11	1.50	.44	.09**	9.64	**
JR (R)	I	.28	.32	.04	.52	.35	.03*	2.78	–
	II	.13	.17	.04	.41	.20	.03*	2.41	–
JN (P)	I	.16	.24	.08	.93	.27	.03*	2.49	–
	II	.11	.17	.06	.64	.20	.03	2.27	
D^2	I	.20	.25	.05	.58	.26	.01	.80	–
	II	.14	.20	.06	.66	.21	.01	.76	–
JP (F)	I	.13	.19	.07	.78	.19	.00	.05	–
	II	.13	.28	.15	1.95	.29	.01	.32	–
JP (S)	I	.18	.22	.04	.45	.23	.01	.79	–
	II	.20	.27	.07	.96	.27	.00	.04	–
Supervisor's Report									
VE (S)		.10	.30	.20*	2.53	.33	.03*	2.77	*
JN (P)	I	.08	.11	.03	.30	.18	.07**	5.18	*
	II	.19	.27	.08	.97	.31	.03*	2.64	*
JN (W)	I	.14	.19	.05	.55	.23	.04*	3.16	*
	II	.24	.30	.06	.77	.32	.02	1.79	–
Performance		.10	.16	.06	.63	.33	.17**	15.63	**
Success		.19	.30	.11	.146	.41	.11**	11.47	**

[a]To explain newcomer's reports, vertical exchange reported by the supervisor, VE(S) was introduced, while for the supervisor's reports, VE(F) was introduced.
[b]Test of regression coefficients for the VE(S) and VE(F). The F statistics show results of the significance test for R^2.

*p < .05.
**p < .01.

more explanatory power after the effect of the structural variables was controlled. Especially, it was found that among the background variables, the AS potential factor made the greatest (in terms of a standard unit) contribution to the VE(S). This finding indicates that the newcomers' potential remains as a major source of variance in VE(S), even after the effect of the structural variables of the organization are controlled. For the other dependent variables, the contribution of the background variables ranged from .04 to .15 percent. Furthermore, examinations on R_d^2 values revealed that for each dependent variable, the original explanatory power of personal variables, as determined in Tables 53 and 54, remained as it was or with little loss, even after the effect of the structural variables had been controlled. In other words, the R_2^2s were found to be almost identical with the simple summation of the two R^2s obtained based on structural and personal variables independently. This result implies that the structural and personal background variables constitute two independent sources which help account for the variance in outcomes of the career development process.

The results shown on the last four columns in Table 55 clearly indicate that vertical exchange can be the third independent source of variance. More precisely, significance tests for R_d^2s indicate that the supervisors' report on vertical exchange, VE(S) made significant contributions to the VE(F) and the OC, RD, JN(R) and JN(P) scales even after the structural and background variables were controlled. This result suggests that the hypotheses (a) and (c) advanced earlier were supported. Likewise, focal newcomer's vertical exchange, VE (F) contributed significantly to explaining the supervisor's reports with respect to the VE(S), JN(P), JN(W), Job Performance, and Success Potential scales, after controlling for the effect of the structural and background variables. This result indicates that the hypotheses (b) and (d) were also supported by empirical evidence. Moreover, the t statistics shown on the last column in Table 55 indicate that significant contributions of the VE variables are mostly supported by the significant regression coefficients for the VE variables themselves.

In sum, (1) the VE(S) failed to contribute extra explanatory power to the D^2 and Job Problem scales reported by the newcomer, while the VE(F) contributed significantly to almost all the variables reported by the supervisor. This result indicates that (2) the supervisor can do very little in terms of vertical exchange to prevent his newcomer from experiencing deficiency needs and job problems under the constraints "given" by the structural and personal background conditions. Although, he can make a significant influence upon the vertical exchange, organizational commitment, role disillusionment, and job need receiving experienced by the newcomer even under such constraints. (3) Supervisor's initiation in the vertical relation is determined partly by the personal background of his subordinate (especially subordinate's potential) and partly by the initiative of the subordinate to engage in an exchange relation with him. However, the influence of personal background variables (20 percent) is far stronger than the initiative of the subordinate (3 percent). (4) Nonetheless, the newcomer's behaviors on vertical exchange seem to have a very consistent impact upon his supervisor. Especially, the VE(F) alone accounts for 17 and 11 percent of the variances in job performance and success potential respectively, after the effect of structural and background variables is controlled. (5) The above findings may suggest that if the process of vertical exchange can be initiated by the newcomer, the impact of his initiative seems to be greater (or more extensive) than that of the supervisor's initiative.

Table 55 displays that by putting all 19 causal variables together, they can explain a minimum of 18 percent to a maximum of 44 percent of the variance (R_3^2) in outcomes measured at Wave 4. To increase the explanatory power of the regression equation, we may need more sophisticated measures on structures of the work unit and the newcomer's tasks. For example, Pugh and his associates (1968) proposed that the structure of a work unit can be better summarized by the following six dimensions: specialization, standardization, formalization, centralization, configuration, and flexibility. In addition, Hackman and Lawler (1971) suggested that the quality of the newcomers' tasks may be represented by the following four "core" dimensions: variety, autonomy, task identity and feedback. Regarding personal background variables, the recommendation is made to rate the newcomer's personal history blank, to collect much information on his educational quality and achievement, and to evaluate his expectations, higher-order need strength, and self-esteem prior to employment, for the purpose of increasing predictive power of background variables on outcomes after employment. All these suggestions will be subject to exploration in future studies.

II. Causal Relationships Between Leader-Member Exchanges and Job Performance

The results displayed in Table 55 indicate that the VE(F) alone can explain 17 percent of variance in job performance when structural and personal background variables are held constant. These results imply that the effect of vertical exchange upon job performance is independent of the structural variables of the organization and personal background variables on a "concurrent" basis of analysis. The results displayed in

Tables 44 and 45 in Chapter VII further indicate that the VE(FY) effect upon job performance is also independent of the other two factors, the RD(FY) and the AS potential, on a "predictive" basis of analysis. These findings suggest that: (1) the function of a vertical exchange relation for organizational career progress is independent of other determinants of progress examined in the present study, and (2) vertical exchange may be a cause of job performance. The term "cause," is used for the present analysis to denote that vertical exchange relates to job performance over time intervals and its relationship is not spurious.

To examine the "causal" relationship between vertical exchange and job performance, a cross-lagged path analysis (Heise, 1970) and a dynamic correlation analysis (Vroom, 1966) were performed. These analyses required that two causally related variables be measured at two different points in time, so that the analyses can determine which variable has control over what is happening between the two time periods. For brevity, seven waves of monitoring involved in our longitudinal study were collapsed (except for the first wave monitoring) into the following three time periods on a year basis: the first year (combination of Waves 2 and 3), the second year (Waves 4 and 5), and the third year (Waves 6 and 7). Based on this reduced time dimension, cross-lagged and test-retest correlations were calculated between vertical exchange and performance ratings. Figure 40 displays the results of this analysis. Figure 40 clearly shows that between any two successive points, vertical exchange (VE) predicts job performance (JP) more strongly than job performance predicts vertical exchange. For example, between the first and the second year, the VE(1) → JP(2) correlation was found to be .26, while the one for JP(1) → VE(2) was .09. Likewise, between the second and the third year, the correlations were .34 for the VE(2) → JP(3) and .24 for the JP(2) → VE(3) relationships. The same relationships hold true for the success potential (SP) scale.

The cross-lagged correlations shown in Figure 40 may be considered as substantial evidence to conclude it is vertical exchange that causes differences in job performance and success potential, rather than the other way around. However, the evidence is not persuasive enough until we can show that the observed correlations are not spurious. Because, it is very likely that some exogenous variables uncontrolled for in the present study can be the true cause of the observed correlations. To check for the possibility of this spurious correlation, dynamic correlation and path analyses were attempted based on the data given in Figure 40.

For the purpose of analyses, the time series displayed in Figure 40 was divided into three different phases: from the first to the second year, the second to the third year, and the first to the third year. For

Figure 40

Cross-Lag Correlation Coefficients Between
Vertical Exchange and Performance Ratings

<u>Job Performance</u>

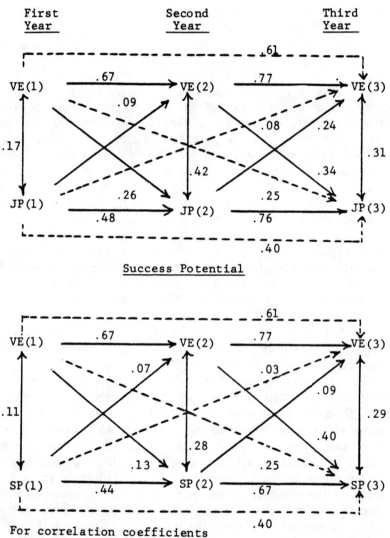

<u>Success Potential</u>

For correlation coefficients
with .22 or greater, p<.05;
with .28 or greater, p<.01.

each time phase, dynamic correlations and path coefficients were computed based on the procedure displayed in Figure 41. In Figure 41, X-odds (X_1 and X_3) represent measures of vertical exchange, while X-evens (X_2 and X_4) represent the measures of a criterion variable. According to Sheridan and his associates (1975), a raw cross-lagged correlation as shown in Figure 40 (for example, a .26 correlation between VE(1) and JP(2)) reflects two different influences: (a) the direct effect that the initial values of each variable have on the later values of the opposite variable, i.e., VE(1) $\rightarrow$ E(2) and JP(1) $\rightarrow$ JP(2), and (b) the direct effect due to the concurrent initial relationship between the two variables, plus the test-retest reliability of each variable, i.e., VE(1) $\rightarrow$ JP(1) $\rightarrow$ JP(2), and JP(1) $\rightarrow$ VE(1) $\rightarrow$ VE(2). This implies that the reason why the correlation (.26) for VE(1) $\rightarrow$ JP(2) becomes greater than the correlation (.09) for JP(1) $\rightarrow$ VE(2), may be attributed to the greater test-retest reliability of the VE measure (.67) relative to the one of the JP (.48). If this is true, the .26 correlation coefficient suggesting a seemingly significant causal effect of vertical exchange upon job behavior may be judged spurious. For this kind of problem, Heise (1970) suggested that the causal inferences should be based on the path coefficients between four measures.

As the computational formula suggests, path coefficients are derived by adjusting raw cross-lagged correlations in terms of test-retest reliability and concurrent correlations. In other words, path coefficients (P_{ij}) represent the direct effect between the VE and JP variables, removing any indirect effect due to different measurement reliability (Sheridan, et al., 1975). Sheridan and his associates suggested that path coefficients can be interpreted in the following manner. (1) If P_{41} is nonzero and P_{32} is zero, then vertical exchange determines the criterion variables. (2) If P_{32} is nonzero and P_{41} is zero, then the criterion variable determines vertical exchange. (3) If both P^{41} and P^{32} are nonzero, there is evidence that the vertical exchange and the criterion variables are mutually dependent. (4) If both P_{31} and P_{42} are nonzero, and P_{41} and P_{32} are zero, then there is evidence that vertical exchange and performance are mutually independent. The interpretation of the result, now depends on the decision as to what are zero and nonzero path coefficients. Since there are no objective standards to guide us in this decision, Sheridan and his associates (1975) suggested that the criterion, $P_{ij} \geq ,30$ where zero-order correlations would be significant at P<.01 level, may be established as the level of nonzero path coefficients.

A dynamic correlation is based on the correlation coefficient between the two change scores. For the present study, it is computed by correlating the change in X-odds (X_3-X_1) with the change in X-evens (X_4-X_2). A spurious dynamic correlation is considered less likely to occur

Figure 41

Path Analysis for Panel Data

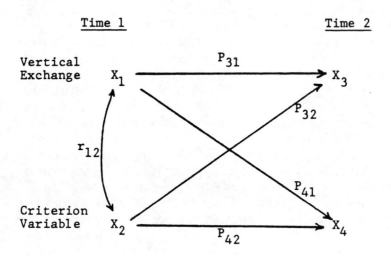

Computational formula:

$$P_{31} = \frac{r_{13} - r_{12}\, r_{23}}{1 - r_{12}^2}$$

$$P_{32} = \frac{r_{23} - r_{12}\, r_{13}}{1 - r_{12}^2}$$

$$P_{41} = \frac{r_{14} - r_{12}\, r_{24}}{1 - r_{12}^2}$$

$$P_{42} \quad \frac{r_{24} - r_{12}\, r_{14}}{1 - r_{12}^2}$$

than a spurious static correlation based on a single point in time. Because for an exogenous variable to cause a spurious correlation between change scores, it would have to make a change in different directions or amounts among the subjects and also be correlated with changes in both X-odds and X-evens (Vroom, 1966; Sheridan, et al., 1975). However, it is likely that a dynamic correlation may be an artifact when the tendency for measurements at time-two is to regress toward the mean of the measurements at time-one. Whenever this bias of measurement happens, negative correlations can be expected between the initial values (X_1 for example) and change scores (X_3-X_1) on the same variable (Campbell and Stanley, 1963), suggesting that the direction and the amount of change is a decreasing function of the initial value. This regression toward the mean actually occurred in the present study. That is, change scores for both vertical exchange and performance ratings between the first and second year were found negatively correlated with the first year values of each variable. Likewise, change scores from the second to the third year were also negatively correlated with the second year values for each variable. Moreover, this measurement bias could not be corrected even after all the variables were standardized. To correct for this measurement bias, Vroom (1966) suggested that residual gain scores be used to control for the effect of initial values on each variable. For the present analysis, corrected dynamic correlations were computed as partial correlations between the change scores on two variables, holding the initial scores on both variables constant. By doing this, a problem of serially correlated data was solved, i.e., correction removed a portion of the changes that could have been linearly predicted from the initial scores. Moreover, since we knew already that the exogenous variables examined in the preceding section have substantial independent effects upon both vertical exchange and the criterion variables, the effects of these variables were also controlled before computing the dynamic correlations. The following 11 structural and personal variables were controlled: AS potential, personality type, *Conne*, age, three dummy variables for educational background, job type, and three dummy variables for work location. Correlations displayed in Figure 40 were also subject to adjustment by controlling the above exogenous variables when path coefficients were computed.

Table 56 displays the results of the dynamic correlation analysis. Cross-lagged correlations represent simple correlation coefficients between vertical exchange and the criterion variables across time. On the other hand, standardized dynamic correlations denote correlation coefficients based on the standardized scores. Standardization was made to adjust mean differences among different time periods for each variable.

Table 56

Correlation Coefficients Between Vertical Exchange
and Job Performance (I) and Success Potential (II)
Based on the First-, Second-, and Third-Year Reports
(N = 80)

| | Time Period | | | | | |
| | First to Second Year | | Second to Third Year | | First to Third Year | |
Correlation	I	II	I	II	I	II
Cross-lagged	.26*	.13*	.34**	.40**	.25*	.25*
Standardized Dynamic	.30**	.22*	.24*	.15	.18	.13
Corrected Dynamic	.32**	.22	.25*	.15	.19	.25*

* p < .05.
** p < .01.

Then, corrected dynamic correlations were computed using change scores derived from the standardized measures, holding exogenous variables and the first year values for vertical exchange and criterion variables constant. Table 56 suggests that significant dynamic correlations exist between vertical exchange and job performance for the successive time periods (the first to the second year, and the second to the third year), but not for the two extreme time periods (from the first year to the third year). On the other hand, between vertical exchange and success potentials, corrected dynamic correlations reached a significance level for the period between the two extreme years, but not for the periods between the successive years. The results shown in Table 56 suggest that although some correlations have dropped to a nonsignificance level due to the correction, there exists a consistent causal influence between vertical exchange and the criterion variables through-out the first three years for career development within the DEPART organization.

Table 57 displays the results of the path analysis. The hypothesis that states vertical exchange is the cause of variation in job performance, is represented by the P_{41} path, while the P_{32} path represents an alternative hypothesis that states job performance is the cause of vertical exchange. As discussed earlier, correlation coefficients displayed in Figure 40 were corrected using the 11 exogenous variables before they were put into the formula to compute the path coefficients. Table 57 indicates that at all

Table 57

Path Coefficients Between Vertical Exchange
and Performance Ratings

VE Path for:	First to Second Year	Time Period Second to Third Year	First to Third Year
Job Performance			
P_{31}	.67	.81	.62
P_{32}	−.02	−.09	−.02
P_{41}	.20	.10	.19
P_{42}	.43	.71	.37
Success Potential			
P_{31}	.67	.80	.62
P_{32}	−.01	−.14	−.04
P_{41}	.08	.23	.21
P_{42}	.43	.61	.37

time periods, the coefficients for the P_{32} path are the smallest for both job performance and success potential. On the other hand, the P_{41} path corresponding to the hypothesis for the present study displayed positive, non-zero coefficients consistently at three different time periods, but none of them reached the significance level ($P_{ij} \geq .30$) proposed by Sheridan and his associates (1975). It is clear from the computational formula shown in Figure 41 that the P_{41} is partly a function of the r_{24}, test-retest reliability of the criterion variable, for the given cross-lagged correlation. This indicates that the greater the test-retest reliability, the smaller the P_{14} for a given r_{14}. In fact, for the present study, test-retest reliability for criterion variables remained at a very high level, even after the effect of exogenous variables was removed: e.g., for job performance, reliabilities are .48, .75, and .41 for the 1st to 2nd, the 2nd to 3rd, and the 1st to 3rd year, respectively. The high test-retest reliabilities which gave rise to the high path coefficients for P_{31} and P_{42}, suggest that the relationship between vertical exchange and the criterion variables are more mutually independent than causally connected.

Relatively small coefficients for the path P_{41} may raise a question that the significant dynamic correlations shown in Table 56 might be spurious.   Since dynamic correlations were corrected for serial correlations, we cannot argue that the significant dynamic results might be biased by the high test-retest reliability.   There is a reasonable doubt that some exogenous variables that were not controlled in the present study might have caused seemingly significant dynamic correlations.   But, it is also reasonable to assume that the P_{41} path coefficients shown in Table 57 may be just strong enough to produce significant dynamic relationships between vertical exchange and the performance ratings as displayed in Table 57.   Especially, considering the fact that the results displayed in Tables 56 and 57 were obtained after controlling many important exogenous variables, it will be concluded that dynamic correlations are authentic, i.e., criterion variables were influenced by vertical exchange, rather than the other way around.

Chapter IX

A Process of Integrating

In the preceding chapters, the focus of analyses has been predicting outcomes of the process of career development. Results of these analyses revealed that the quality of the vertical exchange relation the newcomer experienced with his immediate supervisor during the first year of his organizational life had high predictive validity for outcome variables. Moreover, vertical exchange was found to have an independent causal effect upon outcomes, even after the influence of other determinants (exogenous as well as other factors competing with vertical exchange) had been partialed out. Results also indicated that the potential of the newcomer identified upon recruitment, using the assessment center method, had stronger predictive power for a set of outcomes called career outcomes, compared to the one of vertical exchange. For this chapter, an organizational implication of these findings will be discussed focusing upon the organization's mechanism of integrating the progress into a system of effective human resource utilization. To do this, conceptualization on the *organizational process* of career progress will be attempted based on the model advanced by Schein (1971). Then, relationships between his model, and functions of vertical exchange and potential factors will be examined.

I. Organizational Processes of Career Progress

Schein (1971) proposed a set of concepts to analyze the "career movement" in the organization. His approach, called a *sociopsychological theory of career development,* is based upon the following two dimensions involving a person's career movement within the organization: (1) the career seen as, "a set of attributes and experiences of the *individual* who joins, moves through, and finally leaves an organization," and (2) the career as "defined by the *organization*—a set of expectations held by individuals inside the organization which guide their decisions about whom to move, when, how, and at what speed" (Schein, 1971, 401–402). Parallel to the above dimensions are the concepts of *innovation* and *acculturation.* Innovation corresponds to a process of influence of the individual upon the organization, while acculturation denotes a process of influence of the organization upon the individual. According to Schein, career movements take place as a result of a series of individual-organization interactions in which each party endeavors to influence the other. Movements can be conceived of as processes of crossing either one, or a combination of, the following three structural boundaries of the organization.

(1) *Hierarchical boundaries* which separate the hierarchical levels from one another. Passage of this boundary corresponds roughly to the notion of increasing or decreasing one's rank or level in the organization.

(2) *Inclusion boundaries* which separate individuals or groups who differ in the degree of their centrality. Boundary passage of this dimension corresponds to the notion of one's degree of being more or less "on the inside."

(3) *Functional or departmental boundaries* which separate departments, divisions, or different functional groupings from one another. Crossing these boundaries corresponds to the notion of changing one's function or one's division in the organization.

Schein presented relationships between these boundaries by using a three-dimensional model of the organization as shown in Figure 42. He pointed out that career movement is the process of boundary passage involving some combination of the above three dimensions. The degree of difficulty in boundary passage may vary depending upon: (1) the number of boundaries, (2) the degree of permeability of each boundary, and (3) the type of filtering properties. Schein continued that the variation in these boundary conditions may come from differences in types, and administrative policies of the organization, e.g., tall vs. flat organization, very choosy in membership selection but highly permeable for internal inclusion, or vice versa, differences in policies on human resources utilization (training, rotation, promotion, etc.) and so forth.

According to Schein's theory, career progress for our sample newcomers during the first three years in the DEPART organization can be best described as a process of passing "inclusion boudaries." As Table 12 indicates, the newcomers experienced few departmental moves. At the end of the third year, newcomers were promoted from the Grade 2 to the Grade 3 level. But, this hierarchical move occurred for everyone, thus no variation was created in the speed of passing hierarchical boundaries. Thus, if we follow Schien's theory of career movement, it must be the differences in an "inclusion" dimension among newcomers that explain variations in the outcomes measured in our study.

For the newcomer to the organization, passing inclusion boundaries implies a process of achieving his own role position interdependent with

Figure 42

A Three-Dimensional Model of Career Development

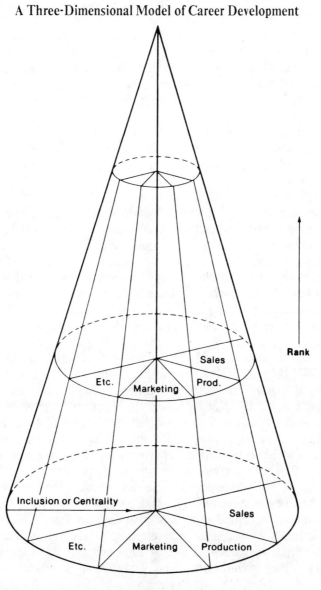

Source: from Shein, E. The Individual, the Organization, and the Career: A Conceptual Scheme. Journal of Applied Behavioral Science, 7, 1971.

roles of the established members in his work unit (Katz and Kahn, 1966). Studies on "role-making" processes (Dansereau, 1975; Graen, 1976) discussed in Chapter IV suggest that increasing interdependent role relations with the immediate supervisor, lead the newcomer to an elevated role position called the "in-group" member. Their findings further indicate that the high leader-member relation measured in terms of "negotiating latitude" enabled the high negotiating member to move into a more "inside" position in terms of inclusion boundaries for the work unit.

A vertical exchange scale used for the present study exemplified more clearly the boundary-spanning function that this particular measure of leader-member relations played. First of all, vertical exchange itself denoted the strength of the interdependent (or "contingent") relationship between the supervisor and his subordinate. Thus, the higher the level of vertical exchange: (a) the more understanding, trust, support, and flexibility the supervisor shows his subordinate, and (b) the more job latitude, authority, and chances for contribution the subordinate receives from his supervisor. Second, results presented in Chapter VI indicated that vertical exchange may have an inclusion function such that the high vertical exchange members acquire a greater amount of resources (or exchange outcomes) and a higher level of role outcomes as well as career outcomes, compared to those with the low or intermediate vertical exchange.

An examination on the effect of exogenous variables presented in Chapter VIII helps us evaluate the inclusion function of vertical exchange in terms of rigidity (number of barriers, permeability, and filtering properties; Schein, 1971) of its boundary. First, the results displayed in Table 51 and 52 indicated that none of the structural variables play a predominant "filtering" function for the vertical relations between the supervisor and his subordinate. However, for the newcomer, structural barriers as a whole accounted for about 20 percent ($R = .45$) of the variance in vertical exchange. This percentage was found to be twice as high as that for the supervisor ($R = .32$), indicating that from the eyes of the subordinate, structural aspects of his career role stand in his way as barriers difficult to "permeate" for reaching his supervisor. Second, the results displayed in Tables 53 and 54 indicated that the supervisor uses the personal background data of his subordinate as a boundary to the vertical relation ($R = .44$), more systematically than does the subordinate ($R = .32$). Especially, potential of the subordinate and one of the educational background variables (private versus public university) characterized the filtering properties for the inclusion boundary of the supervisor's exchange. The above result is very interesting when we consider the fact that the information on newcomer's potential assessed upon recruitment was kept confidential from the supervisors. Third, Table 55 suggested that the structural and background variables combined (R_2^2), explain 26 and 30 percent of the variance in vertical exchange reported by the newcomer and the supervisor respectively. Although for both attempts the regression equations failed to reach a significant level, the effect of the filtering properties seems to be substantial relative to the "net" contribution of the endogenous VE variables.

Generally speaking, the results discussed above indicate that except for the AS potential factor, and a college dummy variables whose effect was hard to explain, none of the exogenous variables displayed a single, most significant filtering effect upon the path of vertical exchange. Given the diversified effects of exogenous variables, the following four variables were subject to further examination as to their impact upon vertical exchange. For these variables, the results of sign tests presented in Chapter VIII suggested that they have a consistent effect not only upon vertical exchange but also upon all other dependent variables reported by the newcomer and his supervisor. (1) Personality type: a consistent positive effect of personality type preferred by the DEPART organization implies that this variable might have been used as a criterion to include newcomers into an "inner circle." If this is true, it is expected that a personality type of the newcomer dichotomized into the Epileptic versus others may have a significant effect upon vertical exchange reported by the newcomer and his supervisor during three years. (2) Job type: The result of a sign test indicated that those newcomers with nonsales type jobs may be in a better position to pass the inclusion boundary in terms of vertical exchange with their supervisors. If this is true, the job type factor will show a consistent effect upon vertical exchange reported across all time periods. (3) Work location: In Table 51, the work-location dummy variable, Kobe showed a consistent pattern of effects, in contrast to Tokyo, upon the newcomers' reports. In addition, the dummy variable for Kyoto displayed significant contributions to Job Needs reported by the supervisors in Table 52. These findings suggest that there might be a systematic difference among organizations operating in different regions with respect to the "climate" on inclusion boundaries. (4) Supervisor change: As mentioned frequently, newcomers changed vertical exchange partners during the first three years. For those newcomers who experienced disruptions in dyadic relations, old ties were broken and the new process of passing inclusion boundaries had to be repeated with new supervisors. This suggests that the more frequently the newcomer changes a partner in dyadic exchange, the less likely are the chances for him to establish the "in-group" relationship with his supervisor.

The above four hypotheses were tested using a repeated-measure ANOVA design with each of the boundary conditions taken as an independent variable, and vertical exchange and job performance measured at five different time periods as dependent variables. Results of the analysis indicated that the first three factors, personality type, job type and work location, do not have any systematic effect upon the dependent variables. On the other hand, frequency of supervisor change experienced by the newcomer produced a significant result. Next, the effect of supervisory changes revealed by the ANOVA study will be discussed in more detail.

1. Instability of a Vertical Dyad Linkage

Table 58 displays frequency of the supervisor changes which occurred to the newcomer after the first year. Supervisor changes took place for all newcomers during the first year because of the temporary assignments during the probationary period, and job rotation thereafter within the department of their formal assignment. However, Table 58 indicates that changes in dyadic relations occurred rather frequently even after the first year, especially between the First Year and Wave 4 (39 percent), and between Wave 6 and Wave 7 (64 percent). Table 58 also displays that after the first year 44 percent of newcomers experienced the change of supervisors more than twice, 40 percent of them once, and only 16 percent of them maintained the same supervisor, by the end of the third year. As Table 12 indicates, these changes took place mainly within the department of original assignment. However, information on the nature of supervisor changes – who has moved (the supervisor moved in, or the newcomer moved out?), and for what reasons (promotions, job rotations, or business needs?) – is not available. The impact of the supervisor change may be different depending upon how the change actually occurred. Therefore, for the present analysis the effect of supervisor changes will be examined at the most generalized level: i.e., the effect of instability of dyadic relations upon the newcomer's progress during the early phases of career development.

Table 59 displays the test-retest reliability of factor scales calculated separately for those who experienced supervisor changes and those who did not, between the First Year and Wave 4, and between Wave 6 and Wave 7. For the period between the First Year and Wave 4, newcomers who experienced supervisor changes showed significantly lower test-retest reliabilities in severity of dyadic problems and in receiving leadership support, compared to the one registered by those who maintained the

Table 58

Frequencies of Changing Supervisors

I. Frequency Between Waves

	Wave 3 to Wave 4	Wave 4 to Wave 5	Wave 5 to Wave 6	Wave 6 to Wave 7
Changed	31	19	7	51
Same	49	61	73	29
Percent Changed	39%	24%	9%	64%
Total N	80	80	80	80

II. Number of Times of the Supervisor Change after the First Year (N = 80)

Zero Times	One Time	Two Times	Three Times
13	32	29	6
(16%)	(40%)	(36%)	(8%)

III. History of the Supervisor Change

Change Group		First Year to Wave 4	Wave 4 to Wave 5	Wave 5 to Wave 6	Wave 6 to Wave 7
Zero	(n = 13)	0	0	0	0
One Time	(n = 32)	7	6	2	17
Two Times	(n = 29)	18	9	3	28
Three Times	(n = 6)	6	4	2	6
Total	(N = 80)	31	19	7	51

Table 59

Test-Retest Reliability for Those Who Experienced Change in the Dyadic Combination Between the First Year and Wave 4, and Between Wave 6 and Wave 7

Factor Scale	First Year to Wave 4			Wave 6 to Wave 7		
	C (31)	UC (49)	Total (80)	C (51)	UC (29)	Total (80)
Newcomer's Report						
Vertical Exchange	47	69	62	29*	72	45
Job Problem: Frequency						
Dyadic Problems	33	64	52	39	63	46
Climate Problems	51	60	55	62	55	60
Job Problem: Severity						
Dyadic Problems	44	72	63	52	71	58
Climate Problems	46*	75	65	62	68	64
Job Need: Receiving						
Leadership Support	65	77	72	70	79	73
Job Enrichment	35*	73	58	22*	76	44
Job Need: Preferred						
Leadership Support	68	62	63	67	47	60
Job Enrichment	35	51	42	59	57	57
Role Disillusionment						
Role Content	40	69	67	63	53	62
Profitability	66	67	67	63	53	62
Organizational Commitment						
Value of Organization	63	75	69	64	65	64
Risk of Committing	75	67	70	62	55	56

Table 59 (continued)

Test-Retest Reliability for Those Who Experienced Change in the Dyadic Combination Between the First Year and Wave 4, and Between Wave 6 and Wave 7

Factor Scale	First Year to Wave 4			Wave 6 to Wave 7		
	C (31)	UC (49)	Total (80)	C (51)	UC (29)	Total (80)
Supervisor's Report						
Vertical Exchange	56	59	58	-04*	67	21
Job Need: Providing						
Leadership Support	48	65	57	06*	55	25
Job Enrichment	26*	65	47	11*	57	31
Job Need: Preferred						
Leadership Support	40	66	54	41	69	52
Job Enrichment	11*	70	46	06*	74	40
Job Performance	30*	64	51	33*	72	46
Success Potential	27	59	44	21*	62	36

Figures denote Pearson correlation coefficients with decimal points omitted.

C   Changed supervisor.
UC   Unchanged supervisor.

*Correlation for the Change group is different from the one for the Unchange group at the $p < .05$ level of significance.

same supervisors during that period. However, for other variables the reliability coefficients for the newcomers' reports did not show any significant differences between the change and nonchange groups. On the other hand, reliability for the supervisor's reports indicated that when the newcomer changes supervisors for one reason or another, reports of the "new" supervisor on his subordinate show considerable discrepancy from those of the "old" supervisor. Especially, in Table 59 supervisors' reports suggested that there exists a significant difference in test-retest reliability for job enrichment (for both providing and preferred dimensions) and job performance between the change and nonchange groups.

Discontinuity of supervisors' reports upon changes in dyadic relations seems to be much more severe between Wave 6 and Wave 7. For that period, almost all reliabilities calculated for the change group showed significantly lower coefficients compared to those for the nonchange group. Moreover, the coefficients themselves dropped to a nonsignificance level except for leadership support preferred and job performance for the supervisor change group. During the same time period, the newcomers' reports displayed a significant difference in reliability coefficients only for vertical exchange and job enrichment received between the change and nonchange groups. The differential effect of supervisor change between the newcomers' and the supervisors' reports is primarily attributable to continuity or discontinuity of reporters. That is, the 51 supervisors who made reports on their newcomers at Wave 7 were different persons from those who did so at Wave 6. This implied that for the 51 supervisors, the test-retest reliability denotes a "between-reporters" correlation, while for all newcomers and the remaining 29 supervisors it denotes a "within-reporters" correlation. Nonetheless, between-reporters test-retest reliability for job performance remained at significance level as follows: a .30 correlation between the First Year and Wave 4 (p < .05), and a .33 correlation between Wave 6 and Wave 7 (p < .01). This result indicates that despite the change of supervisors, the newcomers' job performance tends to remain static between the two monitoring periods.

In sum, Table 59 indicates that the relatively low level test-retest reliability for the supervisors' reports can be attributable to the discontinuity of reporters. When the within-reporter consistency is maintained, supervisors' reports produced just as high test-retest reliability as the one for newcomers' reports. Second, it seems that the nature of supervisor change which occurred between Wave 6 and Wave 7 is different from that which occurred between the First Year and Wave 4. For the former, changes are not only more extensive, but are also more disruptive: supervisors' reports have lost consistency from the preceding period completely in both vertical exchange and job needs providing scales. Also, the newcomers' reports on vertical exchange and job enrichment showed a significant difference in reliability reflecting this change. Third, disruptiveness of the supervisor change which occurred between Wave 6 and Wave 7 was confirmed by the ANOVA results: that is, means for vertical exchange, leadership support and job enrichment reported by change supervisors during that time period were all found significantly lower ($p < .01$) compared to those reported by the noncharge supervisors. However, the performance ratings and all of the newcomers' reports showed no such differences. Four, the above results suggest that, in general, changing a partner of vertical exchange has a negative effect upon responses that follow immediately after the change. Results of regression analyses displayed in Tables 51 and 52 also indicated a systematic positive effect of maintaining a dyadic partnership upon both newcomers' and supervisors' reports at Wave 4. These findings confirm the "short-term" negative effect of changing a supervisor.

2. Supervisor Change as an Exclusion

A "long-term" effect of changing supervisors was examined using information on the number of times a supervisor change occurred during the period after the first year for each newcomer. It was hypothesized that those newcomers who experienced frequent supervisor changes may have been deprived of chances to pass inclusion boundaries through vertical exchange with their supervisors, compared to those who could have a relatively stable partnership with their supervisors throughout the research periods after the First Year. This hypothesis was tested using a number of times of supervisor change, shown in Table 58, as an independent variable, and vertical exchange and job performance measured at five different points in time as dependent variables for the repeated-measure analysis of variance design. However, this design of analysis represented neither a true "control group" design (comparison between the change and nonchange groups), nor a simple "ex post facto" design (Campbell and Stanley, 1963). Rather, it denoted a "summary" of a series of ex post facto studies (or control group studies) that should be performed at each time period based on historical information on supervisor changes. Thus, ANOVA probabilities implied validity of *description*, instead of *prediction*, on the effect of frequency of changing supervisors.

Figure 43 displays the result of ANOVA on vertical exchange reported by the supervisors at five different time periods, using the four newcomer groups based on frequencies of their changing supervisors

Figure 43

Vertical Exchange Reported by the Supervisor for the Four
Newcomer Groups Based on Frequency of Their Changing
Supervisors after the First Year: C_3 (Changed Three Times),
C_2 (Twice), C_1 (Once), and C_0 (No Change)

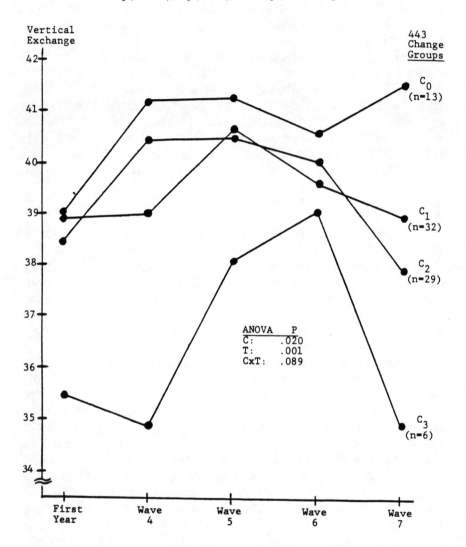

after the first year. Figure 43 clearly displays that those newcomers who have experienced the most frequent changes in vertical dyad linkages (the C_3 group) received the lowest level of vertical exchange reported by their supervisors across all time periods. On the other hand, those who could maintain the same supervisor until the end of the third year (the C_0 group) had vertical exchange reported by their supervisor at the highest level over time, while those who changed once (C_1) or twice (C_2) stayed between the above two extreme groups.

Two interesting findings must be pointed out. First, Figure 43 indicates that those who eventually had to change supervisors three times by the end of the third year were different from other group members, even from the beginning of the process. That is, the C_3 group members could not pass inclusion boundaries in terms of vertical relationships with their supervisors during the starting year of their career. The ANOVA test applied to the First Year data separately indicated that the supervisor's treatment of C_3 group newcomers, in terms of vertical exchange, is significantly lower ($p < .01$) than that for the other group members. The fact that all C_3 members changed supervisors for the Wave 4 period (see Table 58, III) may indicate that they were spun out from the vertical relation during the First Year and "passed" to the hand of other supervisors for the Wave 4 period to start new relations. Figure 43 indicates that this change made the situation worse; the C_3 group members were placed in the most peripheral position under the new supervisors at Wave 4. The situation after Wave 4 again coincided with their history of supervisor changes. The level of vertical exchange was the highest at Wave 6 during which the vertical linkages for the C_3 group members showed relative stability just once within three years. But, vertical relations were again exacerbated at Wave 7, because all C_3 group members were deported from old ties and passed to the new supervisors during the period between Wave 6 and Wave 7.

The next point of interest is a divergence among change groups during Wave 6 and Wave 7. In Table 59, we found that the supervisor change between Wave 6 and Wave 7 was highly disruptive. According to Figure 43, disruption occurred because supervisor change between Wave 6 and Wave 7 reinforced the preceding trend. That is, the C_3 and C_2 group members, all of whom changed their supervisors during that period (see Table 58, III), had a lower level of vertical exchange at Wave 7 reported by their new supervisors, while the C_0 group colleagues had high and increasing vertical exchange at the same time period. An ANOVA performed to examine the above group differences produced a highly significant group effect ($p < .001$) based on the Wave 7 data.

Figure 44 displays the result of a repeated-measure ANOVA applied to job performance. A pattern of mean differences is basically

Figure 44

Job Performance for the Four Newcomer Groups Based on
Frequency of Their Changing Supervisors after the First Year:
C_3 (Changed Three Times), C_2 (Twice), C_1 (Once), and C_0 (No Change)

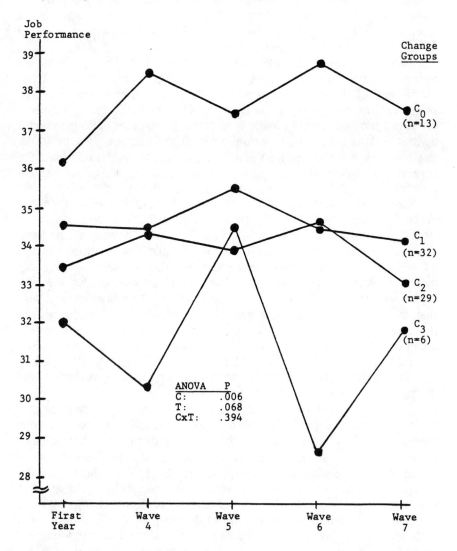

the same as the one for vertical exchange: the C_0 group members received the highest ratings and the C_3 group members the lowest ratings over time, while the C_1 and C_2 group members stayed between the above two groups. Again, ANOVA tests conducted separately based on the First Year and Wave 7 data produced significant group effects (both at $p < .01$ level) upon job performance.

Table 60 displays a summary of the supervisors' reports based on the four change groups. For this part of the analyses, supervisors' responses were aggregated over the six different time periods and were divided by the number of monitoring points. Then, these composite measures were subject to one-way analysis of variance based on the four supervisor change groups. The results shown in Table 60 indicate that the number of times of changing the supervisor had a systematic negative effect upon outcomes of career progress reported by the supervisor. Especially, mean differences were found to be most conspicuous between the two contrasting groups, the C_0 and the C_3, while between the C_1 and C_2 groups the differences seemed to be less clear. However, the same design of analysis administered for the newcomers' reports did not produce any significant results, although a pattern of mean differences among the four groups looked consistent with the one for the supervisors' reports. For example, the means for vertical exchange and role disillusionment reported by the C_3, C_2, C_1 and C_0 newcomers were found to be 27.8, 32.2, 32.0 and 33.8 ($p < .201$), and 39.0, 42.3, 40.4 and 44.2 ($p < .211$), respectively.

In summary, the results presented in this section may point to the following conclusions about the relationship between supervisor change and inclusion boundaries. (1) Instability of the dyadic partnership during the first three years for career development can be characterized as a failure to pass inclusion boundaries in terms of the vertical exchange relation with the supervisor. Especially, for a small group of newcomers (the C_3 group), low vertical exchange and poor job performance during the first year triggered the vicious circle of low VE $\rightarrow$ supervisor change $\rightarrow$ low VE, for the later course of their career development. (2) On the other hand, a small group of newcomers (the C_0 group) who could move deeply into vertical exchange relations with their supervisors, were identified as those having quite a stable dyadic partnership across three years. For these newcomers, the cycle of events was just the opposite of the one for the C_3 group colleagues. That is, high vertical exchange and job performance during the first year strengthened the partnership between the newcomer and his supervisor to a stronger resource-exchange relationship for the next phase of role development. Then, vertical exchange for the subsequent phases made it possible not only to maintain high job performance for the newcomer, but also to

Table 60

Supervisor's Reports Averaged over Time Based on the Newcomer Groups in Terms of Number of Times of Supervisor Change During Three Years: C_3 (Three Times), C_2 (Twice), C_1 (Once), and C_0 (No Change)

Supervisor's Report	Means	for the	Change	Group	ANOVA Probability
	C_3 (n = 6)	C_2 (n = 29)	C_1 (n = 32)	C_0 (n = 13)	
Vertical Exchange	35.8	38.9	38.8	40.1	.020
Job Need: Providing					
Leadership Support	20.8	23.3	23.3	25.0	.029
Job Enrichment	23.3	25.2	26.3	27.8	.001
Job Performance	30.5	32.6	33.3	36.2	.007
Success Potential	9.5	10.3	10.5	11.4	.018

resist outside intervention to divorce the established dyadic linkage between the supervisor and his subordinate. Thus, by the end of the third year, the difference between the most included (C_0) and the most excluded (C_3) became very wide, especially from the eyes of the supervisor. (3) However, the number of times of supervisor change did not necessarily have a significant relationship with the AS potential and career outcomes, although a pattern of mean differences seems to be consistent with previous findings. For example, the mean AS scores for the C_3, C_2, C_1 and C_0 group members were found to be 46.5, 48.8, 50.2, and 50.8 ($p < .606$), respectively, while those for the Potential Index were 48.8, 49.8, 50.1, and 50.8 ($p < .433$), respectively. This result suggests that although the stability of the dyadic relation affects the level of vertical exchange, it does not necessarily determine career outcomes. Rather, the result suggests that vertical exchange itself determines both outcomes and dyadic stability for the career progress simultaneously.

3. Vertical Exchange as a Measure of Inclusion

To examine the role of vertical exchange of facilitating newcomers in passing inclusion boundaries for their career development during the first three years, the "cumulative" effect of vertical exchange upon outcomes was examined using methods of univariate and multivariate analyses of variance. For these analyses, it was assumed that those newcomers who had been within an inner inclusion circle, in terms of vertical exchange throughout all of the research period, would show a systematically different set of outcomes derived from the inside position of leader-member relations. Figure 45 illustrates the hypothetical relationship between the inclusion boundaries and the outcomes of development. When the level of inclusion increases from X_1 to X_2, it is hypothesized that the outcome level will shift from Y_1 to Y_2. To what extent a unit change in X is associated with an increase in Y may depend on: (1) the total amount of resources available to the leader's discretion, and (2) the leadership strategy regarding how to establish a linkage between outcomes and the inclusion level (Graen and Cashman, 1975; Oldham, 1976).

The result presented in Chapter VI suggests that the role of the first-year vertical exchange can be interpreted as a facilitator for passing inclusion boundaries for the subsequent time periods. Moreover, we have learned that vertical exchange based on any of the other monitoring points after the first year tends to have stronger predictive validity of job performance and career outcomes, compared to the one based on the first year (see Tables 23 and 27). These results indicate that the function of vertical exchange, as a facilitator for passing inclusion boundaries, has been operating continuously and with a cumulative effect wave by wave

Figure 45

Inclusion Boundaries and Outcome Levels

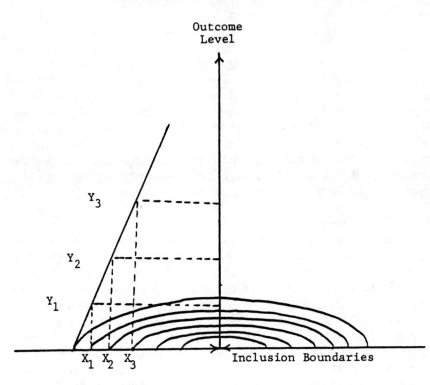

throughout all three years. Thus, it is assumed that the vertical exchange scale aggregated over the six different monitoring periods will be a strong measure of inclusion that the newcomer achieved during the first three years in the DEPART organization.

The above hypothesis was examined in the following manner. First, vertical exchange scores reported by the newcomer on and after Wave 2 were summed and divided by a number of monitoring points to construct an aggregated vertical exchange scale. Then, using this aggregated scale, newcomers were classified into the following three groups which served as a factor for the multivariate analysis of variance: Low (n = 27), Mid (n = 26), and High (n = 27) VE groups. Second, the outcome variables reported by the newcomer and his supervisor were also transformed into aggregate scales in the same manner as that applied to vertical exchange. Then, following the diagram illustrated in Figure 4, outcome measures were grouped into the following three sets for the MANOVA study: exchange outcomes, role outcomes, and career outcomes. Finally, within each outcome set, three VE groups were subject to comparison with respect to equality of mean vectors. The null hypothesis on equality of mean vectors was evaluated using Bartlett's chi-square approximation to the distribution of Wilks lambda (Tatsuoka, 1971). Whenever the null hypothesis was rejected the univariate analysis of variance was performed to find which outcome variables in a given set made a difference among the VE groups.

Table 61 displays results of multivariate and univariate analysis of variance applied to a set of exchange outcomes. Examination on equality of mean vectors for the newcomers' reports among three VE groups indicated that three groups are systematically different (MANOVA P < .001) with respect to the level of exchange outcomes achieved during the first three years for career progress. In Table 61, the High VE group members' who are considered to have been in the innermost position, reported that they received the highest leadership support and job enrichment over three years, and also the highest job challenge given during the Wave 7 period. Moreover, for the High VE group members, the average level of job problems experienced during three years was the lowest in terms of both frequency and severity of the problems encountered. On the other hand, for the Low VE group members, the situation was found just the opposite. They received the most meager support and job enrichment opportunities during three years. Thus, by the end of the third year they reported that their roles were less central to the operation of their work unit and task demands on their jobs were less challenging. Also, they experienced the highest level of job problems throughout the research period. In Table 61, the Mid

Table 61

Univariate and Multivariate Analysis of Variance on Exchange Outcomes
Based on the Vertical Exchange Groups, Using Measures Aggregated over
Five Different Time Periods (N=80)

| Outcome Variables | Mean for the VE Groups | | | ANOVA | ω2 |
	Low (n=27)	Mid (n=26)	High (n=27)		
Newcomer's Report					
Job Need: Receiving					
Leadership Support	13.9	18.7	21.9	.001	.606
Job Enrichment	16.7	20.7	24.5	.001	.435
Job Challenge					
Centrality	15.9	22.2	26.6	.001	.325
Task Demand	13.9	17.3	21.1	.001	.250
Job Problem: Frequency					
Dyadic Problems	33.4	30.8	27.9	.001	.244
Climate Problems	20.5	19.3	17.9	.018	.075
Job Problem: Severity					
Dyadic Problems	35.6	34.2	31.5	.028	.064
Climate Problems	19.7	19.3	16.9	.096	.034
Probability for the MANOVA Test:				.001	
Supervisor's Report					
Job Need: Providing					
Leadership Support	21.9	23.7	24.6	.001	.159
Job Enrichment	25.1	26.2	27.8	.001	.135
Job Challenge					
Centrality	24.1	26.5	27.6	.001	.038
Task Demand	20.1	21.7	21.7	.210	.014
Vertical Exchange	37.3	39.0	40.1	.001	.143
Probability for the MANOVA Test:				.018	

VE newcomers reported that the overall level of exchange outcomes was mediocre: their inclusion level seemed to be "deeper" than that for the Low VE group, but not deep enough compared to their High VE colleagues.

A MANOVA test performed for the supervisors' reports on exchange outcomes produced results to support the findings discussed above: Bartlett's approximation to the Wilks lambda ($\lambda = .750$) calculated for testing equality of mean vectors, yielded a chi-square ($\chi^2 = 21.5$) large enough to reject the null hypothesis at the (p < .018) level of significance. Within the supervisors' reports, a pattern of mean differences among three VE groups clearly confirmed what the newcomers reported. That is, supervisors indicated that they provided the highest level of leadership support, job enrichment, and job challenge to the High VE subordinates, followed by the Mid and Low group members. Moreover, vertical exchange reported by the supervisor was found consistent with what the newcomer reported on the same subject. This finding suggests that an agreement existed between the newcomer and his supervisor regarding the average level of inclusion of the newcomer into the resource system of their work unit over the three-year period for career progress. The results of univariate tests indicated that all outcomes examined in Table 61 are associated with vertical exchange, except severity of climate problems, and task demand reported by the supervisor. The result implies that the inclusion function of vertical exchange is very systematic in determining the level of exchange outcomes.

The omega squares (ω^2) (Fleiss, 1969; Vaughan and Corballis, 1969; Winer, 1971) reported in Table 61 suggest that vertical exchange is most closely associated with Job Need Receiving followed by Job Challenge, and Job Problem within outcomes reported by the newcomer. Based on the aggregated measures, vertical exchange "explained" (Fleiss, 1969) about 61 and 44 percent of variance in leadership support and job enrichment received respectively by the newcomer. Another important resource outcome, job challenge, also showed a close association with vertical exchange: i.e., about 33 and 25 percent of the variance was explained for centrality and task demand respectively. The association between vertical exchange and supervisors' reports became weaker. In Table 61, ω^2s for the supervisors' reports ranged from .014 to .159, indicating that "between" subjects the VE scale may explain maximally about 16 percent of the variance in one of the exchange outcomes.

The same design of analysis was employed to examine the effects of vertical exchange upon role outcomes. In Figure 4 role outcomes were defined as a set of newcomers' work attitudes (attitudes toward his organization, his career role, and the task itself) and immediate organizational outcomes of his role behaviors (performance ratings). Table 62 displays the results of the analysis conducted for a set of attitude variables reported by the newcomer. In Table 62, Job Satisfaction is based on an instrument administered at Wave 7 while all other scales are based on the aggregated scores. Both ANOVA and MANOVA tests produced highly significant results indicating that the level of inclusion measured by the aggregated vertical exchange is systematically connected with personal outcomes of career development for the newcomer. That is, the High VE group members reported that the organization has been much more valuable for them compared to the report made by their Mid and Low VE colleagues. Also, they experienced the lowest level of disillusionment (the highest level of feeling of staying) with respect to their role content and profitability of their organization, followed by the Mid and Low VE group members. Two different measures of job satisfaction produced a consistent pattern of mean differences. First, in terms of need deficiency (D^2) the High VE members reported the lowest level with respect to both leadership support and job enrichment, followed by their Mid and Low VE colleagues. Second, job satisfaction measured at Wave 7 using a 7-item instrument confirmed what the newcomers reported in terms of discrepancy scores, i.e., the High VE members reported the highest level of job satisfaction followed by the Mid and Low VE members.

Estimates of omega squares displayed in Table 62 indicate that the aggregated vertical exchange can explain about 14 to 54 percent of the variance in most of the important attitude scales administered for our study. The VE factor was found most strongly associated with the newcomer's disillusionment on the content of his role, followed by need deficiency, job satisfaction, and organizational commitment variables.

Finally, a set of career outcomes were subject to the analysis for examining the extent to which passing inclusion boundaries would lead to the achievement of the most complex criterion outcomes of career progress. Table 63 displays the results of this analysis. Job performance and success potential scales aggregated over six monitoring periods were included in a set of career outcomes for the MANOVA test, together with the original four career outcome measures evaluated at the end of the third year. The MANOVA results indicate that vertical exchange that the newcomer experienced with his supervisor during three years explains career outcomes with a very high level of significance (p < .001). The High VE group members were found to have been rated at the highest level by their supervisors with respect to job performance and success potential followed by the Mid and Low VE members. Furthermore, by the end of the third year, the High VE group members

Table 62

Univariate and Multivariate Analysis of Variance on Role Outcomes Based on the Vertical Exchange Groups, Using Measures Aggregated over Five Different Time Periods (N=80)

| Outcome Variables | Mean for the VE Groups | | | ANOVA | ω2 |
	Low (n=27)	Mid (n=26)	High (n=27)		
Organizational Commitment					
Value of Organization	37.7	41.7	44.6	.001	.139
Risk of Committing	14.3	13.9	15.7	.120	.029
Role Disillusionment					
Role Content	36.1	41.3	47.5	.001	.539
Profitability	28.0	29.8	31.2	.032	.061
Need Deficiency					
Leadership Support	26.9	11.2	7.0	.001	.331
Job Enrichment	10.8	3.9	1.4	.001	.267
Job Satisfaction	14.1	16.2	20.3	.001	.258
Probability for the MANOVA Test:				.001	

Table 63

Univariate and Multivariate Analysis of Variance on Job Performance and Career Outcomes Based on the Vertical Exchange Groups, Using Measures Aggregated over Five Different Time Periods (N=80)

| Outcome Variables | Mean for the VE Groups | | | ANOVA | ω^2 |
	Low (n = 27)	Mid (n = 26)	High (n = 27)		
Job Performance	31.1	33.6	35.1	.001	.153
Success Potential	10.0	10.7	10.7	.063	.044
Right Type	8.7	9.5	10.6	.009	.091
Potential Index	48.1	49.7	52.9	.002	.132
Performance Index	47.5	49.5	51.4	.089	.036
Bonus	1398	1397	1409	.042	.055
Probability for the MANOVA Test:				.001	

showed a significantly high level of achievement in terms of Right Type ratings, Potential Index, Performance Index and the amount of Bonus, compared to their Low and Mid VE colleagues. Although two of the outcome measures failed to reach a significance level for the ANOVA tests, vertical exchange still had a strong effect upon career outcomes as a whole. The omega squares reported in Table 63 indicate that the explanatory power of the VE scale for career outcomes seems to be weaker compared to the one for the other outcome sets. The ω^2s ranged from .036 for the Performance Index to .153 for aggregated job performance.

Evidence raised in the percent analysis suggests that the level of vertical exchange is closely associated with a newcomer's position for inclusion into a structure of the work unit. Results displayed in Tables 61, 62, and 63 tell us that vertical exchange relates systematically to the level of resource outcomes, role outcomes, and career outcomes achieved by the newcomer during the three years. These results provide evidence to support the following proposition about the role of vertical exchange: as a facilitator for passing inclusion boundaries, vertical exchange functions in such a manner that the higher the level of vertical exchange, the deeper one gets into the structure of resource allocation within the work organization. As a result, the deeper one gets, the higher becomes the level of outcomes from the process of career development.

II. Organizational Consequences of Career Progress

In Chapter I, it was emphasized that the organization must distribute its limited resources to enhance commitment and investment of the individual on the one hand, and to increase the value of human capital to the organization on the other. As Locke (1976) suggested, the supervisor is an "agent" for practicing this organizational requirement. According to him, the supervisor, as an agent, can act as a "value facilitator" for his subordinate to help him attain the desired values associated with his organizational roles, i.e., (a) task-related values: interesting and challenging work, help in attaining work goals, freedom from interruption, good equipment, and (b) *rewards for task performance*: promotion, pay raises, verbal recognition, and so on. The results presented in the preceding chapters indicated that the value facilitating role of the supervisor can be best performed through vertical exchange relations between the supervisor and his subordinate. In previous discussions, the function of vertical exchange in facilitating the process of the newcomer's career progress has been explored within the boundary of a "lower" level vertical dyad linkage, i.e., the relation between the newcomer and his immediate supervisor. However, past studies suggest that interpersonal processes at a lower level are often influenced by the "upper" level structure, i.e., the supervisor-boss relation (Pelz, 1952; Likert, 1961; Wager, 1965). For example, Pelz (1952) reported that the amount of influence the manager (as a subordinate) claimed with his superior moderates the correlation between the manager's behavior (as a supervisor) toward his subordinates and subordinates' reactions to his treatment. Wager (1965) documented the Likert linking-pin thesis, reporting that the leader who has influence with his superior was found to be more effective in using a supportive leadership style toward his subordinates. Cashman and his associates (1975) conducted a study to explore the impact of the quality of upper vertical exchange upon the dyadic relations at the lower level. They found that the supervisor's position in his vertical relation with the boss had a significant effect upon the behaviors of the supervisor and his subordiante. Especially, it was reported that for the low exchange subordinate reporting to the low supervisor in his vertical relation with his boss, the level of satisfaction was exacerbated relative to the other subordinates (see Figure 2, Chapter IV).

For the present study, it is assumed that the value-facilitating function will be best performed by the supervisor who can link the resources of the upper unit in which he is a member, with those of the lower unit in which he is a leader. A linking-pin function of the supervisor merges the two resource environments to facilitate resource transactions across overlapping work units. Under this situation, the leader will try to exploit the potential "external" (upper-unit) resources to meet the "internal" demands for extra opportunities by his unit members. On the other hand, the same supervisor may try to utilize the given internal resources to an optimal extent in order to achieve the goals of his work unit so that his influence with his boss will be stronger within the upper work unit. The above two assumptions allow us to formulate the following hypotheses to be tested in the present study. (1) Within the upper work unit, the supervisor who has a high level vertical exchange with his boss will be provided "valuable" resources by his boss, and he will also show higher job satisfaction and performance. (2) Generally, the supervisor's position on vertical exchange with his boss will have a significant effect upon the resource conditions (job needs receiving and job challenge) for the newcomer subordinate. (3) Especially, the amount of resources and job peformance will be the highest for the newcomer having high vertical exchange with his supervisor who also enjoys a high vertical relation with his boss.

The first hypothesis simply states that the function of vertical exchange will remain the same regardless of the level of managerial hierarchy to which a dyadic relation belongs. The second hypothesis indicates that the upper vertical exchange may overrule the leader-member relation at the lower level. On the other hand, the third hypothesis suggests that interpersonal processes between the supervisor and his subordinate are basically independent of those between the supervisor and his boss, but the combined effect between the two processes may make a significant difference upon the subordinate (but not upon the boss). The study conducted at Wave 7 provided us with data to test the above hypotheses. During that monitoring period, the same set of questionnaires as those used for the supervisor-subordinate dyad were administered to survey the supervisor-boss dyadic relationships. Under this sampling design, the supervisors who are in a linking-pin position were asked to fill out two different questionnaires: one from the standpoint of a "supervisor" vis-à-vis his newcomer, and another from the standpoint of a "subordinate" vis-à-vis his boss. See Figure 5 for the hierarchical structure of the work unit to which this design of the questionnaire survey was administered.

Following the same method of analysis as advanced by Cashman and his associates (1975), the lower level dyadic unit was "interlocked" with the upper level dyadic unit for the analysis of variance study. First, the vertical exchange reported by the newcomer at the Wave 7 monitoring point was transformed into a dichotomous scale in order to classify the subordinate newcomer into the two (High versus Low) VE groups in the lower level. Likewise, the vertical exchange reported by the supervisor "as a subordinate vis-à-vis his boss" was also converted into a dichotomous scale in order to classify the subordinate supervisor into the two VE groups in the upper level. Combining the above two VE factors produced the following classification system for the two-way analysis of variance with a factorial design: (a) the 18 Low VE subordinates reporting to the Low VE supervisor (the Low-Low dyad), (b) likewise, the 18 Low-High dyads, (c) the 18 High-Low dyads, and (d) the 18 High-High dyads. To get a proportional distribution among subgroups, random sampling had to be made since the original distribution was biased toward the Low-Low and High-High cells due to a slight positive correlation between the two VE scales ($r = .09$). Then, reports derived from participants within each unit were subject to the analysis as dependent variables for the ANOVA test. Table 62 displays the results of the analyses for the dependent variables corresponding to the upper level dyadic relations (see Appendix C for the other upper-level results).

The results shown in Table 64 clearly indicate that vertical exchange

Table 64

ANOVA Results on the Supervisor-Boss Reports
Based on the Interlocked Vertical Exchange
at the Wave 7 Monitoring Period (N=72)

| Variable | Mean for the VE Group[a] | | | | Probability | | |
| | Lower Level | | Upper Level | | Lower Level | Upper Level | Inter-action |
	Low VE (n=36)	High VE (n=36)	Low VE (n=36)	High VE (n=36)			
Supervisor's Report							
Vertical Exchange	38.1	38.1	34.7	41.6	.066	.001	.966
Job Need: Receiving							
Leadership Support	25.5	25.3	23.5	27.3	.687	.001	.687
Job Enrichment	26.8	25.4	23.3	28.9	.070	.001	.445
Job Challenge							
Increased Centrality	28.5	28.9	26.4	31.1	.688	.001	.649
Task Demand	22.0	23.1	21.2	23.9	.212	.002	.709
Job Satisfaction	21.3	21.7	19.2	23.8	.677	.001	.488
Boss's Report							
Job Performance	36.7	37.4	35.2	38.8	.497	.001	.978
Success Potential	10.8	11.4	10.4	11.9	.096	.001	.689
Right Type	10.9	11.2	10.4	11.4	.510	.007	.693

[a]Classification for the ANOVA Test was based on the 18 subjects for each VE subgroup: i.e., the Low-Low, Low-High, High-Low, and High-High groups.

does function within the upper level between the supervisor and his boss in just about the same manner as we have seen between the newcomer and his subordinate within the lower level. This result provides evidence to support the first hypothesis. That is, within the upper dyadic linkage, the supervisor who had a High vertical exchange with his boss acquired a significantly higher level of resources (leadership support, job enrichment, and job challenge) in addition to a higher level of job satisfaction, compared to his colleagues who had Low exchange relations with their bosses. Furthermore, reports by the bosses indicated that the High VE supervisors were rated significantly higher in job performance, success potential, and right-type scales, compared to their Low VE colleagues. Table 64 also shows that the vertical exchange processes taking place between the supervisor and his boss were not affected at all by what was going on at the lower level between him and his newcomer subordinate.

Table 65 displays the results of the same analysis applied to the dyadic relations at the lower level. Vertical exchange reported by the newcomer at Wave 7 had the same pattern of effects upon resource outcomes, job satisfaction, and performance ratings, as we have already discovered based on the first-year vertical exchange scale. Results displayed in Table 65 indicate that hypothesis (3) rather than (2), is more relevant in explaining the effect of the upper structure upon the relationship between the newcomer and his supervisor. That is, the level of vertical exchange that the supervisor maintained with his boss in upper dyadic relations was found to have no generalizable effect upon the resource outcomes reported by his newcomer subordinate. But, it did have such an effect upon the newcomer's job performance ($p < .053$), indicating that those newcomers working under the supervisors who have high vertical exchange relations with their bosses, tend to show a higher level of job performance "in general" (i.e., irrespective of the newcomers' exchange positions with their supervisors), compared to those working under the Low VE supervisors (see Figure 46).

Table 65 indicates that the vertical exchange at the upper level has a systematic effect upon the resource outcomes at the lower level, in interaction with vertical exchange at the lower level. Figure 47 displays this pattern of interaction. In Figure 47, the newcomer's report of task demand on his job appears to be the highest for the High-High group, relative to the other group members. This indicates that High VE newcomers reporting to the supervisors who themselves also enjoy High exchange relations with bosses, have an outstanding position regarding the amount of task demands associated with their jobs at the end of the third year.

Table 65

ANOVA Results on the Newcomer-Supervisor Reports
Based on the Interlocked Vertical Exchange
at the Wave 7 Monitoring Period ($N=72$)

Variable	Mean for the VE Group[a]				Probability		
	Lower Level		Upper Level		Lower Level	Upper Level	Inter-action
	Low VE (n=38)	High VE (n=38)	Low VE (n=38)	High VE (n=38)			
Newcomer's Report							
Vertical Exchange	28.5	39.9	34.3	34.1	.001	.868	.063
Job Need: Receiving							
Leadership Support	18.1	22.3	19.8	20.7	.001	.436	.070
Job Enrichment	19.3	26.6	23.4	22.5	.001	.323	.058
Job Challenge							
Increased Centrality	18.7	25.3	21.4	22.5	.001	.491	.048
Task Demand	15.3	20.0	16.8	18.6	.001	.154	.003
Job Satisfaction	14.6	19.8	17.1	17.3	.001	.868	.272
Supervisor's Report							
Job Performance	32.4	36.3	33.1	35.5	.002	.053	.605
Success Potential	10.6	11.4	10.8	11.2	.065	.456	.534
Right Type	9.0	10.4	9.3	10.1	.009	.145	.703

[a]Classification for the ANOVA test was based on the 18 subjects for each VE subgroup: i.e., the Low-Low, Low-High, High-Low, and High-High groups.

Figure 46

Newcomer's Job Performance Based on
the Interlocked Vertical Exchange Between
the Lower and Upper Levels (N=72)

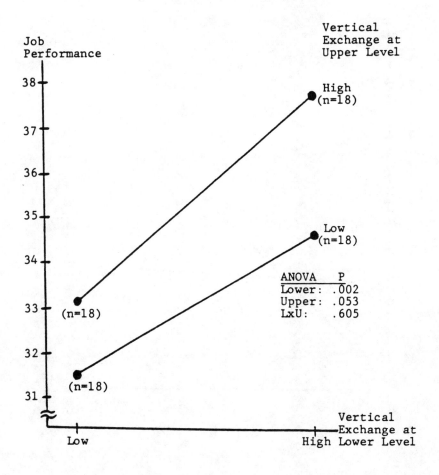

Figure 47

Task Demand Reported by the Newcomer
Based on the Interlocked Vertical Exchange
Between the Lower and Upper Levels (N = 72)

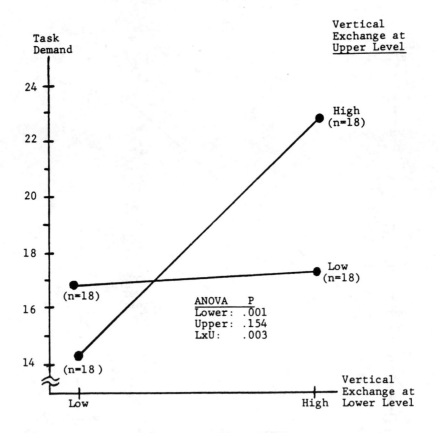

In Figure 47, the position for the High-High group of newcomers looks more conspicuous because of contrasting position that their Low-High group colleagues display. That is, the level of job challenge in terms of task demands appears to be the lowest for the Low VE newcomers reporting to the High VE supervisors. An explanation for this contrasting situation may be the following. In Table 64, the High VE supervisors reported that they had a significantly larger amount of resources received from their bosses compared to their Low VE supervisors. However, the subordinate's report indicated that some of the High VE supervisors may "hold" all these resources without delegating any of them to the subordinate. Thus, for those newcomers working under the non-delegating supervisors, the level of vertical exchange with their supervisors showed the lowest level and the task demands of their jobs seemed least challenging. This situation might have been created, because: (1) the supervisor did not trust his newcomer subordinate, and thus did everything by himself, (2) the supervisor might be very protective of his position; he was afraid of losing any part of the resources given by his boss to his newcomer subordinate, and (3) more than that; the exacerbated position of the Low-High newcomers on task demand as shown in Figure 47, suggests that the supervisor might have taken away a part of the subordinate tasks to make himself look good, or to "enrich" his own supervisory position in the eyes of his colleagues and his superior at the upper level. Either one of the above three incidents or a combination of them may occur only when the supervisor has High vertical exchange with his boss. Otherwise, the newcomer's position in vertical exchange with his supervisor makes no significant difference upon the level of task demands for his job.

Figure 48 displays the mean job enrichment received by the newcomer based on the four vertical exchange groups. Although the interaction effect between the lower and upper vertical exchange failed to reach a significance level ($p < .058$), a position for the Low-High group members again showed exacerbation relative to the other group members. Moreover, examination of the group means for the other resource outcomes (leadership support and centrality) revealed that the Low-High newcomers always have lowest resource positions like those displayed in Figures 47 and 48. The four resource measures shown in Table 65 (two job need and two job challenge scales) were introduced into the multivariate analysis of variance to see if the interlocked vertical exchange would show a significant interaction effect between the lower and upper level vertical exchange upon a set of resource outcomes (Rao's F-ratio approximation $F(4,65)=2.66$; $p < .040$). This result indicates that resources of the upper level become best available to the newcomer when

Figure 48

Job Enrichment Reported by the Newcomer Based on the Interlocked Vertical Exchange Between the Lower and Upper Levels (N = 72)

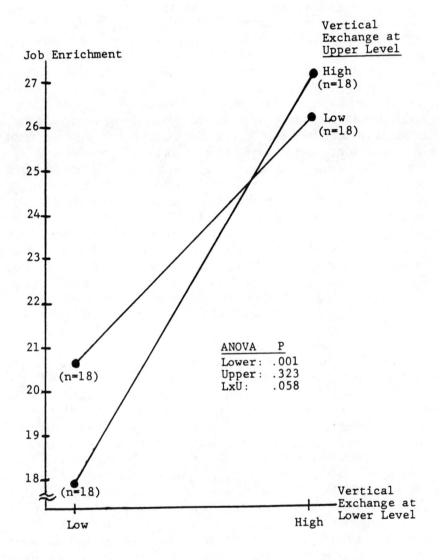

the following two conditions are met: (1) the supervisor has a high level of vertical exchange with his boss, and (2) he is willing to distribute resources acquired from his boss through the high vertical relation to his subordinate in exchange for the latter's contribution to the attainment of group goals.   But, the subordinate's resource position becomes exacerbated when the High VE supervisor refuses transactions between himself and his subordinate.

Results summarized in Tables 64 and 65 may point to the following conclusion about the structure of resource allocation within the overlapping work units.   First, "within" each hierarchical level, the vertical exchange between the leader and his member functions as a facilitator of transactions between resources (or task-related values; Locke, 1976) granted by the leader, and the member's contribution to the work unit in terms of high performance.   Therefore, the higher the level of vertical exchange, the greater the amount of transaction between the member and his leader within each hierarchical level.   Second, there is no general tendency for what the supervisor is doing with his boss to directly affect the exchange relationship between himself and his subordinate in the lower dyad.   The ANOVA results displayed in Table 65 suggest that the main Upper Level effect, in terms of the supervisor's vertical exchange vis-à-vis his boss, does not have any systematic impact upon transactions within the lower level.

Third, transactions "between" hierarchical levels are facilitated when the supervisor played a linking-pin function by promoting exchanges between task-related values and job performance across hierarchical boundaries within the work unit. As shown in Figure 47, the effective linking-pin function of the supervisor provides his subordinate with a very high level of job challenge.   That is, for the linking-pin group (the High-High group in Figure 47): (a) the supervisor himself has a high level resource/performance transaction with his boss buttressed by high vertical exchange, (b) he is also willing to have vertical exchange with his subordinate maintained at a high-level, and finally, (c) this interlocking High-High vertical exchange relation begins to facilitate the *interunit* transactions involving a greater flow of resources and contributions.   These findings about the linking-pin function of the supervisor allow us to construct a generalized view on the structure of resource allocation within the work organization.   Figure 49 illustrates such a structure.

In Figure 49, a linking-pin function is illustrated as an interlocking of two high vertical exchange dyads across the hierarchical boundary. For the other linkages, high level exchange relations (shown using heavy lines) are bounded within either upper or lower level and do not extend

Figure 49

A Structure of Resources Flow Within
the Unit of Work Organization

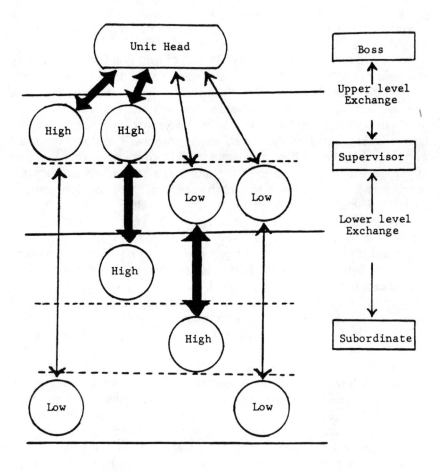

beyond the hierarchical boundary. Moreover, Figure 49 indicates that the newcomer's position within the lower level is a function of the combined effect between the two resource vectors. These findings documented by the present study may provide strong empirical evidence for the notion of the "understructure" of the organization (see Figure 3, Chapter IV) discussed for the study by Cashman and his associates (1975). However, further examinations on the effect of the structure displayed in Figure 49 suggested that it does not necessarily have a significant impact upon the level of career outcomes achieved by the newcomer. That is, among the four career outcomes examined, none of them reflected a significant effect attributable either to the Upper Level factor or to the Lower × Upper interaction. But, Potential Index, Bonus, and Right Type measures produced a significant Lower Level effect. This finding suggests that our sample newcomers were not yet caught tightly by the understructure at the end of the third year, rather they were still "drifting" primarily under the influence of the first-level supervisor for their process of role-making. Of course, drifting does not imply a randomness in the career development process. It has a continuity with the process beginning from the first year. Table 66 displays this continuity.

Table 66

Number and Percentage of Newcomers Recruited into the Wave 7 Understructure from the First-Year Groups Based on the VE (FY) and AS Factors

| VE Understructure at Wave 7 | | First-Year Group | | | |
Lower Level	Upper Level	Low VE Low AS	High VE High AS	Mixed	Total
Low	Low	8 (36%)	5 (20%)	11 (34%)	24
Low	High	6 (28%)	2 (8%)	10 (30%)	18
High	Low	8 (36%)	7 (28%)	5 (15%)	20
High	High	0 (0%)	11 (44%)[*]	7 (21%)	18
Total		22(100%)	25(100%)	33(100%)	N = 80

[*]The percentage is higher than the one for the Mixed Group (21%) at the $p < .05$ level of significance.

Percentages shown in Table 66 denote a selection ratio for the four understructure groups out of the first-year groups defined using the first-year vertical exchange, VE(FY) and the AS potential factors. The results discussed in Chapter VII revealed that those newcomers who have high AS potentials combined with the experience of high vertical exchange during the first year achieved the highest level outcomes for the subsequent periods of career progress, compared to the other group members, especially to the Low VE-Low AS group members. The results displayed in Table 66 suggest that the first-year conditions examined in Chapter VII are also predictive of differentiation of newcomers into the understructure of the organization at the end of the third year. That is, none of the newcomers who came out of the low VE-Low AS first-year group could remain as member of the High-High Structure at Wave 7. On the other hand, from the High VE-High AS group, 44 percent of the newcomers were recruited as members of the most resourceful group at the end of the third year. For the Mixed group (combination of the Low-High and the High-Low first-year groups), the selection ratio was found to be 21 percent. A difference of proportions test (Blalock, 1972) which was attempted to examine the difference between the above two ratios, produced a significant result, indicating that the selection ratio for the High-High first-year group is significantly higher ($p < .05$), compared to the one for the Mixed group. Table 66 also indicates that the Low-Low structural group at Wave 7 recruited more members from the Low-Low first-year group (36 percent), but the result of statistical testing indicated this proportion was not significantly higher compared to the one for the High-High (20 percent) or the Mixed (34 percent) first-year groups.

In sum, the results presented in this chapter point to the following notion of the process of organization career progress. Managerial progress during the early stages in the organization denoted passing inclusion boundaries within the work unit. From the newcomer's point of view, the process of inclusion implied an increasing level of vertical exchange with his supervisor. It was found that to maintain a high level of vertical exchange, a relative stability in the dyadic partnership was imperative. Moreover, there was evidence to suggest that the leader-member relations based on the high level vertical exchange, resist pressures to divorce the partnership. As a result, high vertical exchange reinforced dyadic stability and facilitated the passage of inclusion boundaries. From the standpoint of the organization, inclusion denoted greater transaction between the newcomer and the agent of the organization involving the exchange between resources and contributions. Vertical exchange facilitated this process. Especially, when the supervisor performed a linking-pin function, facilitation was found to be most effective. However, the result of our study suggested that the linking-pin function is available only to a limited group of people, i.e., to those supervisors who connect two vertical dyad linkages across hierarchical boundaries based on the high quality leader member exchange relations. Evidence was raised suggesting that the process of career development predicted based on the first-year conditions, led our sample newcomers into the stage of differentiation based on the understructure of the organization at the end of the third year. However, newcomers were not caught firmly by the understructure, yet they were still in the process of role making primarily bounded within the vertical dyad linkages at the lower level.

Chapter X

Conclusion

1. Role of Vertical Exchange in the Process of Career Development: A Summary of Findings

The vertical exchange measure indicates an efficiency in coordinated behaviors between the two persons working under constraints of the formal organization. First, a factor analysis of the vertical exchange instrument produced the following two dimensions. The first dimension named "dyadic contingency" implied the supervisor's recognition of the subordinate's potentials, his understanding of the subordinate's problems, feedback of his expectations, his willingness to help the subordinate, and exercise of his latitude and flexibility. On the other hand, the second factor, "job latitude" indicated the amount of job latitude given to the subordinate, his contribution, influence, and autonomy on the job. The first dimension refers to trust and understanding between the two persons, while the second one refers to autonomy on the job. The vertical exchange scale used for the present study was constructed by combining the above two dimensions. Therefore, the combined scale implied a set of basic conditions by which the voluntary behaviors between the two individuals were coordinated into a unified activity. Second it was found that the basis of coordination is established by a series of reciprocal behaviors between the supervisor and his subordinate through day-to-day interactions. The result of the analysis indicated that the level of vertical exchange reported by one party is a function of the one reported by the other, being relatively free from the impact of structural variables of the organization and personal background variables of both parties. This finding implied that the level of vertical exchange reflects the amount of interest that one party may have in the other. Third, it was found that vertical exchange determines the level of outcomes from the process of career progress for the newcomer to the organization in a very systematic manner. This result suggests that coordinated behaviors between the leader and his member based on voluntarism and trust, produce desirable outcomes.

Functions that vertical exchange played in the process of management career progress can be summarized as follows:

(1) *Motivation and Learning Functions.* Results presented in Table

38, Chapter VI indicated that the level of vertical exchange reported by the newcomer during the first year of his organizational career has significant predictive validity for all sets of outcomes derived from the process of career progress during the first three years in the organization. Moreover, high test-retest reliability of the first-year vertical exchange indicated that the effect of vertical exchange experienced by the newcomer during the first year penetrated the subsequent time periods, despite the fact that about 85 percent of the newcomers had to change partners for vertical relations during the periods following the first year. This "carry-over" effect of the first-year experience may point to the following motivational and learning functions played by vertical exchange during that time period.

First, it must be noted that all newcomers to the DEPART organization had no prior experience of formal employment. This indicates that working under the bureaucratic structure of the large business organization was a novel experience for them. Thus, they had to learn quickly how to behave in their career role. This learning process posed a host of contingency problems for the newcomers, such as: What are the company expectations? What is the standard for a good job and how does one do it? What are outcomes of high or low performance? What are going to be the targets of their role activities and where is the path to attain them? and how to integrate their career targets with needs and expectations of their supervisors? and so on. These are a set of problems that each newcomer has to solve implicitly or explicitly during the very early stages of his career development. Otherwise, his role activities would lose the anchorage and the perspective for career development. In other words, for the newcomer the first year in the organization is a period in which the basic structure of an "investment function" can be established by learning how to allocate his time and energy in his career role. Evidence presented in this study suggests that those newcomers who could have high vertical exchange relations during the first year solved these contingency problems by coordinating their role activities with those of their supervisors. They could match the target for effort and investment activities with the expectations of their supervisors. This process may have involved newcomer's initiative, (a) to set his goals for role activities, (b) to get his supervisor to recognize these goals, (c) to negotiate with the supervisor for the resources to achieve them, (d) to enhance his endeavor on the job and to get the supervisor's recognition of his performance, and (e) to set higher goals for the next stage of activities. The above processes might have been started by the initiative of the supervisor, but in any event the newcomer learned how to coordinate his activities with those of others. Moreover, as an outcome of experiencing a high level vertical exchange, the newcomer would have acquired skills regarding how to influence other people. The importance of acquiring interpersonal skills has been emphasized by many authors as critical to success in the organization: *interpersonal competence* (Argyris, 1962 and 1970), or *personal impact* (Bray, et al., 1974). It is expected that high vertical exchange relations during the first year gave the newcomer an opportunity to learn how to relate to other people for high performance and progress. And, it is this learning function of vertical exchange that made the first-year experience predictive of outcomes for the subsequent time periods.

A motivational function of vertical exchange appeared very conspicuous when the effect of first-year vertical exchange was moderated by the potential factor of the newcomer. As discussed in Chapter VII, interaction between the two factors produced contrasting motivational effects upon the newcomers, the *success syndrome* effect (Hall and Nougaim, 1968) and the *discouragement effect.* These contrasting effects were caused partly by the "partialness" of the potential factor and partly by the unique character of the manpower development system of the DEPART organization. The success syndrome effect occurred to those who had high potentials for development and at the same time could have a high level vertical exchange at the starting year of their career. For them, motivational processes of career development were characterized by a cycle of mutually reinforcing positive events throughout the three-year period of career progress. That is, (1) high vertical exchange during the first year gave opportunities (leadership support and job enrichment) to a group of high potential newcomers to exercise their potential abilities. Next, (2) a combination of high potential and a resourceful position for role activities enabled this group of newcomers to achieve role outcomes characterized by high job performance and success potential rated by their supervisors, increased organizational commitment, and lowering need deficiency and disillusionment. Then, (3) as a result of achieving these positive outcomes, a group of high potential/high exchange newcomers might have experienced the feeling of "psychological success" (Hall, 1968) or increasing "self-esteem" (Korman, 1967 and 1968). Because of the success in strengthening their role positions both externally and internally, (4) this group of newcomers became more involved in their jobs and expressed a greater desire for higher-order need satisfaction. Then, (5) high job performance and recognized success potential made it possible for the high potential newcomers to engage in high vertical exchange relations with their supervisors for the start of the next phase of activities. Probably because of their high potentials and reinforced needs for growth, a new cycle of events was facilitated toward the higher level of success. Finally, (6) as a result, this particular group of newcomers achieved the highest levels of career outcomes, and had the most challenging tasks by the end of the third year of all their newcomer colleagues. In other words, the high potential newcomers combined with high vertical exchange were plugged into the motivational ladder for "upward spiral" during the first year.

The process of discouragement evolved following just the opposite cycle of events for a group of newcomers who were judged to have high potential but were deprived of the opportunities to realize it due to restricted relations with their supervisors. During the first year, this group of newcomers could not get their supervisors to recognize their potential, expectations, and problems. In addition, their supervisors were reluctant to help them. As a result, these newcomers were most constrained with respect to their latitude on the job regarding authority, influence, and chances of contribution. They reported the lowest amount of resources received from their supervisors. Moreover, they were found to be the most disillusioned, the least committed to the organization, and the most deficient in terms of fulfilling what they wanted on the job throughout the first three years for career progress. The level of job performance also suffered. In fact, it appeared to be lower than that of the low potential newcomers. Thus, they retreated from the task of their role development motivationally: they reported regression in the desire for higher-order need fulfillment relative to the one displayed by the more successful colleagues. Thus, by the end of the third year, their jobs were found to be the least challenging. In addition, the career outcomes achieved by this group of newcomers could only reach the same level as the one achieved by their low potential colleagues by the end of the third year.

In sum, the motivational function of vertical exchange channeled a small group of newcomers into a path for high flying career progress. For the high potential newcomers, the experience of role activities during the first year based on high vertical exchange relations with their supervisors, triggered a cycle of events for success: trust, autonomy, and resources on the job → high job performance → increased commitment, satisfaction and self-esteem → strong need for job enrichment and challenge → increased level of coordination → more trust, autonomy, and so on. On the other hand, for the high potential newcomers who came to accept low vertical relations with their supervisors during the first year, the sequence of events which occured subsequently were quite the opposite. They felt that their potentials were neglected, and that the self-esteem that their potentially high capabilities might have claimed was denied. Thus, the discouragement created by these first-year experiences led about half of the high potential newcomers to a path of a distressing cycle of events. The contrasting effects of the first-year vertical exchange as described above occurred only to a group of high potential newcomers. The contrast was found less conspicuous among a group of low potential newcomers.

(2) *Inclusion Function.* The second function that vertical exchange played in the process of career development was to regulate passage of inclusion boundaries (Schein, 1971) within the work organization. The result of the analysis presented in Chapter IX indicated that the voluntary vertical exchange activities between the newcomer and his supervisor produced differential role positions among newcomers with respect to their "centrality" within the structure of the work organization. The result of analysis indicated that the general level of inclusion measured in terms of the aggregated vertical exchange scores can explain all sets of outcomes associated with the process of career development. Results of MANOVA tests showed that the deeper the level of inclusion, the higher becomes the level of achievement in terms of resource outcomes, role outcomes, and career outcomes. The supervisor's reports suggested that the instability of the dyadic partnership might have a negative impact upon passing inclusion boundaries: the number of times of supervisory change showed a negative effect upon job performance and job needs provided, as well as vertical exchange itself, reported by the supervisor. However, a close examination of the results indicated that instability in dyadic relationships may be a result rather than a cause of the lower inclusion level. That is, it was found that those who experienced very low vertical exchange during the first year were more prone to unstable dyadic relations and lower inclusion levels, compared to those who achieved high vertical exchange at the start of their career. Among our sample newcomers, no variation in the speed of passing hierarchical boundaries was produced during the first three years. However, all results raised by the present study may point us toward prediction that the first hierarchical moves would occur in the near future for the most included newcomers. This hypothesis will be tested by the follow-up study based on company records covering the fourth year, fifth year, and so on.

(3) *Facilitating Vertical Transaction.* From the subordinate's point of view, vertical transaction involved the following two subprocesses: (a) an acquisition of resources from the supervisor for his role activities, and (b) a contribution to help his supervisor and his work unit achieve goals. Results shown in Tables 64 and 65 suggest that the vertical exchange relation is the key to facilitating the above transaction processes. In both

tables, results of the analysis indicated that when the subordinate had a highly coordinated role relationship: (a) he could acquire a larger amount of resources (leadership support, job enrichment, and challenge) sent from his supervisor, (b) the supervisor in turn rated the subordinate's job performance and success potential highly, and (c) he assessed his subordinate as a right-type person for their organization. These findings suggest that the process of resource/performance transaction was facilitated by an increasing level of vertical exchange. Theoretically, vertical exchange can be initiated either by the subordinate or by his supervisor.   However, considering the superiority in both authority and positional resources associated with the supervisory role, it would be easier for the supervisor to take "leadership" in the process of transaction.   Studies conducted by Dansereau and his associates (1975), Graen and Cashman (1975), and Cashman and Graen (1976) suggest that the initiative of the supervisor in the vertical transaction will be better accepted by his subordinate when the supervisor takes a *leadership* strategy based on his expert and reference power, rather than when he takes a *supervision* strategy based on a bureaucratic and coercive power as a basis of influence.

Importance of a supervisor's role as a facilitator of the process of transaction needs to be emphasized. He will be a "sponsor" for the newcomer in the process of career development who provides opportunities for job enrichment and challenge and sends his expectations. He may evaluate the newcomer's behavior and give feedback as to where his subordinate stands and to which direction he is supposed to go. He is responsible for providing the task-related values and resources to help the subordinate develop his role position.   In addition, the task of giving rewards contingent upon the level of job performance achieved by his subordinate must be performed by the supervisor.   Furthermore, he will be primarily responsible for determining the level of career outcomes to be granted to his subordinate by reviewing the quality of investment that his subordinate achieved on a given career role. Finally by performing a role of facilitator, as pointed out above, the supervisor may play an important role for integrating the processes of learning and development into those of task performance. This is a critical function needed to develop the structure for the effective human resource utilization system of the organization.

(4) *Linking-pin Function.* Theoretically, a transaction model based on a single vertical dyad linkage can be interpreted as a special case of a general, linking-pin model that deals with transaction facilitation across hierarchical boundaries involving multiple vertical dyads. Under this generalized model, the role of the supervisor as a facilitator may be

characterized as an "optimizer" (Seashore and Yuchtman, 1967; Campbell, et al., 1970). That is, the linking-pin supervisor as a subordinate vis-à-vis his boss engages in high vertical relations to exploit environmental resources in the upper unit. Then, with these acquired resources, the linking-pin supervisor may facilitate exchange relations with his subordinates in order to induce extra contributions from them to achieve the goals of his work unit. Thus, under this situation the supervisor intersects two different environments ("lower" and "upper") in an attempt to maintain an optimum balance between the two demands: (1) his members' demands for extra resources within the lower level environment, and (2) demands for his (or his group's) contribution to the achievement of goals within the upper level environment.

The results of the analysis based on "interlocked" vertical exchange, suggested that at least the following four types of interunit facilitation were adopted by DEPART supervisors: (a) a group of supervisors trying to optimize dyadic efficiency between the two overlapping units by connecting them with high vertical exchange relations (a linking-pin group), (b) a group of supervisors who tried to maximize the dyadic efficiency within the upper unit by "sacrificing" the one within the lower level (c) those supervisors who facilitated dyadic efficiency within the lower level, but could not initiate the same process within the upper level, and (d) those who failed to link themselves either with their subordinates or with their bosses. These groups represented a part of the "understructure" for distributing the potential resources of the organization. The results of the analysis suggested that the process of career development for our sample newcomers had been under the influence of this understructure since the start of their career, but they were not yet totally captured by the structure at the end of the third year.

2. Systems of Human Resource Development and Interpersonal Processes Within the Organization

In Chapter I, a set of concepts describing the process of human resource development within the organization was presented. Our definition of career development presented in Chapter I indicated that development is a process of increasing the value of one's services by investing in his occupational role and by learning through experience. This definition implied two different processes for career progress occurring within the organization: (a) a process of commitment, investment and achieving high performance on the job (a performance process), and (b) a process of learning, increasing potential, and increasing the value of human assets of the organization (a learning process). A developmental point of view assumed that the individual sets his career targets and goals, and tries to make his role behavior the most instrumental for acquiring skills and knowledge necessary for achieving his goals. On the other hand, demands of the task may require the individual to commit to a given role and invest his time and energy in it so that his performance will contribute to the accomplishment of the goals of the organization. In Figure 1, it is assumed that the role of the organization and the supervisor in the process of career development is to distribute limited resources in order to optimize outcomes from the above two processes. The results presented in this study suggest that a particular aspect of leader-member relations, called vertical exchange, can serve for accomplishing this requirement of the organization. Next, the function of vertical exchange in integrating processes of learning and performance for career progress of our newcomers will be examined.

(1) *Description of the Process.* Integrating functions of vertical exchange in the system of career development displayed in Figure 1 were evaluated in the following manner. First, the high vertical exchange relation helps the newcomer to cope with pressures from the performance process. A key to this process is the understanding between the leader and his member that acquisition (or allocation) of extra resources for role activities is contingent upon the amount of contribution that will be made by the member (or received by the leader). This indicates that valuable performance that the member achieves on a given job provides him with "bargaining" power for acquiring extra resources from the leader. The knowledge of this contingency structure, then, enables the member to commit to his given role, and to invest his time and energy in it to achieve high level job performance. From the supervisor's point of view, support, job enrichment, and challenge given to the member are considered as means to produce the results that help him or his group achieve goals. Thus, the supervisor himself may become more willing to delegate a part of his responsibility to his member with an expectation that the latter will do a good job for him. Under this situation, the member is allowed to take a "bargaining strategy" to cope with performance pressures. As discussed earlier, the nature of bargaining under vertical exchange relations is based upon trust and voluntarism. If the bargaining strategy is a key to promoting the performance process, the following proposition must hold true. (I) Job performance of the member is primarily a function of a level of vertical exchange achieved by the member. Because, as the results presented in previous chapters indicate, high vertical relations enabled the member to acquire means of performance: leadership support, and opportunities for job enrichment and challenge. However, previous analyses also revealed that job performance is determined by (a) the capability of the member (the AS

potential), and (b) stability of dyadic relations over time. Thus, testing of the effect of vertical exchange upon job performance will be attempted by taking into account the effects of these two variables.

In Figure 1, vertical exchange may relate to the learning process in the following manner. Learning implies a process of increasing personal values or the qualifications of the individual toward the attainment of his career goals. The individual member may set up career targets (or a subset of career goals) and use his experiences at work as resources to acquire skills, knowledge, expertise, motivation, and behavioral patterns necessary for achieving the targets. If he succeeds in this attempt, he will choose a next set of targets which is closer to the expected career goals and is more difficult and abstract than the previous targets. Then, as long as his career goals are defined within a framework of the given organization, this value-acquiring process of the individual produces a growth in human assets for the organization. This process of growing personal values may be characterized as "self-directed" activities (McGregor, 1960) of the individual. That is, he will accept targets as his own choosing and his responsibility, find means and resources, be ready to put himself into work, and judge the quality of outcomes by his own standard. Job latitude derived from high vertical exchange between the leader and his member may provide the latter with opportunities to enchance self-directed learning activities on the job. Once the member succeeds in acquiring skills, knowledge, motivations, and behavioral patterns considered valuable in the eyes of the leader, he will "utilize" them by combining the increased personal value of the member with extra responsibilities. This implies that the member may take these extra responsibilities as part of his targets for the effort, and starts the cycle of learning again. If this is the case for our sample newcomers then the following proposition must hold true: (II) growth of personal worth of the newcomer may be explained primarily by the level of vertical exchange that he experienced with his supervisor during the three years. Again, the effect of potentials assessed upon employment and stability in dyadic relations will be accounted for in order to test the above proposition.

Propositions (I) and (II) suggest that under the high vertical exchange relation, the member can formulate his investment function such that the outcomes from both performance and learning processes can be maintained at an optimum level. When the entire processes of career development as displayed in Figure 1 are in full operation over a considerably long period of time, the outcomes from each process at one time period must be the input to determine the level of vertical exchange for the next time period. Therefore, (III) over time the level of vertical exchange is the function of job performance and value of personal resources acquired by the newcomer through experience.

(2) *Results.* The three hypotheses presented above were examined based on the method of regression analysis using the following set of variables. (a) *Vertical exchange:* average vertical exchange scores over six monitoring points (Wave 2 to Wave 7) reported by the focal newcomer (VE-F). (b) *Job performance:* likewise, average performance ratings over six monitoring periods. (c) *Potential Index:* as discussed in the instrument section of Chapter V, this index was developed using information derived from the company's reappraisal of the newcomers' potential conducted at the end of the third year. The reappraisal based on what they called "multiple rater" method, required a team of raters for each newcomer. A rating team commonly consisted of six to seven persons including the superiors (the supervisor and the boss), peers, a personnel staff member, and the focal newcomer himself. Based on the best of their knowledge, a team of raters evaluated the newcomer's potential with respect to technical skills, administrative skills, interpersonal skills, energy, and intelligence. Then, all ratings were aggregated across dimensions and raters into a single Potential Index. For the present analysis, this composite scale was considered as representing the value of personal resources of each newcomer acquired through the three-year experience within the organization. (d) *The AS scale:* newcomer's potential assessed upon recruitment. (e) *Supervisor Change:* The number of times that the newcomer changed a partner of exchange after the first year.

For the first proposition, a regression analysis was run with job performance as a dependent variable and vertical exchange (VE-F), the AS, and supervisor change as dependent variables. For the second proposition, the Potential Index was regressed on the same set of dependent variables as the first one. The hypothesis tested for the above two regressions stated that the VE-F will show a positive, significant contribution to both job performance and Potential Index, holding the AS and Supervisor Change variables constant. For the third proposition, it was hypothesized that both job performance and Potential Index will show positive, significant contributions to the level of vertical exchange, holding the AS and Supervisor Change variables constant. In all three regression equations it was hypothesized that the control variables, the AS and the Supervisor Change, will have positive and negative contributions respectively to all dependent variables. Table 67 displays the results of these regression analyses.

Regression equations No. 1 and 2 shown in Table 67 indicate that vertical exchange reported by the newcomer (VE-F) displayed the hy-

Table 67

Regression Equations for Determining the Relationship Between Job
Performance, Potential Index, and Vertical Exchange (N=80)

Regression				Independent Variable					
	Con	Job Per	Pot Index	AS	Sup Change	VE-F	R	R^2	F
1. Job Performance	23.2**	–	–	.10* (.20)	-1.26** (-.27)	.21** (.29)	.52	.27	9.34
2. Potential Index	34.5**	–	–	.13 (.19)	-.47 (-.08)	.31** (.34)	.44	.19	6.00
3. Vertical Exchange Focal (VE-F)	8.7	.28 (.20)	.25* (.23)	.04 (.05)	-.44 (-.07)	–	.43	.18	4.24

Figures in parentheses denote beta weights.

    * $p < .05$.

   ** $p < .01$.

pothesized effect upon both job performance and Potential Index. Moreover, the VE-F showed the greatest contributions in terms of a standardized unit to the outcomes from both the performance and learning processes.   The AS and Supervisor Change variables also displayed the hypothesized effects, but for the Potential Index regression coefficients of these variables failed to reach a significance level.   This result suggests that personal worth of the newcomer reassessed at the end of the third year can be better explained as an outcome of vertical exchange experiences during three years, rather than as an extension of individual potential identified at the point of employment. This finding implies a strong influence of the vertical exchange experiences upon the process of on-the-job learning during the early phases of career development of the newcomer. Regression No. 3 yielded a result that supports our hypothesis.   Examination of the standardized weights suggested that the average vertical exchange received by the focal newcomer (VE-F) is primarily determined by the level of job performance and reassessed potential of the newcomer. Although the coefficient for job performance ($p < .059$) failed to reach a significance level, its contribution to the VE-F seemed to be as equally important as the one for Potential Index. In fact, a regression run by eliminating the AS and Supervisor Change variables indicated that the explanatory power of the regression equation remained basically at the same level ($R = .42$), with coefficients for both performance and Potential Index showing significant contributions to the VE-F at a $p < .05$ level.

The result of F-tests indicated that all three regressions were significant at the $p < .01$ level. This finding implies that: (a) the structure of career development as illustrated in Figure 1, has been operative for our sample newcomers during the first three years in the DEPART organization, (b) the career development system was primarily regulated by the unique interpersonal relationship called the vertical exchange relation, and (c) the process was partially influenced by exogenous variables, especially by the AS potential factor identified upon recruitment.   However, the potential effect remained less extensive. Rather, it was found that the vertical exchange relation evolved after employment had more systematic influence over the process of career development in terms of both the performance and learning phases.

(3) *Goal Integration.* The results displayed in Table 67 suggest that vertical exchange may claim the fifth integration function in the process of organizational career development.   Traditionally, the *integrationists* viewed this topic either as a problem of incompatibility in the basic nature between the individual and the organization, or as an ultimate answer to solve problems of organizational effectiveness

(McGregor, 1960; Argyris, 1964; Herzberg, 1966; Likert, 1967; Tannenbaum, 1968). However, traditional theories did not necessarily give due considerations to the process of goal integration through career development. According to our framework, the problem of integration denotes effective coping with the pressures of the career environment. Since coping behaviors require the individual to participate in the performance and learning process, effective coping denoted efforts by the individual and the organization to optimize outcomes from the two processes.

For our study, vertical exchange relations between the leader and his member helped integrate the above two subprocesses. First, the high vertical exchange enabled the newcomer to identify his career targets, and to acquire knowledge, skills, motivation, and behavioral patterns which were valued highly by the other members of the organization. Then, these acquired personal values were recognized by the supervisor and "utilized" by him. As a result, the newcomer could strengthen the relationship with the supervisor, and expand the horizon of his career targets. Second, parallel to the above, the process of effective performance evolved. The newcomer invested his time and energy in his tasks for achieving high performance out of the given job. His behavior on the job could produce a significant contribution. Because the high vertical exchange relation made it possible for him to acquire the means (autonomy, support and challenge) for doing a good job. Then, as a result the dyadic relationship between the newcomer and his supervisor was strengthened and further transactions between contributions and resources were encouraged. The integrating function of vertical exchange created an environment for the newcomer in which, (1) he can rely on the potential resources in the environment as a means for realizing his career targets in exchange for contributions that the environment expects of him. On the other hand, (2) from the organizations point of view, integration denoted recognizing and endorsing the career goals of each member flexibly, as being compatible with the structure of resource allocation within the organization. Throughout the process of career development, the leader facilitated the evaluation of the above two perspectives for integration.

3. Concluding Remarks

An early-stage career development within one of the large Japanese business organizations was studied. The result was quite consistent with a theoretical notion on human behavior within the organization. Our sample newcomers were found to be in a process of interpersonal role-making through a leader-member relation called vertical exchange.

Moreover, the results of our study confirmed in a very systematic manner what was reported by the pioneering management progress study conducted by Bray and his associates (1974) at AT&T. As long as the process and the mechanism of organizational career development are concerned, the findings between the two studies are strikingly similar. This is not surprising. Japan, like the United States, has a well-established tradition of corporate career that may be traced back to the era of industrialization which started in the middle of the nineteenth century. In the beginning, status of a corporate career had not received due recognition relative to the one in government office, but the accelerated steps of industrial development made careers in a corporation more and more competitive and prestigious. In a sense our sample newcomers just represented the long history of DEPART men, as did the AT&T people, "Ma Bell."

Implications of findings for the present study can be summarized as follows. First, our study provided evidence to suggest that career development within the organization is determined primarily by what happened "after" employment in the organization, but not "before" employment. The before-employment factors such as AS potentials, and other personal background variables did affect the processes that occurred within the organization after employment, but the effect of these variables was not so extensive as the one caused by the process variable, vertical exchange. This finding may point to the possible shortcomings of deterministic approaches based on the before-employment factors in the study of organizational career development. Second, our study suggests that the nature of progress in the organization may be best characterized by behaviors based on voluntarism and trust. The progress was neither a result of lonesome, "sink-or swim" attempts, nor a result of nurturing under the care of the quasi-family structure in the corporate subculture. It was a result of voluntary reciprocal behaviors between an individual and the organization or an agent of it, aimed at achieving outcomes of mutual interest by exploiting resources that each party was given as "potentials."

Third, the full-potential learning and growth, however, was found occurring only to a small group of our sample newcomers. The quality of vertical exchange relations each newcomer experienced during the first year, interacted with the potential factor to produce differentiation of progress among newcomers for the subsequent time periods. In addition, the "understructure" for resource allocation within the work organization caused further ramifications. However, the pattern of differentiation observed in our study seemed to pose a serious problem to the basic idea of employer-employee relations in the DEPART organization. The results indicated a problem of premature closure of the career development processes within the organization where lifetime employment is a norm of employment. The result presented in Chapter VII clearly documented that progress during the first three years can be predicted in a very systematic manner by the quality of the newcomer's experiences at the starting year based on a combination of the vertical exchange and AS potential factors (see Table 49). This finding implies that progress in the first five years, then in the next five years, and so on, might be determined by what one experienced in the starting year of his career. If this is the case, his entire career in the organization for lifetime commitment becomes doomed by incidents which occurred during the first year. This gloomy picture defies virtues of the lifetime commitment system. Moreover, in the long run premature closure of the career development process will create tremendous inefficiency for a system of human resources utilization. Figure 36 presented in Chapter VII may indicate a token of this inefficiency: the operation of the human resource development system in the DEPART organization during the first three years already created a small high-flying group of newcomers (the High-High group), leaving a large number of other group members under the discouraging and underdeveloped career situations. The further operation of this system, then, may accelerate the differentiation between a small number of highly competent managers and large majority of underutilized managerial talent whose "redevelopment" would be hard to come by, because of the closure of relevant organizational processes and of people's minds for the managerial career development. This question will be explored in the future based on the follow-up studies of the present investigation.

Fourth, the results indicated that the high vertical exchange of the supervisor vis-à-vis his boss can be dysfunctional to the career progress of his newcomer subordinate. As illustrated in Figure 47, it was necessary for a group of supervisors to be involved in the vertical exchange relations with their newcomers at a minimal level, so that they can devote themselves to the dyadic effectiveness with their bosses. These supervisors did not allow their newcomer subordinates to participate in important tasks and decision making. They must have been very eager to make themselves look good in the eyes of their bosses. Maybe they were too busy to be involved in what was going on at the "lower" level. Or, perhaps they could not trust their subordinates. Anyhow they looked very good as "subordinates" in the eyes of their bosses, but did not appear so good as "leaders" from the subordinates' point of view. Thus, subordinates working under this type of supervisor experienced serious constraints in the availability of resources necessary for developing a managerial career. One of the answers to avoid this tragic situation is not to assign the newcomer to one of those sections where the newcomer tends to be left unnoticed by "busy" supervisors. Another approach to this problem may require education and training of the supervisors (Schein, 1964) regarding the skills and knowledge of how to communicate with their subordinates, and how to solve the dilemma of allocating their time and energy between the upper and the lower vertical dyads for optimum dyadic efficiency.

Some methodological problems that might have been involved in our study need to be discussed.

(1) *A Tendency of Regression Toward the Mean.* The results of ANOVA tests in Chapter VI indicated that predictive validity of the VE(FY) scale for the "value of the organization" and "frequency of dyadic problems" was affected by this bias. For both variables, group differences during the first year based on the VE(FY) scale disappeared by the end of the third year, due to the converging trend of the means over time among the three VE(FY) groups. For other variables, predictive validity of vertical exchange seemed to be free from this bias. However, when prediction involves a longer time span than three years, the problem would become more severe.

(2) *Criterion Contamination.* The company policy and practice in the DEPART organization enabled us to avoid serious contamination problems associated with the predictive study. Some results produced for the present study helped us ease the concern. For example, in Table 35, the company's assessment data upon recruitment predicted newcomers' job performance most strongly at Wave 7, while before Wave 7 predictive validity seemed to be sporadic. This result contradicts what might be expected based on the assumption of criterion contamination: i.e, if contamination were involved in prediction, validity would have been the highest during the first year, and would become sporadic for the rest of the time periods. Furthermore, in Table 24 our questionnaire method and company's appraisal displayed only a moderate convergence regarding job performance of the newcomer. This indicates that the two methods can be considered "discriminable" of each other (Lawler, 1967) rather than contaminated by the common bias.

(3) *Range Restriction.* This bias seemed to affect predictive validity of the AS potential scale negatively. This problem occurred probably because: (a) creation of the AS predictor was based on the company's selection test results, and (b) company's promotion policy actually restricted variation in criterion distribution during the three-year research period. For future studies, the following two points need to be considered in order to alleviate the burden of range restriction problems:

(a) assessing recruits' potentials using researchers' own batteries that are relatively independent of the company's selection tests, and (b) covering a time span long enough to obtain sufficient criterion variance for the analysis.

(4) *Effects of Pre-entry Experience.* For our study, some important autobiographic data on sample new recruits were left uncontrolled. This problem may raise a question that the process of career progress within the organization after employment might have been influenced by one of these pre-entry variables. For example, a study conducted by Wakabayashi and his associates (1977) reported that the quality of college experience for the Japanese students is closely related to the development of "career-life orientation." In their study, academic achievement, extra-curricular activities, and the mode of entry to college were found as important factors contributing to the quality of college experience. This finding suggests that it will be rewarding to conduct the career choice and progress studies based on the pre-entry data covering broader aspects of the individual and his experience.

(5) *Ability to Generalize Findings.* The present study may be considered as a "cross cultural validation" of the management progress study conducted by Bray and his associates (1974), and of a series of role making studies reported by Dansereau and his associates (1975) and Graen (1976) based on the American organization and its people. But, strictly speaking, the present study is bounded by several unique conditions regarding: (1) the sample (male, Japanese college graduates), (2) the organization (a large department store), and (3) the time period covered (the first three years). More research will be required to explore the process of career development based upon different samples, organizations, and career stages.

Finally, it must be emphasized that the area of managerial career development needs more research. The design of research may require us to satisfy at least the following four conditions: (1) longitudinal investigation with repeated monitorings, (2) being directed toward predicting outcomes of the developmental process, (3) being able to explain how these outcomes come into being, and (4) to explain the developmental process in terms of its relationship with organizational effectiveness. Furthermore, such research may require a control group design, or a comparative investigation involving multiple organizations for monitorings. The research, however may not require any noble ideas. We just want to know if what we believe we are doing to the people in the organization was performed in the manner we intended.

Appendix A

An English Version of the Questionnaire

Performance Ratings

Item #   Abbreviated Questions

Job Performance

1. Dependability.
2. Alertness.
3. Know-how and judgment.
4. Planning.
5. Interpersonal relations skills.
6. Present level of performance.
7. Interpersonal attraction.
8. Probability of making a significant contribution.
9. Willingness to make contributions to the organization.

Success Potential

1. As a general manager.
2. As a staff specialist.
3. Overall success potential.

The supervisor rated Job Performance of his subordinate using a 5-point scale with response alternatives ranging from "Very much (5)" to "Very little (1)," with "Average (3)," as a midpoint. For Success Potential, response alternatives ranged from "Very high (5)" through "Average (3)" to "Very low (1)."

Organizational Commitment Questionnaire for the Newcomer

Item #	Abbreviated Questions
1.	I am willing to work much harder than other people for the good of this company.
2.	I can tell my friends that this company is a good place to work.
3.	I don't feel a sense of belonging to this company.
4.	If the company wants, I will do my best on any job that I may be assigned.
5.	I think that my personal values and this company's management policies are very similar.
6.	I am proud to tell other people that I am a member of this company.
7.	If I could get a job that I prefer in another company, I think I will move there.
8.	If I could find a company that pays me a slightly higher salary than the present one, I will decide to move.
9.	There is an atmosphere in this company that encourages my best efforts.
10.	If this company's treatment of me becomes even a little worse, I would consider quitting.
11.	Although there are many things to be said about this company, I think that it was a good decision for me to have selected this company.
12.	I do not think that I can gain much by sticking to this company.
13.	I often question this company's personnel policies and practices.
14.	I am committed to this company's success and growth.
15.	I believe that this company is the right one for me to work for.
16.	I think that it was a mistake on my part to have selected this company.

Each item has 7 response alternatives ranging from "Strongly disagree (1)" through "Can't say (4)" to "Strongly agree (7)."

Disillusionment Questionnaire for the Newcomer

Item #	Abbreviated Questions
1.	The content of my present work.
2.	A prospect for future salary increase.
3.	A future prospect of the company growth.
4.	The relative importance of my present work unit within the company.
5.	The flexibility of practices within the company.
6.	The technical competence of my supervisor.
7.	Prospects for future promotions.
8.	Interpersonal relations with my fellow workers.
9.	The company's basic management policies.
10.	Interpersonal relations with my supervisor.
11.	The evaluation of my performance by other people in the organization.
12.	The reputation of the company in the community.
13.	The opportunity for professional development on my present job.
14.	The amount of legitimate authority available in my present job.
15.	The degree of the participation in decision making on my present job.
16.	Present work location (geographical location and conditions).
17.	An overall evaluation about my performance within my present work unit.
18.	Present working conditions (working hours, overtime, physical conditions, holidays, etc.).
19.	The company facilities (recreation facilities, company offered house, facilities for *kenshu*, etc.).

Each item has 7 response alternatives as follows: "Extreme influence (2)," "Slight influence (3)," "No influence (4)," "Slight influence to make me feel like staying with the company (5)," "Moderate influence (6)," and "Extreme influence (7)."

Job Need Questionnaire for the Newcomer and His Supervisor

Item #	Abbreviated Questions
1.	Job Challenge.
2.	Participation in decision making.
3.	Legitimate authority.
4.	Cooperation from peers.
5.	Information about management policies and decisions.
6.	Performance feedback from the immediate supervisor.
7.	Professional development.
8.	Job latitude.
9.	Consideration from the immediate supervisor.
10.	Confidence in my supervisor's technical competence.
11.	Status feedback within the work unit.
12.	Trust in the immediate supervisor.
13.	Attention by the immediate supervisor.
14.	Inside information (including information about various changes and plannings in the organization).
15.	Support from the immediate supervisor.
16.	Influence with immediate supervisor.
17.	Flexibility in choice in work location.

Each question has 5 response alternatives: "Almost none (1)," "A little (2)," "A fair amount (3)," "Quite a bit (4)," and "A great deal (5)." For each question the newcomer was asked to respond regarding, "How much are you Receiving?" and "How much do you Prefer?" The supervisor responded regarding, "How much are you Providing?" and "How much do you think your subordinate Wants?"

Job Problem Questionnaire for the Newcomer

Item #	Abbreviated Questions
1.	Frequent attendance in time-consuming and unfruitful meetings.
2.	Lack of free time because of the busy work schedule.
3.	Not receiving appropriate information from supervisor.
4.	Poor company facilities.
5.	Poor vertical communication.
6.	Understaffing in the work unit.
7.	Inflexibility in top management.
8.	Not given enough opportunity to participate in decision making.
9.	Unfair personnel appraisals.
10.	Inefficient training and development programs.
11.	Personal backbiting among peers.
12.	Supervisor's reluctance to listen to his subordinates' opinion.
13.	Too much emphasis on diploma (*"Gakureki Hencho"*).
14.	Poor horizontal communication.
15.	Supervisor's unfair treatment of his subordinates.
16.	Many unnecessary procedures to get job done ("bureaucratic red tape").
17.	Being assigned to a "dead-end" unit.
18.	Strong seniority system *("Nenkoh Jyoretsu")*.
19.	Many "easy-going" people within the work unit.
20.	Tight budget in the work unit.
21.	Supervisor's interference with private matters of his subordinates.
22.	Lack of opportunity for professional development.
23.	University clique.

Job Problem Questionnaire for the Newcomer (continued)

Item #	Abbreviated Questions
24.	Lack of trust among peers.
25.	Unclear responsibility.
26.	Mistrust in supervisor.
27.	Not given enough authority to get the job done.
28.	Lack of information exchange among peers.
29.	Antagonism between management and union.
30.	Not sure how my job behavior is evaluated.
31.	Salary is inadequate.
32.	Being assigned to disadvantageous work location.
33.	Inadequate procedure for decisions on assignment.

Each item has two parts asking: (1) the frequency of experiencing each problem, and (2) the severity of the problem for job performance. Each question has 5 response alternatives: for the frequency, "Not at all (1)," "Almost never (2)," "Sometimes (3)," "Quite often (4)," and "Almost always (5),", for the severity, "Not a problem (1)," "Minor problem (2)," "Somewhat of a problem (3)," "Important problem (4)," and "Major obstacle."

Vertical Exchange Questionnaire for the
Newcomer and His Supervisor

Item #	Abbreviated Questions

1. How flexible do you believe your supervisor is about changes in your job?

2. What are the chances that your supervisor would like to use his authority to help you solve problems in your job?

3. What are you capable of contributing to your job? How much are you able to contribute now?

4. How well do you feel that your supervisor understands your problems and needs?

5. How much latitude does your supervisor actually have to help you make changes in your job?

6. How well do you feel that your supervisor recognizes your potential?

7. How much influence do you actually have to bring about changes in your job that you want to see?

8. To what extent does your supervisor help you know what he expects you to do in your job? — Does he usually tell you what he expects you to do in your job?

9. How much latitude do you have to get your job done with your own responsibility?

10. To what extent have you been able to define your job and position for yourself?

11. To what extent does your supervisor tell you how satisfied he is with the job you did? — Does he usually tell you how satisfied he is with what you have done?

12. How often do you eat dinner or personally converse with your supervisor after work time?

Each item has 5 response alternatives ranging from "Not at all (1)" to "Almost always (5)." A parallel form of this questionnaire was administered to the supervisor of each newcomer.

Job Challenge Questionnaire for the
Newcomer and His Supervisor

Item #   **Abbreviated Questions**

1.   To do a job that requires technical knowledge and expertise.

2.   To find new aspects of your job and develop them as an integral part of your responsibility.

3.   To ask questions about your job in order to solve the problems for achieving effectiveness on your job.

4.   To represent your work unit in proposing new ideas.

5.   To engage in a task where you are required to exchange information and to maintain close contact with people in other sections for enhancing coordination.

6.   To make an official report either in a written or an oral form.

7.   To play the leadership or supervisory role for your work unit.

8.   To exercise your discretion for judgment and decision making delegated by your supervisor.

9.   To be in a position where you plan and organize for other people within your work unit.

10.   To let other people know about your ideas which you have committed to, and worked out, to increase the profit and effectiveness of the company.

11.   To contribute to development of your organization by devoting your full potentialities allowing little concern with your private matters.

12.   To establish comfortable interpersonal relationships by going out together for a drink with fellow workers, or by paying a visit to your supervisor's home.

13.   To show that you know and you agree to the company policies and practices.

14.   To demonstrate your capacity and the possibility of greater contribution as a result of your endeavor for investing in yourself.

15.   To represent your unit or your company in the business of meeting with people from other companies.

16.   To be assigned to the task in which your skills, expertise, and knowhow are challenged.

17.   To take the responsibility for the organization of a project, or to supervise entire processes for an important task.

Job Challenge Questionnaire for the
Newcomer and His Supervisor (continued)

Item #   **Abbreviated Questions**

18.   To train yourself for supervisory skills and to acquire a style or a "sense" necessary for the executive figure.

19.   To be consulted by your supervisor with business or personal problems.

20.   To get inside information about the company's new policies and future programs.

Both the newcomer and his supervisor were asked to respond regarding the extent to which the newcomer has an opportunity to experience each of the job challenge episodes. Response alternatives ranged from "Not at all (1)" to "Very Often (5)."

Job Satisfaction Questionnaire for the Newcomer

To what extent do you feel satisfied with each of the following items?

Response alternatives:

1	–	A little,	4	–	Moderately high, and
2	–	Lukewarm	5	–	Very much
3	–	A fair amount,			

1.   Your present job.

2.   Your work unit.

3.   The way your supervisor treats you.

4.   Interpersonal relationships with peers.

5.   Your pay level.

6.   The welfare facilities and housing-aid programs of the company.

7.   Overall situation.

Right Type Questionnaire for the Supervisor

1. To what extent do you think that your subordinate feels attracted to the company?

    1.   I think he feels attracted very little.

    2.   I cannot say.

    3.   Lukewarm.

    4.   A fair amount.

    5.   I think he feels very much attracted.

2. To the best of my knowledge;

    1.   I do not think he fits this company very well.

    2.   I can not tell if he fits or mis-fits.

    3.   He seems to fit somehow all right.

    4.   He fits well.

    5.   He is the best fit.

3. If he keeps going his own way as I can see now, in the future;

    1.   To tell the truth, he will be a loser.

    2.   He will just be able to survive.

    3.   He will be in an average position among his colleagues.

    4.   He will move into a fairly high level.

    5.   He will be one of those promising managers.

Appendix B

Factor Analysis: A Summary of Results

Vertical Exchange Instrument

Item Number and Abbreviated Content		Factor Loading F·I	F·II	Communality Estimate (h^2)
F·I: Dyadic Contingency				
6.	Sup recognizes your potential	.75	.32	.65
4.	Sup's understanding of your problems.	.74	.34	.63
8.	Sup tells you what he expects.	.74	.22	.56
2.	Sup's willingness to help you.	.73	.22	.57
5.	Sup's latitude to help change your job.	.73	.23	.55
11.	Sup tells how he is satisfied with your job.	.70	.30	.58
1.	Sup's flexibility in changing your job.	.60	.23	.45
12.	Going out with sup after work.	.52	.17	.31
F·II: Job Latitude				
9.	Your latitude for getting job done.	.18	.69	.42
3.	Chances for your contribution.	.27	.64	.42
7.	How much influence do you have?	.40	.59	.48
10.	Latitude to define job for yourself.	.17	.59	.32
	Percent Variance	66%	34%	

Job Need Instrument

Item Number and Abbreviated Content	Factor Loading		Communality Estimate (h^2)
	F-I	F-II	

F-I: Leadership Support

Item Number and Abbreviated Content	F-I	F-II	(h^2)
9. Sup's consideration of your feelings.	.81	.16	.65
13. Sup's attention to your work.	.80	.31	.72
6. Sup tells how you are doing on the job.	.68	.18	.56
12. Trust given by your supervisor.	.67	.33	.60
15. Willingness of your sup to help you.	.66	.29	.58
10. Confidence in sup's technical skills.	.63	.17	.47
16. Chances that sup adopts your ideas.	.61	.46	.63

F-II: Job Enrichment

Item Number and Abbreviated Content	F-I	F-II	(h^2)
2. Participation in decision making.	.25	.79	.69
1. Doing tasks I really want to do.	.29	.71	.59
8. Putting your ideas into work.	.20	.71	.55
3. Enough authority to get job done.	.27	.63	.55
7. Learning expertise and knowhow.	.15	.62	.45
5. Access to information on new plans.	.11	.58	.44
14. Quick information on changes.	.32	.51	.44

Residual Items

Item Number and Abbreviated Content	F-I	F-II	(h^2)
4. Assistance and cooperation from peers.	.30	.34	.25
11. Feedback on performance.	.53	.18	.47
17. Assignment to the tasks of my preference.	.23	.31	.24
Percent Variance	52%	48%	

Job Problem Instrument

Item Number and Abbreviated Content	Factor Loading			Communality Estimate (h^2)
	F-I	F-II	F-III	

F-I: Dyadic Problems and Constraints

5.	Poor vertical communication.	.75	.13	.24	.67
8.	Lack of opportunities for participation	.75	.27	.04	.71
3.	Sup does not give proper instruction.	.61	.22	.10	.57
14.	Poor horizontal communication.	.58	.26	.11	.58
27.	Lack of authority.	.58	.42	.09	.63
26.	Uncomfortable relation with the sup.	.54	.39	.08	.67
16.	Many nonessential procedures.	.52	.12	.37	.50
7.	Top lacks flexibility and decisiveness	.50	.24	.33	.61
20.	Insufficient budget.	.48	.24	.33	.53
30.	Ambiguity of how I am doing on the job.	.46	.18	.20	.49
22.	Poor opportunity for learning expertise.	.41	.22	.24	.41

F-II: Organizational Climate

11.	Backbitings among peers	.31	.71	.02	.62
13.	Overestimating values of education.	.16	.67	.21	.57
23.	University clique in the company.	.18	.67	.24	.60
21.	Sup's intrusion into my privacy.	.11	.58	.21	.50
15.	Sup shows favoritism to his subordinates.	.36	.56	.17	.59
17.	Stuck in shady section of the organization.	.25	.54	.19	.55
18.	Rigid seniority system.	.19	.49	.31	.55
19.	Seeing many easy-going people.	.42	.45	.22	.51

Job Problem Instrument (continued)

Item Number and Abbreviated Content		F-I	Factor Loading F-II	F-III	Communality Estimate (h^2)
F-III: Shortage of Resources					
32.	Being in disadvantageous work location.	-.01	.21	.70	.62
33.	Little chance for changing assignment.	.21	.16	.58	.60
4.	Poor company facilities	.11	.20	.56	.45
31.	Low salary.	.09	.23	.48	.44
6.	Understaffing.	.35	-.09	.43	.41
Residual Items					
1.	Attendance at time-consuming meetings.	.33	.26	.32	.40
2.	Too busy to enjoy my free time.	.31	.05	.39	.44
9.	Unfair personnel appraisals.	.37	.42	.31	.56
10.	Impractical training program.	.41	.40	.20	.48
12.	Sup's reluctance to listen.	.57	47	.14	.68
24.	Lack of trust among coworkers.	.41	.58	.04	.63
25.	Unclear responsibility.	.42	.43	.18	.54
28.	Lack of information exchange among peers.	.51	.47	.05	.56
29.	Unpleasant union-management relations.	.11	.43	.38	.40
	Percent Variance	41%	37%	22%	

Organizational Commitment Instrument

Item Number and Abbreviated Content	Factor Loading		Communality Estimate
	F-I	F-II	(h^2)

F–I: Psychological Value of the Company

15.	The company best fits me for working.	.78	−.37	.74
6.	Proud of being a member of the company.	.77	−.32	.68
11.	It was right to have chosen this company.	.76	−.42	.77
2.	This company is worthwhile working for.	.74	−.44	.74
1.	Willing to work harder than other people.	.72	−.44	.73
16.	It was wrong to have chosen this company.	−.72	.35	.71
9.	Company climate encourages my effort.	.68	−.29	.57
5.	I can agree with company policies.	.62	−.29	.54
14.	I really wish company to develop.	.56	−.11	.37

F–II: Risk of Committing

8.	Move to another company for better pay.	−.20	.71	.55
7.	Move to another company for better job.	−.28	.67	.49
10.	Quit if employment conditions worsen.	−.31	.67	.54
13.	Feel questionable about company's treatment.	−.41	.47	.43

Residual Items

3.	No identification with the company.	−.56	.39	.52
4.	Do my best in any job.	.28	−.52	.43
12.	Nothing good will happen from hanging on.	−.67	.44	.37
	Percent Variance	63%	37%	

Disillusionment Instrument

Item Number and Abbreviated Content		Factor Loading		Communality Estimate (h^2)
		F-I	F-II	
F-I: Role Content				
15.	Degree of participation.	.79	.30	.75
14.	Amount of authority given.	.78	.17	.71
1.	Content of your present job.	.69	.28	.64
6.	Supervisor's treatment.	.69	.19	.72
10.	Consideration from your supervisor.	.59	.14	.66
17.	Recognition within your work unit.	.59	.49	.71
4.	Importance of your work section.	.53	.47	.61
13.	Opportunities for learning.	.50	.20	.39
8.	Relationship with peers.	.45	.38	.46
F-II: Profitability of the Organization				
2.	Chances of pay increase.	.23	.72	.65
3.	Future prospects of the company.	.29	.65	.57
18.	Working conditions.	.12	.62	.53
12.	Reputation of the company.	.22	.61	.55
19.	Company facilities.	.08	.53	.43
9.	Company policies and practices.	.22	.52	.49
5.	Flexibility of the organization.	.39	.46	.46
Residual Items				
7.	Chances of promotion.	.72	.32	.68
11.	Evaluation of your work by others.	.59	.39	.64
16.	Location of your present work place.	.14	.34	.22
	Percent Variance	52%	48%	

Job Challenge Instrument

Item Number and Abbreviated Content	Factor Loading F-I	F-II	Communality Estimate (h^2)

F-I: Increased Centrality

		F-I	F-II	h^2
10.	To express your ideas to help company.	.74	.28	.65
13.	Agreement with company policies.	.67	.15	.53
18.	To learn supervisory skills and style.	.67	.27	.56
19.	To be consulted about decisions.	.65	.22	.50
20.	To get inside information.	.55	.25	.48
11.	To contribute your maximum effort.	.50	.38	.47
14.	To demonstrate your capability.	.42	.37	.43

F-II: Task Demand

		F-I	F-II	h^2
16.	Doing tasks that challenge your expertise.	.21	.76	.63
1.	To do tasks requiring technical skills.	.08	.74	.59
5.	To engage in coordinating tasks.	.34	.65	.61
6.	To make an official report.	.20	.65	.53
2.	To tap new aspects in your job.	.30	.62	.60
4.	To represent your section.	.39	.59	.60
3.	To solve your job problems.	.30	.49	.48
8.	To exercise your discretion.	.50	.46	.61

Residual Items

		F-I	F-II	h^2
7.	To play a leadership role.	.56	.19	.50
9.	Planning and organizing for others.	.64	.37	.63
12.	To tighten interpersonal relations.	.55	.13	.37
15.	To engage in business negotiations.	.24	.52	.41
17.	To organize a project.	.48	.41	.51
	Percent Variance	52%	48%	

Appendix C

ANOVA Results Based on the Interlocked Vertical Exchange

Newcomer-Supervisor (Lower Dyad) Reports Based on the Interlocked Vertical Exchange at the Final Wave of Research (N=72)

Variable	Mean for the VE Group								Probability		
	Lower VDL		Upper VDL		Interaction				Lower VDL	Upper VDL	Inter-action
	Low	High	Low	High	LL	LH	HL	HH			
Newcomer's Report											
Vertical Exchange	28.5	39.9	34.3	34.1	29.5	27.4	39.1	40.8	.001	.868	.063
Job Need: Receiving											
Leadership Support	18.1	22.3	19.8	20.7	18.7	17.5	20.9	23.8	.001	.436	.070
Job Enrichment	19.3	26.6	23.4	22.5	20.7	17.9	26.2	27.1	.001	.323	.058
Job Challenge											
Increased Centrality	18.7	25.3	21.4	22.5	19.7	17.6	23.1	27.4	.001	.491	.048
Task Demand	15.3	20.0	16.8	18.6	16.3	14.3	17.3	22.8	.001	.154	.003
Job Problem: Frequency											
Dyadic Problem	32.9	29.3	30.9	31.3	32.4	33.3	29.3	29.2	.009	.757	.695
Climate Problem	20.4	17.2	18.8	18.8	20.2	20.6	17.3	17.1	.001	.925	.684
Job Problem: Severity											
Dyadic Problem	32.9	32.8	32.5	33.1	33.0	32.7	32.0	33.6	.965	.735	.627
Climate Problem	20.2	19.0	19.4	19.8	20.2	20.2	18.5	19.4	.324	.719	.686
Role Disillusionment											
Role Content	39.0	47.2	43.5	42.7	40.9	37.0	46.1	48.4	.001	.539	.019
Profitability	29.8	31.6	31.2	30.2	30.8	28.7	31.6	31.7	.094	.372	.298
Organizational Commitment											
Value of Organization	41.0	44.0	42.8	42.2	42.9	39.2	42.8	45.2	.094	.716	.083
Risk of Committing	15.6	15.8	16.4	15.0	16.2	15.1	16.6	14.9	.882	.150	.745
Need Deficiency											
Leadership Support	14.8	8.7	11.5	11.9	13.9	15.6	9.2	8.3	.107	.916	.054
Job Enrichment	9.0	2.3	5.4	5.9	9.1	9.0	1.8	2.8	.003	.844	.808
Job Satisfaction	14.6	19.8	17.1	17.3	15.1	14.1	19.2	20.4	.001	.868	.272

Newcomer-Supervisor (Lower Dyad) Reports Based on the Interlocked Vertical Exchange at the Final Wave of Research (N=72) (continued)

Variable	Mean for the VE Group								Probability		
	Lower VDL		Upper VDL		Interaction				Lower VDL	Upper VDL	Interaction
	Low	High	Low	High	LL	LH	HL	HH			
Supervisor's Report											
Vertical Exchange	38.6	39.3	38.1	39.8	37.9	39.3	38.3	40.3	.425	.049	.690
Job Need: Providing											
Leadership Support	23.1	24.8	23.1	24.7	22.3	23.8	23.9	25.6	.074	.094	.929
Job Enrichment	26.1	26.5	25.5	27.1	25.4	26.7	25.7	27.4	.532	.046	.796
Job Challenge											
Increased Centrality	25.6	27.1	25.3	27.5	25.1	26.2	25.4	28.9	.268	.094	.366
Task Demand	21.1	21.6	21.0	21.7	20.9	21.2	21.1	22.2	.542	.429	.626
Job Performance	32.4	36.3	33.1	35.5	31.5	33.3	34.7	37.8	.002	.053	.605
Success Potential	10.6	11.4	10.8	11.2	10.3	10.9	11.4	11.4	.065	.456	.534
Right Type	9.0	10.4	9.3	10.1	8.6	9.5	10.1	10.7	.009	.145	.703

Entry for the subgroups, LL, LH, HL, and HH, consists of 18 subjects each.

Supervisor-Boss (Upper Dyad) Reports Based on the
Interlocked Vertical Exchange at the
Final Wave of Research (N=72)

Variable	Lower VDL		Upper VDL		Interaction				Lower VDL	Upper VDL	Inter-action
	Low	High	Low	High	LL	LH	HL	HH			
Focal Supervisor's Report											
Vertical Exchange	38.1	38.1	34.7	41.6	34.7	41.6	34.7	41.6	.425	.049	.690
Job Need: Receiving											
Leadership Support	25.5	25.3	23.4	27.3	23.7	27.3	23.2	27.3	.687	.001	.687
Job Enrichment	26.8	25.4	23.3	28.9	24.3	29.3	22.4	28.5	.070	.001	.445
Job Challenge											
Increased Centrality	28.5	28.9	26.4	31.1	26.4	30.6	26.4	31.5	.688	.001	.649
Task Demand	22.0	23.1	21.2	23.9	20.6	23.5	21.9	24.2	.212	.002	.709
Job Problem: Frequency											
Dyadic Problem	29.0	31.0	32.3	27.7	30.4	27.5	34.1	27.9	.095	.001	.188
Climate Problem	19.5	19.9	20.4	19.1	19.7	19.4	21.2	18.7	.686	.189	.294
Job Problem: Severity											
Dyadic Problem	33.1	32.6	33.4	32.3	32.0	34.2	34.7	30.4	.740	.529	.054
Climate Problem	22.2	20.9	22.0	21.0	21.8	22.6	22.2	19.5	.316	.451	.196
Role Disillusionment											
Role Content	48.3	47.3	44.9	50.7	45.1	51.4	44.7	50.0	.445	.001	.686
Profitability	33.7	33.8	32.6	34.9	32.3	35.1	32.8	34.7	.978	.028	.646
Organizational Commitment											
Value of Organization	47.6	48.2	46.0	49.8	45.3	49.9	46.6	49.8	.717	.019	.666
Risk of Committing	18.4	17.7	17.2	18.9	17.2	19.7	17.2	18.2	.452	.076	.452
Need Deficiency											
Leadership Support	2.6	4.6	5.1	2.2	3.2	2.1	7.0	2.3	.082	.011	.123
Job Enrichment	2.4	3.4	4.7	1.1	3.9	1.0	5.5	1.2	.469	.008	.624
Job Satisfaction	21.3	21.7	19.2	23.8	18.7	23.9	19.6	23.7	.677	.001	.488

Supervisor-Boss (Upper Dyad) Reports Based on the
Interlocked Vertical Exchange at the
Final Wave of Research (N=72) (continued)

Variable	Mean for the VE Group								Probability		
	Lower VDL		Upper VDL		Interaction				Lower VDL	Upper VDL	Inter-action
	Low	High	Low	High	LL	LH	HL	HH			
Boss's Report											
Vertical Exchange	42.3	43.3	41.8	43.8	41.2	43.4	42.4	44.2	.213	.013	.747
Job Need: Providing											
Leadership Support	28.2	27.3	26.6	28.9	27.3	29.1	25.9	28.7	.202	.002	.509
Job Enrichment	28.3	28.0	27.5	28.8	27.7	28.9	27.3	28.7	.653	.058	.967
Job Challenge											
Increased Centrality	32.9	32.9	31.8	34.0	31.2	34.6	32.3	33.5	.999	.031	.311
Task Demand	26.2	25.1	25.5	25.9	25.9	26.6	25.1	25.2	.320	.727	.803
Job Performance	36.7	37.4	35.2	38.8	34.9	38.4	35.6	39.2	.497	.001	.978
Success Potential	10.8	11.4	10.4	11.9	10.2	11.5	10.6	12.2	.096	.001	.689
Right Type	10.9	11.2	10.4	11.6	10.4	11.4	10.5	11.8	.510	.007	.693

Entry for the subgroups, LL, LH, HL, and HH, consists of 18 subjects each.

Bibliography

Albrecht, P.A.; Glaser, E.M.; and Marks, J.; Validation of multiple-assessment procedures for managerial personnel. *Journal of Applied Psychology,* 1964, *48,* 351–60.

Alderfer, C.P. *Existence, relatedness, and growth: Human needs in organizational settings.* New York: Free Press, 1972.

_____. An experimental test of a new theory of human needs. *Organizational Behavior and Human Performance,* 1969, 4, 142–75.

Argyris, C. *Integrating the individual and organization.* New York, Wiley, 164.

_____. *Interpersonal competence and organizational effectiveness.* Homewood, Ill.: Dorsey, 1962.

_____. *Intervention theory and method: A behavioral science view.* Reading, Mass.: Addison-Wesley, 1970.

_____. *Personality and organization.* New York: Harper, 1957.

Atkinson, J.W. *An introduction to motivation.* Princeton, N.J.: Van Nostrand, 1964.

_____., and Feather, N.J. *A theory of achievement motivation.* New York: Wiley, 1966.

Barnard, C. *The functions of the executive.* Cambridge, Mass.: Harvard University press, 1938.

Becker, H.S. The career of the Chicago public schoolteacher. *American Journal of Sociology,* 1952, *57,* 470–77.

_____. Notes on the concept of commitment. *American Journal of Sociology,* 1960, *66,* 32–40.

_____. Personal changes in adult life. *Sociometry,* 1964, *10,* 40–53.

_____. Geer, B., Hughes, E., and Straus, A. *Boys in white.* Chicago: University of Chicago Press, 1961.

Bender, J.M. What is "typical" of assessment center? *Personnel,* 1973, *50.*

Bennis, W.G.; Berlew, D.E.; Schein, E.H.; and Steele, F.I. *Interpersonal dynamics.* Homewood, Ill.: The Dorsey press, 1973.

Bentz, V.J. Validity of Sears assessment center procedures. In W. C. Byham (Chm.), *Validity of assessment centers.* Symposium presented at the American Psychological Association, Washington, D.C., September. 1971.

Berlew, D.E., and Hall, D.T., The socialization of manager: Effects of expectation on performance. *Administrative Science Quarterly,* 1966, *11,* 207–33.

Blake, R.R., and Mouton, J.S. *The managerial grid.* Houston: Gulf, 1964.

Blalock, H.M., Jr. *Casual inference in nonexperimental research.* New York: Norton, 1964.

_____. *Social statistics.* New York: McGraw-Hill, 1972.

Blau, P.M. Patterns of interaction among a group of officials in a government agency. *Human Relations,* 1954, *7,* 337–48.

Brager, G. Commitment and conflict in a normative organization. *American Sociological Review,* 1969, *34,* 482–91.

Bray, D.W.; Campbell, R.J.; and Grant, D.I. *Formative years in business: A long-term AT&T study of managerial lives.* New York: Wiley, 1974.

_____., and Campbell, R.J. Selection of salesmen by means of an assessment center. *Journal of Applied Psychology,* 1968, *52,* 36–41.

_____., and Grant, D.L. The assessment center in the measurement of potential for business management. *Psychological Monograph,* 1966, *80,* Whole No. 625.

Brim, O., and Wheeler, S. *Socialization after childhood.* New York: Wiley, 1966.

Brislin, R.W.,; Lonner, W.J.; and Thordike, R.M. *Cross-cultural research methods.* New York: Wiley, 1973.

Brummet, R.L.; Flamholtz, E.G.; and Plye, W.C. Human resource measurements. *The Accounting Review,* 1968, *43,* 217–24.

Campbell, D.T., and Fiske, D.W. Convergent and discriminant validity by the multitrait-multimethod matrix. *Psychological Bulletin,* 1959, *56,* 81–107.

_____., and Stanley, J.C. *Experimental and quasi-experimental designs for research.* Chicago: Rand McNally, 1963.

Campbell, J.P.; Dunnette, M.D.; Lawler, E.E.; and Weick, K.E., Jr.; *Managerial behavior, performance and effectiveness.* New York: McGraw-Hill, 1970.

Caplow, T. *Principles of organization.* New York: Harcourt Brace, 1964.

Cashman, J.; Dansereau, F.; Graen, G.; and Haga, W.J. Organizational understructure and leadership: A longitudinal investigation of the managerial role making process. *Organizational Behavior and Human Performance,* 1976, *15,* 278–96.

_____., and Graen, G. The nature of leadership in the vertical dyad: The team building process. *Organizational Behavior and Human performance,* in press.

Dansereau, F.; Graen, G.; and Haga, W.J. A vertical dyad linkage approach to leadership within formal organizations. *Organizational Behavior and Human Performance,* 1975, *13,* 46–78.

Davis, F. Professional socialization as subjective experience: The process of doctorial conversion among student nurses. In H. Becker, B. Geer, D. Riesman, and R. Weiss (eds.), *Institutions and the person.* Chicago: Aldine Publishing Co., 1968, 235–51.

Dicken, C.F., and Black, J.D. Predictive validity of psychometric evaluations of supervisors. *Journal of Applied Psychology,* 1965, *49,* 34–47.

Dornbusch, S.M., The military academy as an assimilating institution. *Social Forces,* 1955, *33,* 316–21.

Dunnette, M.D.; The assessment of managerial talent. In P. McReynolds (ed.), *Advances in psychological assessment (II).* Palo Alto: Science and Behavior Books, Inc., 1971.

_____. A note on the criterion. *Journal of Applied Psychology,* 1963, *47,* 251–54.

_____.; Arvey, R.D.; and Banas, P.A. Why do they leave? *Personnel,* 1973, May-June, 25–39.

Fiedler, F.E. *A theory of leadership effectiveness.* New York: McGraw-Hill, 1967.

Finkle, R.B., Managerial assessment centers. In M.D. Dunnette (ed.), *Handbook of industrial and organization psychology.* Chicago: Rand McNally, 1976, 861–88.

Fleishman, E.A., and Peters, D.R. Interpersonal values, leadership attitudes and "managerial success." *Personnel Psychology,* 1962, *15,* 127–44.

Fleiss, J.L. Estimating the magnitude of experiment effects. *Psychological Bulletin,* 1969, *72,* 273–76.

French, J.R., and Raven, B.H. The basis of social power. In D. Cartwright (ed.), *Studies in social power.* Ann Arbor, Michigan: University of Michigan Press, 1959.

Georgopoulus, B.S.; Mahony, G.M.; and Jones, N.W. A path-goal approach to productivity. *Journal of Applied Psychology,* 1957, *41,* 345–53.

Ghiselli, E.E. Dimensional problems of criterion. *Journal of Applied Psychology,* 156, *40,* 1–4.

_____, and Haire, M. The validation of selection tests in the light of the dynamic character of criteria. *Personnel Psychology,* 1960, *13,* 225–31.

Glaser, B. *Organizational careers: A sourcebook for theory.* Chicago: Aldine Publishing Co., 1968.

_____. *Organizational scientists: Their professional careers.* New York: Bobbs-Merrill, 1964.

Glaser, R.; Schwarz, P.A.; and Flanagan, J.C. The contribution of interview and situational performance procedures to the selection of supervisory personnel. *Journal of Applied Psychology*, 1958, *42*, 69–73.

Gouldner, A. Cosmopolitans and locals: Toward an analysis of latent social roles I. *Administrative Science Quarterly*, 1958, *2*, 281–306.

_____. The norm of reciprocity: A preliminary statement. *American Sociological Review*, 1960, *25*, 161–79.

Gouldner, H.P. Dimensions of organizational commitment. *Administrative Science Quarterly*, 1960, *4*, 468–90.

Graen, G. Instrumentality theory of work motivation: Some experimental results and suggested modifications. *Journal of Applied Psychology Monograph*, 1969, *53*, Whole No. 2, Part 2.

_____. Role-making processes within complex organizations. In M.D. Dunnette (ed.), *Handbook of industrial and organizational psychology.* Chicago: Rand McNally, 1976.

_____., and Cashman, J. A role making model of leadership informal organizations: A developmental approach. In J.C. Hunt and L.L. Larson (eds.), *Leadership frontiers.* Kent: Kent University Press, 1975, 143–66.

_____.; Cashman, J.F.; Ginsburgh, S.; and Schiemann, W. Effects of linking-pin quality upon the reality of working life of lower participants: A longitudinal investigation of the managerial understructure. *Administrative Science Quarterly*, 1977, *22*, *491–504.*

_____.; Dansereau, F.; and Minami, T. Dysfunctional leadership styles. *Organizational Behavior and Human Performance*, 1972, *7*, 216–36.

_____.; Orris, J. B.; and Johnson, T. Role assimilation processes in a complex organization. *Journal of Vocational Behavior*, 1973, *3*, 395–420.

_____., and Schiemann, W. Assessing the structure and functioning state of the leader-member exchange: A vertical dyad linkage approach. Mimeographed paper, 1977.

_____., and Schiemann, W. Leader-member agreement: A vertical dyad linkage approach. *Journal of Applied Psychology*, 1978, *63*, 206–12.

Grant, D.L., and Bray, D.W. Contributions of the interview to assessment of management potential. *Journal of Applied Psychology*, 1969, *53*, 24–34.

_____., and Katkovsky, W. Contributions of projective techniques to assessment of management potential. *Journal of Applied Psychology*, 1967, *51*, 226–32.

Greenwood, J.M., and McNamara, W.J., Interrater reliability in situational tests. *Journal of Applied Psychology*, 1967, *51*, 101–6.

Grusky, O. Career mobility and organizational commitment. *Administrative Science Quarterly*, 1966, *10*, 488–503.

Guion, R.M. Criterion measurement and personnel judgment. *Personnel Psychology*, 1961, *14*, 141–49.

_____. Recruiting, selection, and job replacement. In M.D. Dunnette (ed.), *Handbook of industrial and organizational Psychology.* Chicago: Rand McNally, 1976, 777–828.

_____. Synthetic validity in a small company: A demonstration. *Personnel Psychology*, 165, *18*, 49–63.

Hachman, J.R., Lawler, E.E. Employee reaction to job characteristics. *Journal of Applied Psychology*, 1971, *55*, 259–86.

_____., and Oldham, G.R. Development of the job diagnostic survey. *Journal of Applied Psychology,* 1975, *60,* 159–70.

Haga. W.J.; Graen. G.; and Dansereau, F. Professionalism and role making within a service organization: A longitudinal investigation. *American Sociological Review,* 1974, *39,* 122–33.

Hall, D.T. Identity changes during the transition from student to professor. *The School Review,* 1968, *76,* 445–69.

_____. The theoretical model of career subidentity development in organizational setting. *Organizational Behavior and Human peformance,* 1971, *6,* 50–76.

_____., and Nougaim, K.E. An examination of Maslow's need hierarchy in an organizational setting. *Organizational Behavior and Human Performance,* 1968, *3,* 12–35.

_____., and Schneider, B. Correlates of organizational identification as a function of career and organizational style. *Administrative Science Quarterly,* 1972, *17,* 340–50.

_____.; Schneider, B.; and Nygren, H. T. Personal factors in organizational identification. *Administrative Science Quarterly,* 1970, 15, 176–90.

Hamner, C., and Tosi, H. Relationship of role conflict and role ambiguity to job-involvement measures. *Journal of Applied Psychology,* 174, *4,* 497–99.

Hardesty, D.L., and Jones, W.S. Characteristics of judged high potential management personnel: The operations of an industrial assessment center. *Personnel Psychology,* 1968, *21,* 85–98.

Heise, D.D. Causal inference form panel data. In E.F. Borgatta and G.W. Bohnstedt (ed.), *Sociological Methodology.* San Francisco: Jossey-Bass, Inc., 1970, 3-27.

Herzberg, F. *Work and the nature of man.* Cleveland: World, 1966.

Hilton, A.C.; Stanley, F.B.; Parker, J.W.; Taylor, E.K.; and Walker, W.B. The validity of personnel assessments by professional psychologists. *Journal of Applied Psychology,* 1955, 287-93.

Hinrichs, J.R. The attitude of research chemists. *Journal of Applied Psychology,* 1964, *48,* 287–93.

_____. Comparison of "real life" assessment of management potential with situational exercises, paper-and-pencil ability tests, and personality inventories. *Journal of Applied Psychology,* 1969, *53,* 425–32.

Hogue, J.P.; Otis, J.L.; and Prien, E.P. Assessments of high-level personnel: VI. Validity of predictions based on projective techniques. *Personnel Psychology,* 1962, *15,* 335–44.

Hollander, E.P. Conformity, status, and idiocyncrasy credit. *Psychological Review,* 1958, *65,* 117–27.

_____., and Julian, J.W. Contemporary trends in the analysis of leadership process. *Psychological Bulletin,* 1969, *71,* 387–97.

Homans, G.C. Social behavior as exchange. *American Journal of Sociology,* 1958, *63,* 597–606.

House, R.J. A path goal theory of leader effectiveness. *Administrative Science Quarterly,* 1971, *16,* 321–38.

_____., and Dessler, G. The path-goal theory of leadership: Some post hoc and a priori tests. In J.G. Hunt and L.L. Larson (eds.), *Contingency approaches to leadership.* Carbondale, Ill.: Southern Illinois University Press, 1974.

_____., and Mitchell, T.R. Path-goal theory of leadership. *Journal of Contemporary Business,* 1974, *5,* 81–97.

_____., and Rizzo, J. R. Role conflict and ambiguity as critical variables in a model organizational behavior. *Organizational Behavior and Human Performance,* 1972, *7,* 465–505.

Hrebiniak, L.G., and Alutto, J.A. Personal and role-related factors in the development of organizational commitment. *Administrative Science Quarterly,* 1972, *17,* 555–73.

Hughes, E.C. Institutional office and the person. *American Journal of Sociology,* 1937, *43,* 404–13.

Jacobs, T. *Leadership and exchange in formal organizations.* Alexandra, Va.: Human Resources Research Organization, 1970.

Janowitz, M. *The professional soldier: A social and political portrait.* New York: Free Press, 1960.

Jennings, E.E. *The mobile manager.* Michigan University *Graduate School of Business Administration,* 1967.

Johnson, T.W., and Graen, G. Organizational assimilation and role rejection. *Organizational Behavior and Human Performance,* 1973, *10,* 72–87.

Kahn, R.L.; Wolfe, D.M.; Quinn, R.P.; and Snoek, J.D. with Rosenthal, R.A. *Organizational stress: Studies in role conflicts and ambiguity.* New York: Wiley, 1964.

Katz, D., and Kahn, R.L. *The social psychology of organization.* New York: Wiley, 1966.

_____.; Maccoby, N.; Gurin, G.; and Floor, L.G. *Productivity, supervision, and morale among railroad workers.* Ann Arbor, Mich.: University of Michigan, Survey Research Center, Institute of Social Research, 1951.

_____.; Maccoby, N.; and Morse, C. *Productivity, supervision, and morale in an office situation.* Ann Arbor, Mich.: University of Michigan, Survey Research Center, Institute of Social Research 1950.

Kaufman. M. *The forest ranger.* Baltimore: Johns Hopkins Press. 1960.

Korman, A.K. "Consideration," and "Initiating Structure," and organizational criteria: A review. *Personnel Psychology,* 1966, *19,* 349–61.

_____. The predictive validity of managerial performance: A review. *Personnel Psychology,* 168, *21,* 295–322.

_____. Self-esteem as a moderator of the relationship between self-perceived ability and vocational choice. *Journal of Applied Psychology,* 1967, *51,* 65–67.

Kornhauser, W. *Scientists in industry: Conflict and accomodation.* Berkley: University of California Press, 1962.

Kraut, A.I., and Scott, G.J. Validity of an operational management assessment program. *Journal of Applied Psychology,* 1972, *56,* 124–29.

Laurent, H. Cross-cultural cross-validation of empirically validated tests. *Journal of Applied Psychology,* 1970, *54,* 417–23.

_____. Early identification of managers. *Management Record,* 1962, *24,* 33-38.

Lawler, E. E. *Motivation in work organization.* Monterey, Calif.: Brooks/Cole, 1973.

_____. The multitrait-multirater approach to measuring managerial job performance. *Journal of Applied Psychology,* 1967, *51,* 369–81.

_____. *Pay and organizational effectiveness: A psychological view.* New York: McGraw-Hill, 1971

_____., and Hall, D.T. Relationship of job characteristics to job involvement, satisfaction, and intrinsic motivation. *Journal of Applied Psychology,* 170, *50,* 305–12.

Levinson, H.; Price, C.R.; Munden, H.J.; and Solley, C.M. *Men, management, and mental health.* Cambridge: Harvard University Press, 1962.

Lewin, K. *Field theory in social science.* New York: Harper, 1951.

Likert, R. *Human organization: Its management and value.* New York: McGraw-Hill, 1967.

_____. *New patterns of management.* New York: McGraw-Hill, 1961.

Locke, E.A. Motivational effects of knowledge of results: Knowledge or goal setting? *Journal of Applied Psychology,* 1967, *51,* 324–29.

_____. The relationship of intentions to level of performance. *Journal of Applied Psychology*, 1966, *50*, 60–65.

_____. Toward a theory of task motivation and incentives. *Organizational Behavior and Human Performance*, 1968, *3*, 157–89.

McClelland, D.C.; Atkinson, J.W.; Clark, R.A.; and Lowell, E.L. *The achievement motive*. New York: Appleton-Century-Crofts, 1953.

McConnel, J.J., and Parker, T.C. An assessment center program for multi-organizational use. *Training and Development Journal*, 1972, *26*, 6–14.

McGregor, D. *The human side of enterprise*. New York: McGraw-Hill, 1960.

Mansfield, R. Career and individual strategies. In J. Child (ed.), *Man and Organization*, New York: Wiley, 1973, 107–32.

Maslow, A. H. *Motivation and personality*. New York: Harper, 1954.

_____. *Toward a psychology of being*. Princeton, N. J.: Van Nostrand, 1962.

Megginson, L.C. Management selection, development, and motivation in the United States. *Management International*, 1963, *2*, 96–106.

Merton, R. K. *Social theory and social structure*. New York: Free Press, 1957.

Mills, T. Human resources – Why the new concern? *Harvard Business Review*, 1975, 120–34.

Newcomer, M. *The big business executive*. New York: Columbia University Press, 1955.

Oldham, G.R. The motivational strategies used by supervisors: Relationships to effectiveness indicators. *Organizational Behavior and Human Performance*, 1976, *15*, 66–86.

Orihara, H. "Test Hell" and alienation: A study of Tokyo University freshmen. *Journal of Social and Political Ideas in Japan*, 1967, *10*, 225–50.

Pamplin, J.N. Executive selection in private enterprise and the federal government: An analysis and comparison. Unpublished master's thesis, University of Maryland, 1959.

Parsons, T., Bales, R.F. (eds.). *Family, socialization, and interaction process*. Glencoe, Ill.: Free Press, 1955.

Pelz, D.C. Influence: A key to effective leadership in the first-line supervisor. *Personnel*, 1952, *9*, 3–11.

_____. and Andrews, F.M. *Scientists in organizations*. New York: Wiley, 1966.

Platt, J. R. Strong inference. *Science*, 1964, *146*, 347–52.

Porter, L. W. Job attitudes in management: I. Peceived deficiencies in need fulfillment as a function of job level. *Journal of Applied Psychology*, 1962, *46*, 375–84.

_____. Job attitudes in management: II. Perceived importance of needs as a function of job level. *Journal of Applied Psychology*, 1963, *47*, 141–48.

_____. A study of perceived need satisfaction in bottom and middle management jobs. *Journal of Applied Psychology*, 1961, *45*, 1–10.

_____.; Crampon, W.; and Smith, F.J. Organizational commitment and managerial turnover: A longitudinal study. *Organizational Behavior and Human Performance*, 176, *15*, 87–98.

_____. and Henry, M.M. Job attitudes in management: V. Perceptions of the importance of certain personality traits as a function of job level. *Journal of Applied Psychology*, 1964, *48*, 31-36.

_____., and Lawler, E.E. *Managerial attitudes and performance*. Homewood, Ill.: Richard Irwin, 1968.

_____., and Lawler, E.E. Properties of organization structure in relation to job attitudes and job behavior. *Psychological Bulletin*, 1965, *64*, 23-51.

_____.; Lawler, E.E.; and Hackman, J.R. *Behavior in organizations*. New York: McGraw-Hill, 175.

Prien, E.P. Assessments of high-level personnel: V. An analysis of interviewers' predictions of job peformance. *Personnel Psychology,* 1962, *15,* 319–34.

Pugh, D.S.; Hickinson, D.J.; Hinings, C.R.: and Turner, C. Dimensions of organizational structure. *Administrative Science Quarterly,* 1968, *13,* 65–91.

Riesman, D. *The lonely crowd.* New Haven, Conn.: Yale University Press, 1950.

Roadman, H.E. An industrial use of peer ratings. *Journal of Applied Psychology,* 1964, *48,* 211–14.

Sano, K. *Bunshō kansei-hō tesuto kaisetsu.* Tokyo: Kaneko *Shobō,* 1969.

_____. *Seikaku no shindan.* Tokyo: Dainippon Tosho, 1970.

_____. *Tamenkansatsu no hassō.* Tokyo: Tokuma Books, 1975.

Seashore, S.E., and Yuchtman, E. Factorial analysis of organizational performance. *Administrative Science Quarterly,* 1967, *12,* 377–95

Schein, E.H. The individual, the organization, and the career: A conceptual scheme. *The Journal of Applied Behavioral Science,* 1971, *7,* 401–26.

_____. How "Career Anchors" hold executives to their career paths. *Personnel,* 175, *52,* 11–24.

_____. How to break in the college graduate. *Harvard Business Review,* 1964, *42,* 68–76.

_____. *Organizational psychology.* Englewood Cliffs, N.J.: Prentice-Hall, 1965.

_____. Organizational socialization and the profession of management. *Industrial Management Review,* 1968, *9,* 1–16.

_____. and Lippitt, G.L. Supervisory attitudes toward the legitimacy of influencing subordinates. *Journal of Applied Behavioral Science,* 1966, *2,* 199–29.

Schiemann, W.A. A structural versus an interpersonal approach to organizational communication. Unpublished doctoral dissertation, University of Illinois, Champaign-Urbana, 177.

Schuler, R. The effects of role perceptions on employee satisfaction and performance moderated by employee ability. *Organizational Behavior and Human peformance,* 1977, *18,* 98–107.

_____. Role perceptions, satisfaction and performance: A partial reconciliation. *Journal of Applied Psychology,* 1975, *60,* 683–87.

Sheldon, M.E. Investments and involvements as mechanisms producing commitment to the organization. *Administrative Science Quarterly,* 1971, *16,* 143–50.

Sheridan, J.E.; Downey, H.K.; and Stocum, J.W. Testing causal relationships of House's path-goal theory of leadership effectiveness. In J.G. Hunt and L.L. Larson (eds.), *Leadership Frontiers.* Kent, Ohio: Kent State University Press, 1975, 61–80.

Smith, P.C. Behaviors, results, and organizational effectiveness: the problem of criteria. In M.D. Dunnette (ed.), *Handbook of industrial and organizational psychology.* Chicago: Rand McNally, 1976, 745–75.

Stodgill, R.M., and Coons, A.E. *Leader behavior: Its description and measurement.* Ohio State University, Bureau of Business Research, Business Research Monograph No. 88, 1957.

_____. and Shartle, C.L. and Associates. *Patterns of administrative performance.* Ohio State University, Bureau of Business Research, Business Research Monograph No. 81, 1956.

Stouffer, S.A., et al., *The American Soldier.* Princeton, N. J.: Princeton University Press, 1949.

Sumiya, M. The function and social structure of education: Schools and Japanese university. *Journal of Social and Political Ideas in Japan,* 1967, *10,* 117–38.

Super, D. *The psychology of careers.* New York: Harper, 1957.

Tannenbaum, A.S. *Control in organizations.* New York: McGraw-Hill, 1968.

_____. Control in organizations: Individual adjustment and organizational performance. *Administrative Science Quarterly*, 1962, *1*, 236–57.

Tatsuoka, M.M. *Multivariate analysis: Techniques for educational and psychological research.* New York: Wiley, 1971.

Thomson, H.A. Comparison of predictor and criterion judgments of managerial performance using the multitrait-multimethod approach. *Journal of Applied Psychology*, 1970, *54*, 496–502.

Thorndike, R. L. *Personnel selection.* New York: Wiley, 1949.

Tosi, H. Organizational stress as a moderator of the relationship between influence and role response. *Academy of Management Journal*, 1971, *14*, 7–20.

_____., and Tosi, D. Some correlates of role conflict and ambiguity among public school teachers. *Journal of Human Relations*, 1970, *18*, 1068–75.

Vaughan, G.M., and Corballis, M. Beyond tests of significance: Estimating strength of effects in selected ANOVA designs. *Psychological Bulletin*, 1969, *72*, 204–13.

Vogel, E.F. *Japan's new middle class.* Berkeley and Los Angeles: University of California Press, 1963.

Vroom, V.H. Comparison of static and dynamic correlational methods on the study of organizations. *Organizational Behavior and Human Performance*, 1966, *1*, 55–70.

_____. *Work, and motivation.* New York: Wiley, 1964.

Wager, L.W. Leadership style, influence, and supervisory role obligations. *Administrative Science Quarterly*, 1965, *9*, 391–420.

Wakabayashi, M.; Graen, G.; Samo, K.; Minami, T.; and Hashimoto, M. Japanese private university as a socialization system for future leaders in business and industry. *International Journal of Intercultural Relations*, 1977, *1*, 60–80.

Wallace, S.R. How high the validity? *Personnel Psychology*, 1974, *27*, 397–407.

Webb, E.J.; Campbell, D.T.; Schwartz, R.D.; and Secherest, L. *Unobtrusive measures: Nonreactive research in the social sciences.* Chicago: Rand McNally, 1966.

Weick, K., Jr. *The social psychology of organizing.* Reading, Mass.: Addison-Wesley, 1969.

Whyte, W.F. *Money and motivation: An analysis of incentives in industry.* New York: Harper, 1955.

Whyte, W.H. *The organization man.* New York: Simon and Schuster, 1956.

Wilensky, H.L. Work, careers, and social integration. *International Social Science Journal*, 1960, *12*, 543–60.

Winer, B.J. *Statistical principles in experimental design.* New York: McGraw-Hill, 1971.

Wollowick, H.B., and McNamara, W.J. Relationship of the components of an assessment center to management success. *Journal of Applied Psychology*, 1969, *53*, 348–52.

Worbois, G.M. Validity of externally developed assessment procedures for identification of supervisory potential. *Personnel Psychology*, 1975, *28*, 77–91.

Ziller, R.C. Individualization and socialization. *Human Relations*, 1964, *17*, 341–60.

Index of Names

Subject Index